WITHDRAWN
NDSU

Bullets and Bureaucrats

Recent Titles in
Contributions in Military History
SERIES EDITOR: THOMAS E. GRIESS

The Leavenworth Schools and the Old Army: Education, Professionalism, and the Officer Corps of the United States Army, 1881-1918
Timothy K. Nenninger

In Peace and War: Interpretations of American Naval History, 1775-1978
Kenneth J. Hagan, editor

Pacifying the Plains: General Alfred Terry and the Decline of the Sioux, 1866-1890
John W. Bailey

Divided and Conquered: The French High Command and the Defeat of the West, 1940
Jeffery A. Gunsburg

The Army and Civil Disorder: Federal Military Intervention in Labor Disputes, 1877-1900
Jerry M. Cooper

History of the Art of War Within the Framework of Political History, The Germans
Hans Delbrück, translated by *Walter J. Renfroe, Jr.*

The Art of Leadership in War: The Royal Navy From the Age of Nelson to the End of World War II
John Horsfield

A Wilderness of Miseries: War and Warriors in Early America
John E. Ferling

Iron Arm: The Mechanization of Mussolini's Army, 1920-1940
John Joseph Timothy Sweet

American Sea Power in the Old World: The United States Navy in European and Near Eastern Waters, 1865-1917
William N. Still, Jr.

A Hollow Threat: Strategic Air Power and Containment Before Korea
Harry R. Borowski

The Quest for Victory: The History of the Principles of War
John I. Alger

Men Wanted for the U.S. Army: America's Experience with an All-Volunteer Army Between the World Wars
Robert K. Griffith, Jr.

Bullets and Bureaucrats
The Machine Gun and the United States Army, 1861-1916

David A. Armstrong

Contributions in Military History, Number 29

GREENWOOD PRESS
WESTPORT, CONNECTICUT • LONDON, ENGLAND

Library of Congress Cataloging in Publication Data

Armstrong, David A.
   Bullets and bureaucrats.

   (Contributions in military history, ISSN 0084-9251 ; no. 29)
   Bibliography: p.
   Includes index.
   1. United States. Army—Procurement—History—19th century. 2. United States. Army—Procurement—History—20th century. 3. Machine-guns. I. Title. II. Series.
UC263.A75   355.8'2424'0973   81-7226
ISBN 0-313-23029-3 (lib. bdg.)   AACR2

Copyright © 1982 by David A. Armstrong

All rights reserved. No portion of this book may be reproduced, by any process or technique, without the express written consent of the publisher.

Library of Congress Catalog Card Number: 81-7226
ISBN: 0-313-23029-3
ISSN: 0084-9251

First published in 1982

Greenwood Press
A division of Congressional Information Service, Inc.
88 Post Road West
Westport, Connecticut 06881

Printed in the United States of America

10 9 8 7 6 5 4 3 2 1

CONTENTS

	Illustrations	vii
	Preface	ix
	Introduction	xi
I.	Promise Denied and Opportunity Lost, 1861-1863	3
II.	A Bold Step Forward, 1863-1866	32
III.	Inertia Takes Over, 1866-1880	51
IV.	In Pursuit of Perfection, 1881-1897	72
V.	Combat and Its Results, 1898-1901	96
VI.	From Stepchild Invention to Standard Equipment, 1901-1906	125
VII.	A Failed Experiment, 1907-1909	151
VIII.	A Mistake and Its Consequences: The Benet-Mercie, 1909-1913	171
IX.	An Inadequate Staff and a Minimal Solution, 1914-1916	189
X.	Conclusion	209
	Bibliographical Notes	217
	Index	227

ILLUSTRATIONS

1. Brig. Gen. James Wolfe Ripley, chief of ordnance, 1861-1863 — 8
2. Ager "Coffee Mill" gun — 16
3. Patent model of 1862 Gatling gun — 33
4. Brig. Gen. Alexander B. Dyer, chief of ordnance, 1864-1874 — 35
5. Gatling gun, model 1865 — 37
6. Billinghurst and Requa battery gun, cal. .50 — 39
7. Vandenburgh volley gun, cal. .50, with eighty-five barrels — 41
8. Brig. Gen. Stephen Vincent Benet, chief of ordnance, 1874-1891 — 66
9. A Gatling battery at Fort McKean, Dakota Territory — 81
10. Lieut. John Henry Parker — 97
11. Working a Gatling gun while almost hidden in the deep grass in front of Santiago — 102
12. Parker's command during the siege of Santiago — 103
13. Maj. Gen. William Crozier, chief of ordnance, 1901-1918 — 127
14. German Maxim gun, model 1908 with sled mount — 173
15. Benet-Mercie machine gun, model 1909, with tripod mount added when the gun proved unstable when fired from the bipod mount — 176

PREFACE

Since the beginning of warfare, fighting men have recognized that in battle the side with superior weapons will be victorious, other factors being equal. Despite universal understanding of the value of superior arms, systematic efforts to gain military advantage through the organized development of new weapons and methods of employing them are a recent phenomenon. Traditionally soldiers have been satisfied with a thorough knowledge of the physical details of a particular arm and an understanding of its employment; few fighting men have speculated upon how they might improve a weapon or use it in a more effective and efficient manner. Because they had little interest in the development of novel weapons and doctrine, military leaders seldom attempted to accelerate the creation of new arms and concepts for their use.

In 1861 the United States Army was offered a prototype machine gun, an early representative of the new machine weapons that emerged in the second half of the nineteenth century. For more than five decades, however, machine guns were of only peripheral interest to the American military. Study of its failure to use the machine gun reveals that the army lacked the bureaucratic, fiscal, and above all the intellectual capacity needed to recognize, explore, and exploit the potential of novel weapons. Unable to assimilate this promising weapon in the years before World War I, the American army had limited success in adapting its structure and doctrine to the requirements of machine warfare.

Many individuals and organizations deserve my thanks for their valuable advice and assistance. Professor Theodore Ropp and Professor I. B. Holley, Jr., contributed valuable ideas and trenchant criticism in the course of this study's development. Col. Thomas E. Griess and Col. Roy K. Flint demonstrated their interest in the work in a most concrete fashion by giving me the time to complete it. The staffs of several archives and libraries deserve special recognition: Wilhelmina Lemen and Elizabeth M. Graham, Duke University Library; John Taylor, National Archives of the United States; Joyce Eakin, Col. George Pappas, and Col. James B. Agnew, United States Army Military History Research Collection; and Marie Capps, United States Military Academy Archives; all gave freely of their time and expertise. I owe a debt of gratitude to my wife, Lynne, whose patience and enthusiasm for my work was unflagging. Any errors of omission or commission found in this work are solely my responsibility.

INTRODUCTION

To the soldiers waiting in the trenches, it seemed as if the guns had been firing for an eternity; suddenly the week-long barrage paused and the Somme front was quiet. In this brief moment of peace—0730 hours, July 1, 1916—the three thousand men of 103 Brigade (Tyneside Irish), Thirty-fourth Division, left their trenches and began to walk down the open slopes of the Avoca Valley toward the division front line a mile away. Loaded with at least sixty-six pounds of equipment, weapons, rations, and personal gear, these green soldiers, members of Field Marshal Kitchener's New Army, plodded forward in waves. As the Tynesiders advanced, German machine guns hidden in high ground overlooking the Avoca Valley swept them with a storm of fire. Sheltered in deep dugouts, the German gun crews survived the British barrage; now they cut down the ranks of Irishmen as if they were wheat. When 103 Brigade reached the front-line trench, two of its four battalions were gone, but the surviving members of the remaining battalions kept going. By the time that the remnants of the brigade crossed the 500 yards of no-man's-land and reached the German trench, which was by then in British hands, enemy machine guns and artillery had reduced the assault force to a handful. After a brief pause in the captured works, the survivors, all fifty of them, set off toward the brigade objective, the village of Contalmaison, which lay in the distance. A corporal's guard was all that remained of a brigade attack across open ground in the face of deadly accurate artillery and machine-gun fire. Incredible as it seems, the disaster that befell the Tynesiders was only a small part of a debacle that cost the British Fourth Army 57,470 officers and men on July 1. The official historian's laconic note "For this disastrous loss of the finest manhood of the United Kingdom and Ireland there was only a small gain of ground. . . ." is an ironic epitaph for what was the most costly single day in the history of the British army.[1]

Gen. Sir Henry Rawlinson, the commander of the Fourth Army, made two basic mistakes, which led directly to the disaster on the Somme. First, he assumed that a lengthy bombardment employing more guns and much more ammunition than had heretofore been available to the British would destroy all German defenses. As the fighting on July 1 demonstrated, neither the number nor the type of guns used proved sufficient to the task. Confident that the weight of his artillery preparation would utterly flatten the German fortifications, General Rawlinson believed that the infantry under his command would have to do little more than occupy the position conquered by his guns. Despite the protests of both subordinate commanders and his superior, Gen. Sir Douglas Haig, Rawlinson abandoned the standard system of attacking as skirmishers. In order to insure that the inexperienced infantrymen reached their objectives with a minimum of confusion, Rawlinson decreed that they attack in rigidly organized waves. The survival of the German defenders doomed the attack of the Fourth Army to failure; Rawlinson's abandonment of standard assault tactics transformed failure into catastrophe.[2]

The Somme was not the first nor would it be the last battle in which British generals pitted the courage and stamina of their infantry against German wire, trenches, guns, and men. Nor were the British commanders alone in their failure to solve the trench stalemate. Weakened by a series of failed offensives, the morale of the French army collapsed after the defeat of the Nivelle offensive in April and May 1917. German commanders proved more adept in adjusting their methods to the requirements of machine warfare, but neglect of the tank and the failure of their offensives in 1918 demonstrated their inability to solve the trench deadlock. In what Paul Fussell has called the "most ironic" of wars, European soldiers, members of a society that viewed the mechanical development of its civilization with immense pride, could not solve the tactical and strategic problems created by the products of a generation of technical progress.[3] Condemned to wage siege warfare along a

300-mile front as intricately fortified as any medieval castle, the generals could do little better than try to bludgeon a path through the enemy works with ever-increasing amounts of men and materiel. Unprepared for the kind of war thrust upon them in the autumn of 1914, these men continued to use nineteenth-century methods in the first of the machine wars of the twentieth century.[4]

If few of the generals grasped the capabilities and limitations of the machine weapons that industry had produced, none of them understood the processes by which these arms had come into being. Further complicating the situation was the fact that, with the possible exception of the German army, soldiers had not paid sufficient attention to the tactical problems posed by the firepower of modern rifles, machine guns, and artillery. For the generals of the Edwardian era, efficient mobilization was the acid test of their ability to cope with the demands of technology, and in August 1914, all of them passed the test. But, as the fighting in the fall of 1914 demonstrated, machine weapons in unprecedented numbers drastically altered the nature of battle. Unused to thinking deeply about technology and its effect upon the nature of battle and unable to draw upon past experience for guidance, the generals could not educate themselves in the midst of a war; consequently, they and their men were forced to "muddle through." The result was wholesale carnage, which consumed a generation of young men and crippled Western Europe.

In the years following the end of what had already begun to be called the Great War, a number of thoughtful soldiers began to explore the relationship between technology and warfare. Motivated largely by a desire to solve the deadlock that had prevailed in France, Guilio Douhet, J.F.C. Fuller, Basil Liddell-Hart, and Charles DeGaulle developed a set of ideas that promised to allow soldiers to restore mobility to warfare. Together with the practical work of Heinz Guderian, Giffard Martel, Hugh Trenchard, the faculty of the U.S. Army Air Corps Tactical School, and other less well-known figures, these theories gave the generals the instruments that they needed to avoid the impasse of 1914-1918.

Although military interest in technology increased rapidly in the years before World War II, military historians have been slow to turn their attention from the dramatic events of the battlefield and campaign to consideration of the relationship between the soldier, his weapons, and the industry that produces them. Of the few historical works that explore the development of weapons, perhaps the best known is I. B. Holley, Jr.'s, *Ideas and Weapons*, a masterful study of the American army's attempts to develop an effective aerial weapon in the period from 1907 to the end of World War I. Less well known is Holley's *Buying Aircraft: Materiel Procurement for the Army Air Forces*, a volume in the *United States Army in World War II* series sponsored by the Department of the Army. Published more recently, Dennis Showalter's *Railroads and Rifles: Soldiers, Technology and the Unification of Germany*, a study of the relationship between technology and the Prussian army in the three decades before Moltke's crushing defeat of the Austrians at Königgrätz in 1866, adds a new dimension to our understanding of how Europe's most modern army dealt with the first fruits of the technology of the Industrial Revolution. All of these studies demonstrate the critical role of bureaucracy in the integration of novel weapons into the doctrine and organization of the military.

Chronologically this study bridges the decades that separate the Prussian army of 1866 and the embryonic American air service of 1907. Technologically, the machine gun rests between European breech-loading rifles and artillery and the Wright biplane, which the War Department purchased in 1908. The Dreyse needle gun and Krupp's new artillery were advanced forms of traditional weapons, while the airplane was a novel device with little precedent in military experience. Like the airplane, the machine gun was, in its final form, a novel weapon, but particularly in its early versions it was not markedly different from conventional artillery pieces. Not as obviously different or as glamorous as the airplane, the machine gun became a sort of military oddity—a weapon that had considerable power but did not fit established tactical and organizational concepts. Relegated to a position of obscurity, the machine gun remained an object of peripheral interest for most soldiers until the events of the Great War thrust it into military prominence.

Within the American army there were substantial obstacles to attempts to fit the machine gun into the combat arms. After the Civil War the army returned to its traditional missions of defending the nation's coasts and policing its frontiers; protected by oceanic

Introduction   xv

moats and having no rivals in the hemisphere, the United States enjoyed a generation of peace and free security. Accordingly the government let the army shrink in size and reduced military expenditures to a minimum. In these circumstances the army bureaucracy flourished, as it was not intended to be an instrument for promoting the effectiveness of the nation's land forces but was designed around the much older bureaucratic rationale of assuring tight control of public funds. As insurance against unnecessary expenditures, Congress erected a system of statutes that controlled not only the size but also the exact structure of the American army. Dominated by the need for economy and bound to a procrustean legal bed, the military dozed and its armament rusted.

Jarred from its slumber by the Spanish-American War, the army began a long overdue program designed to modernize its structure, armament, and methods. Hampered by statutory restrictions and lacking expertise within its new staff organization, the American military could not respond adequately to the organizational and doctrinal challenges posed by weapons like the machine gun. Caught with its methods and thinking in transition between the nineteenth and twentieth centuries, the army of the United States was as unprepared for machine warfare in 1917 as the European powers had been in 1914.

NOTES

1. James E. Edmonds, comp., *History of the Great War: Military Operations*, vol. 5, pt. 1 (London, 1932), p. 483. The account of the Tyneside Brigade's attack was drawn from chap. 15 of this work and from Martin Middlebrook's *The First Day on the Somme* (New York, 1972), pp. 120-26.

2. This account is drawn from Middlebrook, *The First Day on the Somme*, chap. 16. See also Edmonds, *History of the Great War*, pp. 484-93.

3. Paul Fussell, *The Great War and Modern Memory* (New York, 1973), p. 8.

4. See the chapter titled "Big Battalions: The Napoleonic Legacy" in John Terraine's *The Western Front, 1914-1918* (London, 1964) for a discussion of this failure.

Bullets and Bureaucrats

I
PROMISE DENIED AND OPPORTUNITY LOST, 1861-1863

Experts sometimes miss the point. As J.F.C. Fuller once said, the main characteristic of the American Civil War, at least from the point of view of armament, was the "extraordinary inventiveness" displayed. But then, after listing the wide range of weapons developed or proposed, he hastened to other topics and failed to pose the main question concerning the weaponry of the Civil War. In a conflict marked by the inventiveness Fuller cites, why did both sides end the war armed with substantially the same type of weapons with which they had started four years earlier? There were, to be sure, startling advances in the technology of violence as the account of the duel between the *Monitor* and the *Merrimack* graphically illustrates. Yet despite a spate of military inventions unprecedented in American and perhaps world history, virtually all the field armies of the Civil War spent more than three years battering each other to exhaustion with the muzzle-loading rifles and cannon of 1861.[1]

What happened? Why were new ideas not translated into concrete additions and improvements to the panoply of the Civil War soldier, particularly those who fought for the Union? Was this failure the product of inefficiency and conservatism within the Union Ordnance Department, or was it due to the imperfect states of these new and untried arms? Examination of the wartime experience of the Union army with one of these new weapons, the machine gun, yields some answers to these questions.

The Civil War was fought near the beginning of the acceleration of weapons development that occurred in the last half of the nineteenth century. Discoveries in the applied sciences of chemistry and metallurgy combined with rapid advances in industrial technology and machine design to give inventors new capacity to develop a wide variety of devices with direct or secondary military applications. The key to progress in the design of small arms lay in a series of improvements in ammunition between 1816 and 1884. The invention of the percussion cap in 1815 and the development of the cylindro-conoidal bullet following its invention in 1823 by Lieut. John Norton, Thirty-fourth Cumberland Regiment of Foot, combined with the well-known principle of rifling to give the infantry soldier of 1861 a reliable shoulder arm capable of accurate fire at 400 yards.[2]

Civil War infantrymen fought primarily with a single-shot, muzzle-loading rifle of American or British manufacture. Based upon the design of the U.S. rifle-musket, model 1855, this weapon was a transitional arm that combined the effective range of a modern infantry rifle with a rate of fire of three rounds per minute, which was less than that achieved in the army of Frederick the Great. Among its chief disadvantages was the fact that a soldier could not load it lying on the ground. Thus the infantryman was forced to expose a large target to enemy fire in order to load his weapon. Despite its shortcomings the increased range and accuracy of the rifle-musket drove the cavalry from the battlefield and rendered the infantry and artillery tactics of Napoleon's day obsolete. Rugged, relatively reliable in foul weather, simple to operate and cheap to manufacture, this new weapon with its percussion cap and cylindro-conoidal, expanding "Minie ball" was a principal cause of the extended, often stalemated, character of Civil War combat; together with other products of nineteenth-century technology the percussion rifle gave the world its first "modern" war.[3]

Artillery developments during the Civil War further separated the field artillery from heavy coastal defense and siege guns. New casting techniques and rapid progress in barrel design joined to create such behemoths as the Rodman Columbiads, with bore diameters of 15 and even 20 inches and weights ranging from 49,000 to 116,500 pounds, as well as giant siege mortars such as the 13-inch weapon used to bombard the Confederate works at Petersburg. The situation was very different, however, in the field artillery. Despite the appearance of limited numbers of new fieldpieces such as the British-made Armstrong and Whitworth rifled breechloaders, Civil War field artillery was made up largely of three types of weapons—the smoothbore, 12-pounder, model 1857 Napoleon gun-howitzer and the 3-inch Ordnance and 3-inch 10-pounder Parrot rifled guns. Loaded from the muzzle, these weapons were sturdy and simple to operate and used standard, relatively reliable types of ammunition. Such technical advances as the Rodman method of gun casting permitted the creation of much larger and heavier guns. But because the size of field artillery was governed by the weight limitations of cross-country mobility in an era of animal transport, the Union army used substantially the same weapons from First Manassas to Appomattox.[4]

Despite the relatively static condition of the armaments of the field armies, there seems to have been no great pressure for change. Individual regimental, division, or even corps commanders asked for new weapons such as the Sharps or Spencer breech-loading rifles, but there was never consistent pressure from highly placed commanders for the general improvement of the capabilities of their forces through the issue of new or improved models of basic infantry and artillery weapons. In the Confederate forces, whose main problem was the continued supply of adequate weapons, this lack is understandable, but in the Union armies, where northern industry gave the generals a marked advantage in the quality and quantity of equipment they received, such a lapse is, at the very least, puzzling.[5] Part of the explanation seems to lie in the fact that northern field commanders generally appear to have found the weaponry of their forces satisfactory. Leaders such as George McClellan, Joseph Hooker and Ulysses S. Grant had gained their tactical experience in the Mexican War, and the remarkable increases in range and accuracy of the rifle-musket made it virtually a new type of weapon for them. Indeed, none of these men succeeded in completely solving the tactical problems that the rifle-musket created.[6]

Some change did occur. By 1865 Union cavalry and some infantry units carried breechloaders.[7] Brig. Gen. Alexander B. Dyer, the chief of the U.S. Army Ordnance Department, had concluded that new weapons were needed and that the army could not afford

". . . to stand still and rest content with what we have already attained."[8] Coming at the very end of the conflict, General Dyer's conclusion did not greatly affect the weaponry of the Union armies.

According to its most influential Civil War chief, the organization of the Bureau of Ordnance in 1861 was ". . . only suitable, for an army on a peace establishment. Its strength [was] . . . now entirely inadequate. . . ."[9] At the very time when it was called upon to arm and equip the flood of men responding to Lincoln's first call to arms, the department lost almost one-quarter of its fifty-nine officers to the South. Among the defectors was the exceptionally capable Josiah Gorgas, who was destined to become chief of ordnance for the Confederacy.[10] Transfers to northern field commands by such able men as Oliver Otis Howard and Jesse Reno further reduced the strength of the Ordnance Department. In 1862 the Union army listed only forty-five regular ordnance officers on its rolls. Eventually Congress would permit the use of volunteer officers in ordnance positions with the field armies, and in 1863 federal legislation authorized expansion of the Ordnance Corps to a wartime strength of sixty-four officers.[11]

Manned by a shrinking officer force and deprived of some of its most experienced and able personnel, the Ordnance Department continued to be charged with three major missions. The first was to operate seventeen government arsenals, armories, and depots (eleven more of these installations had been seized by the Confederacy). The second mission was to furnish the Union forces with all ordnance stores including artillery weapons and carriages, small arms and accoutrements, all items of ammunition, harness for horse-drawn artillery, veterinary medicines, and all the tools and materials used in ordnance activities. Finally, ordnance officers were responsible for the test and evaluation of all new items falling into these categories prior to their adoption for issue to the Union armies.[12] Clearly, the handful of technically trained ordnance specialists available in 1861 was overwhelmed with the task of procurement; small wonder they gave so little thought to the problem of improved design.

The chief of ordnance was indeed accurate when he said that the bureau was attuned only to the demands of a peacetime army;

neither ordnance nor any other Union staff bureau had done any systematic logistical planning for war.[13] But of far greater significance than a lack of planning was the general nature of the orientation and experience of the prewar Bureau of Ordnance and its officers. Developed in the period between 1809 and 1861, Ordnance Department procedures and priorities were established by the limited demands of a miniscule force primarily concerned with policing the frontier and coastal defense and by the requirements of a Congress whose overriding concern was fiscal restraint. Understandably enough, blessed as it was with free security and continental isolation, the American army lagged far behind those of European nations in the procurement of new weapons.[14] While an individual such as Maj. Thomas Jackson Rodman, an early student of metallurgy, was capable of making contributions to advances in cannon design and manufacture, the U.S. Army tended to adopt new weapons and methods only after they had been tested, proved, and adopted by the armies of one or more of the major European powers. When tested in the Mexican War and on the frontier, this system had proved to be adequate. Whether such would be the case when Union forces faced those of the Confederacy remained to be seen.

At the begining of the war ordnance affairs were in the hands of Col. Henry K. Craig, an acerbic seventy-year-old whose chief qualification for his post seemed to be that he had held it for ten years. Advanced age and recurring illness soon rendered Craig unfit for active duty, and in April 1861 the next senior ordnance officer, Lieut. Col. James W. Ripley, was promoted over Craig's head to the newly created office of brigadier general, chief of ordnance. Ripley was then sixty-six years old.[15] Recently returned from an unfinished tour of inspection of foreign arsenals, Ripley had a wide range of experience in ordnance work including the superintendency of the key arsenal at Springfield, Massachusetts. Measured against the professional criteria of the day, experience and seniority, Ripley appeared well qualified for his new job. Neither Ripley's health nor the vigor with which he performed his duties reflected his years, but there is little doubt that his advanced age underlay the inflexibility and conservatism that marked his career as chief of ordnance.[16]

Brig. Gen. James Wolfe Ripley, chief of ordnance, 1861-1863. *Courtesy*: U.S. Military Academy Archives.

A member of the ordnance service for forty-seven years at the time of his appointment as its chief, Ripley was intimately familiar with all aspects of departmental administrative procedures, and he firmly believed in following the letter and spirit of all regulations. His devotion to bureaucratic routine had not been shaken by an incident during the Creek War when Gen. Andrew Jackson had threatened to hang him for refusing to fill an irregular requisition submitted by a unit under Jackson's command.[17] Caution, not flexibility, was the lesson Ripley apparently drew from his brush with the epitome of the rough and ready "citizen-soldier." His faith in the importance of procedure undiminished, Ripley continued to rise slowly within his corps.

Assisted by Capt. William Maynadier, a man with fifteen years experience in the intricacies of administrative routine, Ripley set about the task of running his department. Despite the small size and elaborate procedures of the Ordnance Department, its wartime operations were not under tight central control. According to Ordnance Department regulations, any general or field grade officer commanding a field army, a garrison, or a detachment could, upon his own authority, order the issue of any item supplied by the ordnance service. In such a case the officer or enlisted member of the Ordnance Corps who controlled the stocks from which the issue was made was directed to transmit to Ripley's headquarters the order authorizing the issue. Further, in circumstances of urgent necessity any army officer could purchase items normally supplied by the Ordnance Department, submit a report of the purchase and a certificate justifying their necessity, and obtain government reimbursement.[18] Field commanders often resorted to the latter method, particularly in the early stages of the war. These provisions of ordnance regulations helped to meet commanders' needs as the Union rushed to arm its forces in 1861, but large-scale use of such methods substantially reduced central control of ordnance operations by Ripley's office.

During normal operations the commanders of the various arsenals, armories, and depots fabricated or purchased all articles issued by the Ordnance Department. The Quartermaster Department moved the items to the field where they were issued under the direction of the ordnance officer on the staff of the local commander. Returns, reports, and vouchers accounting for issues made during specific periods of time filtered in from the field armies and fixed installations operated by the department. Carefully compiled by a task force of clerks, the information gleaned from these papers enabled the chief of ordnance to see what had gone on in his department in the previous month, quarter, or year.[19] Unlike the peacetime procedure, which placed issues and purchases under the tight control of the chief of ordnance, the wartime system of immediate issue or civilian purchase placed the chief of ordnance in the position of reacting to the actions of his subordinates.[20] These men were, in turn, reacting to the demands of Union forces in the field. The unsynchronized nature of this system made careful planning essential if ordnance operations were to have any semblance of order. Since there was little machinery for coordination and planning within the War Department as a whole, the chief of ordnance was forced to rely upon his personal experience and that of his subordinates for guidance in logistical planning.[21] In 1861 Ripley's experience and that of his principal subordinates had very limited relevance to the situation at hand.

During the spring and summer of 1861 the major ordnance problem was the procurement of weapons, particularly small arms. When General P.G.T. Beauregard's forces fired on Fort Sumter in April, the regular army counted some 16,000 officers and men in its ranks; four months later Lincoln's calls for volunteers had produced an army of 486,000 three-year enlistees. The demand for weapons quickly exhausted existing stocks of modern fire arms. In 1861 the government counted over 600,000 shoulder arms of various types in storage; on paper these reserves seemed more than adequate, but the usefulness of the weapons was illusory. The problem was quality. The vast majority of these guns were smoothbores; perhaps eight in one hundred had rifled bores.[22] Armed with such guns, federal troops would be at a tremendous disadvantage if they faced Confederates armed with rifled weapons firing Minie bullets—a fact that was obvious to soldier, citizen, and politician alike. The armament problem, a military and political bombshell, had to be solved quickly, and the rush to procure arms was on.

The federal government had three ways of obtaining the large numbers of weapons it needed: by increasing the production of government arsenals, a task complicated by Confederate capture of a major small-arms factory at Harpers Ferry, Virginia; by contract with private manufacturers and arms dealers in the United States, and by overseas procurement. All these methods of procurement were used; overseas purchases placed weapons in the hands of troops the most quickly while the economical government arsenals were the slowest to respond to the need for large numbers of arms. Ripley's response to procurement problems was to solve them following precedents, regulations, and laws of the prewar Ordnance Department. Production at the remaining government small-arms factory at the Springfield Arsenal was expanded from eight hundred per month in April to sixty-nine hundred in October 1861, but this had little effect on the immediate supply problem. Procurement from civilian sources was governed by a law enacted in 1809, which required all transactions to be made either by open purchase or after advertisement for bids.[23] Ripley could only depart from this procedure at the risk of subsequent investigation and condemnation by Congress. Rigidly honest and conditioned by years of a penny-pinching routine that put economy above all other considerations, the general adhered to the time-consuming system of competitive procurement prescribed by regulations.

Unable to get enough small arms from the Ordnance Department, the War Department turned to large-scale procurement from both domestic and European sources. These contracts were made by a wide variety of Union agents; they were not supervised by qualified ordnance personnel, were made in violation of the provisions of the 1809 law, and in the case of foreign purchases were often motivated by a desire to deny arms to the Confederate armies. Corruption and fraud were widespread, and Union forces were saddled with large numbers of European arms that the soldiers often considered little better or in some instances even worse than the rusting smoothbores in the federal armories.[24] While congressional investigations uncovered evidence of profiteering, graft, and official corruption, the fact remains that the wholesale procurement of arms authorized by Secretary of War Cameron was the only feasible method of arming vast numbers of Union troops quickly.[25] By refusing to forgo his devotion to peacetime procedures, Ripley lost the chance to guide War Department procurement activities and use the resources of the Ordnance Department to protect the public treasury while getting the weapons necessary to the public interest.

Mired in the minutiae of administrative detail and with only limited control over both the procurement and distribution of weapons and other ordnance items, Ripley's office received an ever-increasing number of suggestions, ideas, and plans for new weapons. The war had deprived him of much of his personal control over both the arsenals, armories, and depots, and the operations of the ordnance supply system, but the chief of ordnance still retained a tight hold on his other major responsibility, the testing and evaluation of new weapons. Imaginative and energetic exercise of his authority in this area might have enabled General Ripley to equip the Union soldier with the best products of the revolution in weapons design then in progress and thus shorten, perhaps drastically, the course of the war.

According to the system outlined in departmental regulations published in 1852, the Ordnance Department depended upon civilian inventors and entrepreneurs to initiate the chain of events that eventually placed new weapons and equipment in the hands of the troops. The process began when the individual promoting the new device sent a letter to the Ordnance Department explaining its uses and requesting that the department conduct an official test of the invention. Further action depended upon whether the Bureau of Ordnance and its chief, to whose desk the application eventually came, thought that the proposal had merit. If the response was positive, the application passed to the secretary of war bearing an endorsement from the chief of ordnance recommending that a board of officers test and evaluate the new device. If the secretary took the advice of his chief expert on weapons, as he usually did, orders were published by the adjutant general convening a board to try the device.[26] Having furnished the War Department a prototype of his invention at his own expense, the inventor waited for the results of the official trials; these results, together with the recommendations of the board of officers, made up an official report, which was sent to the chief of ordnance. After reviewing the official report and considering the needs of the service as he understood them, the chief of ordnance would add his judgment in the form of a summary endorsement to the report. The entire staff action, including the test report and all official correspondence, was passed to the secretary of war for final action and a decision on whether or not to buy the new device.[27] Not only was the process of innovation begun by the civilian inventor, but it depended as much upon his persistence and financial resources as it did upon the merits of his invention.

The system for evaluating inventions was extraordinarily simple. In a more complicated era simplicity may be overvalued, for if the system was easy to operate, it was also readily blocked. The key position in the process was occupied by the chief of ordnance. His interest in a new device ordinarily determined not only whether it would enter the system for evaluation, but also whether or not it would complete its passage through the system successfully.

Shortly after assuming his duties as chief of ordnance, Ripley offered the secretary of war a clear statement of his position on the adoption of new small arms by the Union land forces:

> A great evil now specially prevalent in regard to arms for the military service is the vast variety of new inventions, each having, of course, its advocates, insisting upon the superiority of his favorite arm over all others and urging its adoption by the Government.
> The influence thus exercised has already introduced into the service many kinds and calibers of arms, some, in my opinion, unfit for use as military weapons, and none as good as the U.S. musket, producing confusion in the manufacture, the issue, and the use of ammunition, and very injurious to the efficiency of troops. This evil can only be stopped by positively refusing to answer any requisitions for or propositions to sell new and untried arms, and steadily adhering to the rule of uniformity of arms for all troops of the same kind, such as cavalry, artillery, and infantry.[28]

Ripley also warned Secretary Cameron of the need for strict control of weapons procurement to prevent excessive costs to the government. Especially germane in light of the history of War Department small-arms procurement activities in 1861, this warning had substantial contemporary validity as it was written prior to the First Battle of Bull Run, at a time when many federal officials, including President Lincoln, expected the war to last only a few months.[29] Ripley's concern about the difficulties, particularly in ammunition supply, created by using small arms of varying calibers was valid, but subsequent events demonstrated that he was prejudiced against all new types of weapons, not just small arms. The

War Department system for responding to change was blocked by Ripley's simple but effective refusal to answer, let alone encourage, any proposals for "new and untried arms." By this action the Union chief of ordnance forfeited a major opportunity to strengthen the Union and its armies.

Finding direct access to War Department channels blocked, inventors and their backers turned to alternative methods of gaining official consideration of their products. As the federal government was still relatively small and to a degree run on the basis of personal intervention of a wide variety of public figures—legislators, state and federal officials, senior military officers, and even the president himself, this latter course—direct application to President Lincoln—was the channel used in the earliest efforts to interest the United States in a machine gun.

Abraham Lincoln, who had himself invented a device to lift river boats over shoal water, shared with most American males of the past century a fascination with machines, particularly new machines. As Winston Churchill would do in the future, Lincoln displayed a lively interest in demonstrations of weapons or devices that could strengthen the military forces under his command; after witnessing such a trial he would on occasion intervene directly with the secretary of war to obtain official consideration of the new invention. Other officials also brought new inventions to the attention of the secretary of war. By the spring of 1862 the repeated use of these direct approaches to War Department channels had sensitized both the president and his secretary of war, Edwin M. Stanton, to General Ripley's prejudice against new inventions. As his civilian superiors gradually realized, Ripley was willing to use the administrative machinery of the Ordnance Department to frustrate or delay those projects or inventions that he opposed.[30]

Almost as soon as the war began, the Union army was offered a machine gun. The history of this weapon, which was variously termed the Ager gun, the Union gun, the Union repeating gun, and the "Coffee Mill" gun, illustrated many of the problems that entrepreneurs faced in trying to sell novel weapons—particularly early machine guns—to the army. First, although the fact was often not recognized either by army officers or civilian salesmen, even the early machine gun of rudimentary design represented a new

Promise Denied and Opportunity Lost

weapon with a different type of firepower. There were no direct precedents to govern its test and evaluation or to suggest the optimum method of using it in combat. Prototype machine guns were most often viewed as a species of artillery. Such classification was probably inevitable in view of the very real similarities between the appearance, transportation, ammunition resupply, and crew requirements of early machine guns and those of contemporary light artillery weapons. Tests that compared their capabilities frequently produced results unfavorable to the machine gun and led ordnance officers and others to ignore the military potential that an early machine gun might possess. The practice of using artillery terminology when referring to early machine guns probably further reinforced the official tendency to view the machine gun as a species of artillery and to expect it to perform in the same manner.

Of more immediate importance to the commercial prospects of the machine gun was the fact that it was not bound to the interests of any of the traditional combat arms. Artillery officers saw machine guns as artillery pieces but could not find a role for them that was not adequately filled by an existing weapon-projectile combination. Infantry and cavalry officers could find no place for the heavy, crew-served weapon in their organization. Unlike the salesmen of breech-loading small arms and rifled artillery, the promoters of machine guns had no group within the military to whom they could appeal for support. Thus the entrepreneur trying to merchandise machine guns had first to create an awareness of and appreciation for the unique qualities of his product.

Acceptance of the machine gun was retarded by the fact that a number of different machine guns were offered to the Union army during the Civil War. Probably convinced that he was protecting the government against fraud or the folly of inventors incapable of producing weapons that could fulfill the extravagant claims made for them, General Ripley was able to play off the capabilities of one type of machine gun against those of another. He also used the history of the failure of one machine gun as a reason for not trying the prototype of another. True to its prewar policy of passively waiting for civilian innovation in weaponry, the Ordnance Department missed the opportunity to intervene actively in the development of the machine gun either by encouraging the continued work of an inventor whose device seemed promising or by the more radical approach of devoting departmental resources to the improvement of an existing prototype.

Following its invention by Wilson Ager in 1861, the Union repeating gun was patented in Great Britain. However, the commercial possibilities offered by the Civil War were too great to overlook, and Ager, an American citizen, decided to offer his invention to the service of the United States. In June 1861 a troop of New Yorkers whose disparate accomplishments effectively complemented their purpose arrived in Washington bent on selling Ager's gun to the army. A small-time politician with connections in the capital city, Simeon Draper would provide the necessary entrée to an important political figure, Secretary of State William H. Seward. Knowledge of official procedures and contractual ar-

Ager "Coffee Mill" gun. *Courtesy*: George M. Chinn, *The Machine Gun* (Washington, D.C.: GPO, 1951).

rangements was the province of Orison Blunt, an experienced arms manufacturer and importer who was already engaged in arms procurement for both the Ordnance Department and the Union Defense Committee of New York City. The extensive contacts, credentials, and experience of Draper and Blunt served to offset the obscurity of the actual salesman of the gun, J. D. Mills.[31]

The trio forsook application for an official trial of the weapon through War Department channels and instead sought an audience with the president. Draper and Blunt were remarkably successful; within a week of their arrival in Washington, Lincoln was persuaded to attend a nonfiring demonstration of the Union repeating gun. What the president saw was a weapon, comparable in size to the modern Browning M2 heavy machine gun, with a heavy rifled barrel of .58 caliber attached to a housing that contained the breech mechanism. The breech housing was fastened to a light metal platform, which in turn was attached to the axle of a lightweight artillery carriage; centered on the axle, the gun and its platform were flanked by ammunition boxes, which were also fastened to the carriage axle. Operated by a hand crank, the breech mechanism (patterned after the Colt revolver) received cartridges from a hopper atop the breech housing and fed them into a rotating cylinder, which aligned the cartridge with the barrel, tripped the firing pin and then ejected the spent cartridges into a container. As the metallic self-primed cartridge had not yet been invented, Ager had designed a special steel cartridge case for his gun. Loaded with the contents of the standard paper rifle cartridge, the cylindrical steel case was hand-primed by fixing a percussion cap to a nipple on the rear of the casing. Struck by the similarity between the ammunition hopper atop the gun and the hopper of a contemporary coffee grinder, Lincoln dubbed Ager's invention the "Coffee Mill" gun.[32]

Several days after the demonstration Ripley was persuaded to allow the firing of the Union repeating gun at the Washington Arsenal. Witnessed by a crowd of dignitaries that included five generals, three cabinet officers, the governor of Connecticut, and President Lincoln, the demonstration was accounted remarkable, and the audience—particularly Lincoln—was impressed by the military potential of the new weapon. Lincoln urged Ripley to consider the Ager gun and stated, ". . . I really think it worth the attention of the Government."[33] Mills and his companions returned to

New York convinced that purchase of Ager's invention was assured. Mills became restive, however, over the lack of governmental action and wrote to both Lincoln and Ripley. Lincoln forwarded Mills' letters to Ripley. All of the correspondence was dutifully recorded in the letter registers, filed, and forgotten.[34] Sticking to his policy of refusing to answer letters about new weapons, Ripley clearly meant to ignore explicit presidential interest in the Ager gun.

Stymied, Mills returned to Washington in October 1861 and reestablished contact with the president. Unable to interest Ripley in the Ager gun and unwilling to intrude in military affairs by ordering the chief of ordnance to test the gun, Lincoln ordered ten Union repeating guns from the firm of Woodward and Cox; the price was $1,300 per gun.[35]

After several attempts Lincoln succeeded in interesting his new field commander, Maj. Gen. George B. McClellan, in Ager's invention. Mills offered to sell fifty of his guns to the Union army at a price of $1,200 each. Taken aback by the high cost, McClellan temporized, but after pressure from Lincoln he agreed to buy the guns from a new manufacturer, the American Arms Company, at a price of $735 per weapon. In mid-December the president signed a purchase order for fifty of these guns, but Mills was not out of the woods yet. Ordnance Department action on Lincoln's order lagged; in late February 1862 Mills wrote to the ordnance office and asked that the presidential pledge be translated into a firm contract.[36]

While Ripley conducted a bureaucratic rearguard action against the Union repeating gun, the Union army had its first opportunity to use the weapon in combat. Intrigued by the possibilities offered by the weapon, Col. John W. Geary—politician, Mexican War veteran, and commander of the Twenty-eighth Pennsylvania Regiment of Volunteers—drew two of the Union repeating guns purchased from Woodward and Cox from the Washington Arsenal. Geary's regiment took part in the Union advance under Maj. Gen. Nathaniel P. Banks toward the Shenandoah Valley, and on March 29, 1862, the guns were used against Confederate cavalry at Middleburg, Virginia. According to an eyewitness a squadron of Confederate horse was taken under fire at a range of 800 yards, cut up, and forced to retire by the hand-powered machine guns. Despite this promising showing, Geary shipped the guns back to Washington less than a month later and reported that after several trials the Union repeating gun had proved ". . . inefficient, and unsafe to the operators."[37] The poor quality of the guns produced by the firm of Woodward and Cox ended the first Union attempt to use the machine gun in combat.[38]

Realizing that Ripley limited the commercial opportunities in Washington, J. D. Mills sought to sell the Union repeating gun to the commanders of various Union field forces. A specimen was sent to Maj. Gen. John C. Fremont, the commander of the Mountain Department in Virginia; Fremont arranged for a test of the gun by his chief of artillery, Lieut. Col. John Pilsan, and Lieut. Augustus Otto. Fired at a board fence 60 yards long and 7 feet high from a distance of 400 yards, the gun achieved thirteen hits in seventeen shots; in a second trial 79 of 197 rounds fired hit the target. Almost all of the hits penetrated the 1-inch pine boards of the fence. At 444 yards only twenty-seven of sixty-eight shots hit the fence, but Pilsan and Otto noted that during this trial they had experienced difficulties with the elevating mechanism. Fremont's test board credited the weapon with a maximum range of 800 yards, the distance at which Colonel Geary's guns had engaged the Confederate cavalry.[39]

The two officers recommended that Ager's invention be improved by (1) increasing its caliber from .50 to .90, (2) improving the powder used, (3) modifying the steel cartridges and breech mechanism, and (4) mounting the gun on a tripod and reducing its weight to the point where it would be man-portable. Although they appeared to make sense singly, in combination these recommendations contained major defects. Increase in the caliber complicated ammunition supply, as the gun would no longer use the standard infantry cartridge, and by raising the weight and size of the gun worked against the recommendation that the gun be made man-portable. Reduction in the weight of the gun, on the other hand, was limited by the fact that the weapon was air-cooled and required a heavy barrel to resist the effects of overheating caused by rapid fire.[40] These contradictions reveal the lack of technical background and experience of the report's authors. Neither man was a regular officer who could have been expected to have had the experience necessary to discern the contradictory nature of the recommendations in their report.[41]

Turning to tactical matters, Pilsan and Otto envisioned using the Union gun to attack "solid bodies" of troops and "extended lines [of infantry] as well as cavalry charges." The gun, they believed, would render good service in guarding and defending bridges and defiles; because of its light weight and the ease with which it could be moved, the gun would be particularly useful in mountain warfare—an area of immediate concern to General Fremont.[42]

Interestingly enough, Pilsan and Otto recommended that each federal infantry regiment receive two Union repeating guns. Not only would this action increase the defensive firepower of the infantry, but ". . . in case of a regiment becoming depleted, through sickness, desertion, disaster or otherwise, two repeating guns would restore the disturbed balance, and prove a reliable substitute for its original efficiency."[43] This concept forecast the replacement of the firepower of masses of infantry with the firepower of the machine gun, a step that would finally come during World War I. Although somewhat contradictory in its technical recommendations, the report did contain sound ideas concerning the organizational structure and tactics that would make the machine gun most useful. Favorably endorsed by General Fremont, Pilsan's report was forwarded to General Ripley, who, predictably, ignored it.[44]

Two days before dispatching the test report to Washington, Fremont telegraphed an order for sixteen Union repeating guns directly to Ripley. The aging bureaucrat replied that he had ". . . no Union repeating guns on hand, and am not aware that any have been ordered."[45] The records of his office indicate that Ripley was well aware of the guns that Lincoln had ordered; in fact, two of these weapons had been issued to Colonel Geary's Twenty-eighth Pennsylvania Regiment from the Washington Arsenal and later returned to that post. In reply Fremont asked if Ripley's message had been garbled in transmission and then cited Lincoln's order for fifty Union repeating guns, which had been placed in December 1861. Probably coached by J. D. Mills, Fremont had exposed Ripley's lie. Ripley was trapped and took refuge in silence; he ignored Fremont's second telegram.[46] This maneuver successfully frustrated General Fremont's attempt to acquire the guns for a trial with his forces.

Fremont turned to Lincoln, and on May 15, 1862, the president asked Ripley for Fremont's original requisition for "Coffee Mill" guns. Ripley could not ignore a written request from Lincoln; hence, he resorted to subterfuge and added Colonel Geary's unfavorable report on the Union repeating gun to the requisition Lincoln had requested. The favorable report from Fremont's command remained in the Ordnance office files. This piece of chicanery apparently dampened Lincoln's interest—but not Fremont's. After his defeat by Stonewall Jackson at Cross Keys in the final stages of Jackson's Valley campaign, Fremont ordered two guns from Woodward and Cox. Fremont resigned from the service a few days after placing this order, however, and his forces did not use the Union repeating gun.[47]

Following Fremont's relief from command, military interest in Ager's invention declined, but again an unofficial demonstration of the gun, this time in the western theater, caused a high-ranking Union field commander, Maj. Gen. William S. Rosecrans, to ask the Ordnance Department to send some Union repeating guns to his command. Rosecrans' request was part of his endorsement to a report of the official demonstration. The body of the report contained summaries of the remarks of five general officers who had witnessed the demonstration. All of the generals favored the Union repeating gun, and one, George W. Thomas, estimated that ". . . with [one] well instructed operator it is equal to a company of our best marksmen. . . ."[48] Ripley eventually sent ten guns to the Army of the Cumberland, but the shipment went astray at Nashville and the guns did not reach Rosecrans' forces until after the Battle of Chickamauga.[49] There is no record of their use in combat.

In 1864 Maj. Gen. Benjamin Butler, a gentleman who was as fascinated with machinery as Lincoln and similarly optimistic about its military potential, requisitioned ten of Ager's guns for the Army of the James. Mounted on boats used to patrol the James River, the guns did not excite much interest.[50] Butler's experiment ended army use of the Union repeating gun.

A weapon with substantial military potential, astute and financially sound backing, clever merchandising by the indefatigable J. D. Mills, and even the enthusiastic support of the president, Wilson Ager's machine gun appeared to have an excellent chance of being adopted by the Union army. The most obvious, indeed the key, reason for its failure was the adamantine opposition of the chief of ordnance, James W. Ripley. Convinced that imperfect prototype machine guns were not worth purchasing, the general ignored the desires of the president and the field commanders it was his duty to support. Ripley was successful both in blocking unofficial channels to the War Department and in closing the way to an official Ordnance Department test and evaluation of the Union repeating gun. Without this latter step the weapon could not legally be adopted for general issue to United States forces.

Although a central reason for its failure, Ripley's actions were not the only factor blocking adoption of the weapon. Ager's gun had several major weaknesses: a tendency for the barrel to overheat during sustained firing; its dependence on special steel cartridges, which allowed gas to escape at the breech and which were heavy, expensive, and liable to loss; and the fact that the 800-yard maximum range of the gun was little more than the maximum effective range of the standard infantry rifle-musket. The inventor attempted to remedy the problem of overheating by providing spare barrels and an ingenious air-cooling device and by limiting the rate of fire to 120 rounds per minute.[51] But Ager could not replace the steel cartridges because brass or copper cartridges were not yet commercially available, and since it continued to leak gas at the breech, he was unable to increase the range of the gun. In addition, the shoddy construction of the guns made by Woodward and Cox marred attempts to use the weapon. Still, the chief of ordnance remained primarily responsible for the failure of efforts to secure adoption of the Union repeating gun.

Having experienced General Ripley's opposition to new weapons, Lincoln turned to the head of naval ordnance activities, Adm. John A. Dahlgren, for a professional evaluation of another machine gun. This weapon, the Raphael repeater, was offered to the president in June 1862. Like the Union repeating gun, the Raphael repeater was a single-barrel, carriage-mounted weapon. However, the inventor designed a substantially different breech mechanism. In place of Ager's steel cartridges the Raphael repeater used chambers drilled in steel bars to contain its paper cartridges. As the bar was fed through the breech of the gun, each chamber and the cartridge it contained was aligned with the rear of the gun barrel and the cartridge was fired. Ordnance tests showed that the

Promise Denied and Opportunity Lost

Raphael repeater could fire forty shots in twenty seconds, and because it used a heavy powder charge and a relatively light, .47 caliber bullet, it had a maximum range of 1,800 yards.[52] In range, at least, the Raphael repeater was clearly superior to the Union repeating gun.

Impressed with the results of the test of the Raphael repeater that he and Secretary Stanton had witnessed in early August 1862, Lincoln wrote Stanton, "While I do not order it into the service I think it well worthy of the attention of the Ordnance Bureau and should be rather pleased if it should be decided to put it into the service."[53] According to law the president could not order the army to adopt a new weapon, but the firm expression of presidential desires was directive enough for Stanton, who instructed General Ripley to give the Raphael repeater an official trial. Carried out at the Frankford Arsenal under the supervision of Maj. Theodore T.S. Laidley, the tests failed to produce conclusive results. Laidley found the Raphael repeater to be sturdy and simply designed, but he noted that the gun lacked the accuracy of the rifle-musket and possessed all of the restrictions on movement and requirements for infantry support of conventional artillery pieces without having the "great moral effect of Artillery." Major Laidley concluded his report with the remark that while the Raphael repeater could be used as a defensive weapon or in a manner similar to the French army practice of attaching light rifled guns to each infantry regiment, he did not believe that an entire unit should be equipped with the weapon. Carefully neutral, Laidley did express a definite opinion of the military value of the Raphael repeater; he also furnished considerable ammunition for those who opposed the adoption of the weapon.[54] When the backers of the Raphael repeater offered to sell the government five hundred guns at $850 per weapon, General Ripley advised Secretary Stanton not to accept the offer because of its cost and ". . . the still greater inconvenience of further multiplying the kinds and calibers of artillery in the military Services, already far too great. . . ."[55] In view of Laidley's colorless report the secretary of war had little choice but to accept Ripley's recommendation.

Unlike the Ordnance Department trials, tests of the Raphael gun conducted at the direction of field commanders produced results that definitely favored the weapon. Impressed by a demonstration of the Raphael repeater, Maj. Gen. John Sedgewick, the commander of the Sixth Corps, convened a board of officers to evaluate the weapon. Particularly affected by the apparent defensive power of the machine gun, the board suggested the formation of hundred-man companies armed with eight to twelve Raphael repeaters. Attached to infantry brigades or divisions, these companies could furnish substantial defensive fire when needed. Sedgewick and his superior, Maj. Gen. Joseph Hooker, both of whom were trained artillerymen, reviewed the report and supported its conclusions.[56] Unlike General Ripley, commanders of Union field forces were more concerned with the performance of this machine gun than with any complication it might cause in the supply of ammunition.

The case that Ripley constructed to support his opposition to the recommendations of the Sixth Corps displayed his talent for criticism and an aptitude for arithmetical obfuscation. Noting that the report failed to give a detailed description of the trials of the Raphael repeater and their results, the chief of ordnance proceeded to cite the adverse portions of Major Laidley's official report on the weapon. Ripley further bolstered his argument by referring to unfavorable army experience with the Union repeating gun.

He then cited a proposal made by a Charles Kell to equip the Army of the Potomac with Raphael repeating guns. Kell's scheme called for the assignment of twelve Raphael guns to each of thirteen infantry brigades plus the creation of a regiment of twelve batteries, each armed with twelve Raphael repeaters; each gun would cost $830. The chief of ordnance mixed references to the Kell proposal and the report submitted by the Sixth Corps so that both appeared expensive enough to justify rejection by the War Department. Ripley stated that Kell's offer required the purchase of 1,020 Raphael repeating guns at a cost of $876,000; this figure was so inflated (three hundred guns at a cost of $249,000 were actually called for) that it may well have been a deliberate attempt to mislead the secretary of war. Having totally obscured the real question of whether the Raphael repeating gun was worthy of serious consideration by the Union army, the chief of ordnance recommended that because of its cost Kell's offer should not be accepted ". . . without a better guarantee of commensurate advantages to be derived from it."[57] His comment was particularly ironic, since Ripley had frustrated all attempts to ascertain what such advantages might be.

The history of the Raphael repeater resembled that of the Union repeating gun in many respects; however, there were several major differences. The president succeeded in forcing the chief of ordnance to conduct an official test of the Raphael repeater, but the results of this test were not good enough to overcome General Ripley's prejudice against new weapons. Instead, Ripley used the negative parts of the test report to counter pressure from President Lincoln and to undermine support for the weapon expressed by Union field commanders. Unable to ignore the Raphael repeating gun, General Ripley opposed the weapon within the official system for test and evaluation. His success demonstrated the extent of his control over the selection of armament for the Union forces.

Having carried out his duties in a conservative and thoroughly autocratic manner for more than two years, Brigadier General Ripley was forced to retire in mid-September 1863. Twenty months earlier he had angered President Lincoln with his dilatory handling of a presidential project to build mortar boats for operations against Forts Donelson and Henry. In the same month, Lincoln replaced his ineffectual secretary of war, Simon Cameron, with Edwin M. Stanton, an irascible gentleman as fully determined to have his way as was the autocratic chief of ordnance. On January 24, 1862, only nine days after Stanton's appointment, Lincoln authorized his new secretary to make changes in the Ordnance Department; a day later Maj. Alexander B. Dyer, commander of the Springfield Arsenal, arrived in the capital city. Washington newspapers reported that Dyer was to replace Ripley, but Dyer declined to take the position because he was then in the midst of vastly expanding rifle production at the Springfield Arsenal.[58] Ripley's position had been weakened by reports that defective artillery ammunition had been received at Vicksburg. At length, Lincoln and Stanton decided to remove General Ripley and replace him with Col. George D. Ramsay, the head of the Washington Armory. A new law enabled the president to retire officers who had served for forty-five years or more. On September 15, 1863, Brig.

Gen. James W. Ripley retired after more than forty-nine years of active service.

Affable and eager to please his friend Lincoln, Ramsay lacked his predecessor's domineering manner and bias against new weapons. But he did not have the energy and interest in new arms needed to undertake a large-scale program to equip the Union armies with the most powerful weapons that were available.[59]

General Ripley's record as chief of ordnance is a mixed one. He was obsessed with preserving his hold upon the direction of the Union armament program, and he was a virtual archetype of the administrator whose concern for the details of routine rendered him little more than a glorified clerk. However, under his direction the Ordnance Department did register some notable achievements. The burgeoning Union armies were adequately equipped and armed; if the quality of the arms and equipment issued was initially uneven, it soon reached a uniformly good or even excellent standard.[60] Ripley made a concerted effort to insure the adoption of standard armament for the field forces, and he insisted that all weapons, particularly small arms, be made with interchangeable parts. These measures simplified supply and repair problems, and the requirement for interchangeable parts helped to spur the development of the techniques of mass production by American industry. While he was in office, the Bureau of Ordnance took its first steps toward logistical planning by developing realistic replacement factors for hand weapons it supplied to Union troops.[61] Finally, even General Ripley's severest critics must concede that he made a concerted effort to insure that the transactions made or supervised by his department conformed to the provisions of regulations and that they were conducted in an honest manner.[62]

Unyielding in his opposition to new weapons, Ripley retarded the improvement of the weaponry available to the Union soldier, and he thereby lost a major opportunity to advance the cause of the Union. The dour chief of ordnance was the product of a system wherein promotion to high rank was a function of surviving both the perils of life and of a rigidly enforced system of administrative routine; Ripley was trained by all of his experience to resist change—the one factor that could upset his well-ordered universe. Sixty-six years old when he took office as chief of ordnance, the general had lost both the ability and desire to adapt a change whether in the form of new ideas or new weapons. Ripley was the end product of a military system that had not been seriously challenged for almost half a century, and his attitude toward new weapons was as out-of-date as the smooth-bore muskets that filled the nation's arsenals in 1861.

NOTES

1. J.F.C. Fuller, *Armament and History* (London, 1944), pp. 118-19; Carl L. Davis, *Arming the Union, Small Arms in the Civil War* (Port Washington, N.Y., 1973), pp. ix-x. By the end of the war Union cavalry regiments were equipped with breechloaders, but the infantry remained armed mainly with muzzleloaders.

2. In 1896 Maj. Clarence E. Dutton, Ordnance Corps, observed that "The metallic cartridge . . . is the greatest military invention since the discovery of gunpowder. It is, however, an evolution rather than an invention, embodying a slow accretion of the ideas of many workers and inventors." Theodore F. Rodenbaugh and William L. Haskin, eds., *The Army of the United States* (New York, 1896), p. 134; Bernard and Fawn Brodie, *From Crossbow to H-Bomb* (Bloomington, Ind., 1973), pp. 130-34.

3. Joseph W. Shields, *From Flintlock to M1* (New York, 1954), pp. 69-80; Jack Coggins, *Arms and Equipment of the Civil War* (Garden City, N.Y., 1962), pp. 26-33; Theodore Ropp, *War in the Modern World* (New York, 1962), pp. 180-84.

4. Donald B. Webster, Jr., "Rodman's Great Guns," *Civil War Ordnance—II* (Washington, D.C., 1965), pp. 13-14; Albert Manucy, *Artillery Through the Ages* (Washington, D.C., 1949), pp. 17-21, 60-61; Coggins, *Arms*, pp. 61, 64, 76, 85-86, 96.

5. See Richard N. Current, "God and the Strongest Battalions," in *Why the North Won the Civil War*, ed. David Donald (New York, 1960), p. 15.

6. Manuscript by Jay Luvaas entitled "Civil War Tactics—The Dream." Copy in possession of the author.

7. Coggins, *Arms*, pp. 28, 34-35, 54, 58.

8. U.S., War Department, *The War of The Rebellion: A Compilation of The Official Records of the Union and Confederate Armies* (Washington, D.C.), ser. 3, vol. IV, p. 803 (hereafter cited as *OR*).

9. Ripley to Cameron, June 24, 1861, *OR*, ser. 3, vol. I, p. 292.

10. Gorgas was practically forced into Confederate service by the vindictive action of the Union chief of ordnance, Col. Henry K. Craig. Craig

ordered Gorgas posted from an assignment with the Ordnance Board to much more onerous foundry duty. Gorgas' brilliant career as the Confederate chief of ordnance underlines the magnitude of the error. Frank E. Vandiver, *Ploughshares Into Swords* (Austin, Tex., 1952), pp. 52-53.

11. A. B. Dyer to E. M. Stanton, October 20, 1865, *OR*, ser. 3, vol. V, p. 144; *OR*, ser. 3, vol. I, p. 22 and Ripley to Cameron, June 24, 1861, p. 292; Rodenbaugh and Haskin, *Army*, p. 132; Emory Upton, *The Military Policy of the United States* (Washington, D.C., 1904), p. 262. For a detailed discussion of Ordnance Department personnel problems, see Davis, *Arming*, chap. 1.

12. James A. Huston, *The Sinews of War: Army Logistics 1775-1953* (Washington, D.C., 1966), pp. 168-69; *OR*, ser. 3, vol. I, p. 48; U.S., Ordnance Department, *Regulations for the Government of the Ordnance Department* (Washington, D.C., 1852), pp. 3-4 (hereafter cited as *Regulations*).

13. Huston, *Sinews*, p. 171; Russell F. Weigley, *Quartermaster General of the Union Army* (New York, 1959), pp. 165-66, 204-5.

14. Huston, *Sinews*, p. 171; Davis, *Arming*, pp. 8-9.

15. A. Howard Meneely, *The War Department, 1861: A Study in Mobilization and Administration* (New York, 1928), pp. 109, 113.

16. Dumas Malone, ed., *Dictionary of American Biography*, vol. XV, (New York, 1935), p. 625 (hereafter cited as *DAB*); Robert V. Bruce, *Lincoln and the Tools of War* (New York, 1956), pp. 23-30.

17. Claud E. Fuller, comp., *Springfield Muzzle-Loading Shoulder Arms* (New York, 1930), p. 100.

18. *Regulations* (1852), pp. 3, 15.

19. Ibid., pp. 34-37.

20. In peacetime requisitions for ordnance items passed through command channels to the General-in-Chief of the Army for his review and approval. The secretary of war sent copies of all requisitions to the chief of ordnance who was to ". . . modify and regulate them in such manner as to curtail all extravagancies, to suit them to the exigencies of the service, to existing appropriations, and to just and proper views of economy; and in the performance of this part of his duty, he shall invariably communicate with the General-in-Chief of the Army." Ibid., p. 17. The procedure for processing requisitions is specified in paragraph 67 of *Regulations*. Ibid., p. 16.

21. Weigley, *Quartermaster*, p. 218.

22. Ibid., p. 204; Fred Albert Shannon, *The Organization and Administration of the Union Army, 1861-1865* (Gloucester, Mass., 1965), vol. I, pp. 110-13.

23. Ibid., pp. 113-14; Bruce, *Lincoln*, p. 32; *Regulations* (1852), p. 135.

24. Davis, Arming, pp. 60-64. Davis states that 80 percent of these foreign weapons were ". . . accurate, dependable and of good quality."

25. Shannon, *Organization*, vol. I, pp. 58-60; Huston, *Sinews*, pp. 178-82, 185-86.

26. In 1841 the Ordnance Board, a panel of ordnance officers charged with advising the secretary of war on subjects related to the Ordnance Department, was established. Its principal task was to standardize and modernize the armament of the field, siege, and coastal artillery. With this work completed in 1849 the active role of the board diminished although its function was included in the edition of ordnance regulations published in 1852. Personnel shortages were probably the fundamental reason for the lack of Ordnance Board activity during the Civil War. *Regulations* (1852), pp. 3-4; Rodenbaugh and Haskin, *Army*, p. 129.

27. *Regulations* (1852), pp. 3-4; Bruce, *Lincoln*, pp. 70-71.

28. Ripley to Secretary of War, subject: Notes on subject of contracting for small arms, June 11, 1861, *OR*, ser. 3, vol. I, pp. 264-65.

29. Huston, *Sinews*, p. 189.

30. Lincoln to Stanton, January 24, 1862, Abraham Lincoln, *The Collected Works of Abraham Lincoln*, ed. Roy Basler, vol. V (New Brunswick, N.J., 1955), p. 110; U.S. War Department *Proceedings of a Court of Inquiry . . . to Examine into the Accusations against Brig. and Bvt. Major General A. B. Dyer, Chief of Ordnance*, vol. I (Washington, D.C., 1869), p. 193. (hereafter cited as *Dyer Court*).

31. George M. Chinn, *The Machine Gun* (Washington, D.C., 1951), p. 37; Bruce, *Lincoln*, pp. 118-19.

32. Bruce, *Lincoln*, p. 119; Chinn, *Machine Gun*, pp. 37-39.

33. Bruce, *Lincoln*, p. 120.

34. Ibid., pp. 120-21.

35. National Archives, Record Group (hereafter cited as NA, RG) 156, "Statements of Purchases of Ordnance 1861-67," p. 5.

36. U.S., Congress, House, *Executive Document 99*, 40th Cong., 2d sess., 1868, pp. 736, 996; NA, RG 156, "Register of Letters Received Relating to Inventions 1812-70," p. 94; Bruce, *Lincoln*, pp. 122-23; Chinn, *Machine Gun*, pp. 39-40.

37. Bruce, *Lincoln*, pp. 194-95.

38. British officers visiting McClellan's army during the Peninsular campaign saw fifty Ager guns mounted on horse-drawn carriages. According to their report the workmanship of the guns was defective; the observers rated the weapons as unsatisfactory. Allan Nevins, *The War for the Union*, vol.

1, *The Improvised War, 1861-1862* (New York, 1959), pp. 365-66.

39. Fremont to Ripley, April 28, 1862, with report to Fremont, April 25, 1862, attached, NA, RG 156, "Reports of Experiments 1826-71," vol. 98, entry 49.

40. Ibid.

41. U.S., War Department, *Official Army Register of the Volunteer Force of the United States Army for the Years 1861, '62, '63, '64, '65* (Washington, D.C., 1865), pt. II, pp. 382, 510.

42. Fremont to Ripley, April 28, 1862, with attached report cited previously.

43. Ibid.

44. Ibid.

45. Bruce, *Lincoln*, p. 196.

46. Ibid., pp. 196-97. Union repeating guns also were used during the initial phase of McClellan's Peninsular campaign by a New York infantry regiment. They were later tried by Pennsylvania and New York regiments. Opinion of their performance was mixed, and the chief of ordnance for the Army of the Potomac described the guns as of "inferior workmanship." Ibid., pp. 197-200.

48. Reports of various officers on merits of Union repeating gun, June 6, 1863, NA, RG 156, "Reports of Experiments 1826-71," vol. 98, entry 55.

49. Bruce, *Lincoln*, pp. 250-52.

50. Ibid., p. 283.

51. Chinn, *Machine Gun*, pp. 38-39.

52. NA, RG 156, "Reports of Experiments 1826-71," vol. 98, entry 50; Bruce, *Lincoln*, pp. 208-9. Dahlgren's opinion of the gun is not recorded.

53. Lincoln to Stanton, August 9, 1862, Lincoln, *Works*, vol. V, p. 365.

54. NA, RG 156, "Reports of Experiments 1826-71," vol. 98, entry 50.

55. Ripley to Secretary of War, September 16, 1862, NA, RG 156, "Letters, Endorsements, and Reports Sent to the Secretary of War 1812-89," vol. 13, p. 490.

56. Proceedings of a Board of Officers Convened at Head Quarters, Light Division, April 4, 1863, NA, RG 156, "Reports of Experiments 1826-71," vol. 98, entry 54.

57. Report on the Raphael Repeating Gun to the Secretary of War, April 22, 1863, NA, RG 156 "Letters, Endorsements, and Reports Sent to the Secretary of War 1812-89," vol. 14, pp. 187-88.

58. *Dyer Court*, vol. I, p. 193; Bruce, *Lincoln*, pp. 162-68.

59. Bruce, *Lincoln*, pp. 260-65; Malone, *DAB*, vol. XV, p. 625; F. W. Foster-Gleason, "Two Chiefs of Ordnance," *Civil War Ordnance—II* (Washington, D.C., 1965), p. 26.

60. Bruce, *Lincoln*, p. 34.

61. Felicia J. Deyrup, *Arms Makers of the Connecticut Valley*, Smith College Studies in History, vol. XXXIII, ed. Vera B. Holmes and Hans Kohn (Northampton, Mass., 1948), pp. 193-96; Huston, *Sinews*, pp. 172, 189.

62. Shannon, *Organization*, vol. I, p. 60; Malone, *DAB*, vol. XV, p. 625.

II

A BOLD STEP FORWARD, 1863-1866

During the early years of the Civil War, while Gen. James W. Ripley blocked all attempts to secure adoption of a machine gun by the Union forces, a Southern-born doctor, Richard J. Gatling, developed the first models of the machine gun that would eventually be adopted by the United States Army. Comparison of the records of tests of other prototype machine guns with those of trials of the Gatling gun illustrates the superiority of Gatling's design. These records also demonstrate that in 1864 and 1865 Ordnance Department tests of prototype machine guns were conducted in a fair and painstaking manner but that the weapons were often so flawed in design and construction that they had very little military value.

The initial model of Gatling's gun, patented in 1862, had six barrels, which were rotated around a central axis by the action of a hand crank. The lack of commercially available metallic cartridges forced Gatling to design his gun to use steel casings similar to those used in the Union repeating gun. Charged with a paper cartridge, primed with a percussion cap on a nipple on the rear and then loaded into a drum on top of the gun, the casings were gravity-fed into position behind the gun barrels. As the barrel assembly rotated, the loaded casings were cammed forward against the barrels, fired, and then ejected into a hopper where they were held for reloading.

Presumably inspired at least in part by the design of Samuel Colt's revolver, the Gatling leaked gas at the point where the steel casing joined the rear of the gun barrel. This flaw would be corrected by the development of the self-contained metallic cartridge, which fitted into the rear of the gun barrel and sealed the breech on firing.[1] Multibarrel design and heavy construction required by the state of metallurgy in the 1860s made the Gatling gun, like other early machine guns, too heavy to be carried by hand. Mounted on a carriage similar to that used by light artillery pieces, Gatling guns closely resembled conventional artillery.

Patent model of 1862 Gatling gun. *Courtesy*: Smithsonian Institution.

Surviving Ordnance Department records indicate that Gatling first tried to sell his invention to the federal government in late 1862. His letter was returned by Ripley's office with the remark that since the Ordnance Department had no direct knowledge of the weapon, it was unable to express an opinion concerning its usefulness to the federal service.[2] Ripley used the fact that the weapon had not been tested by the military to deny the weapon the very test it lacked. After this brush with the Ordnance Bureau, Gatling turned to the chief executive of Indiana for help. Governor Oliver Hazard Perry Morton had been an organizer of the Indiana Republican party and was a strong supporter of Abraham Lincoln. Consequently he could claim influence in the War Department, but his earlier contacts with General Ripley had been almost uniformly antagonistic, so Governor Morton's influence did not open Ordnance Department channels to Gatling's invention.[3] Facing War Department apathy, Gatling suffered disaster at home when fire completely destroyed his manufacturing facility, the Eagle Iron Works, and all of the copies of the 1862 version of his invention.[4] Undeterred, the physician-turned-inventor spent the early months of 1863 locating both a new factory and new financial backing for his device. The Cincinnati Type Foundry and the firm of McWhinney, Rindge and Company provided the manufacturing facilities and operating capital he sought. As he had yet to secure a government contract, Gatling's success in securing new financial backing was an important factor in the continued development of his invention.

Having dealt with his money and manufacturing problems, Gatling used the spring of 1863 to demonstrate the capabilities of his invention. Several trips to Washington, together with additional correspondence, represented a renewed assault upon an indifferent War Department.[5] Rebuffed in Washington, Gatling at length persuaded Maj. Gen. Horatio C. Wright, commanding general of the Department of Ohio, to inspect the new weapon. Wright was impressed by the Gatling gun, and the letter he sent the Ordnance Office contained a favorable but cautious description of the gun and its merits. His letter was ignored.[6] Frustrated, Gatling decided to deal directly with field commanders in an effort to market his device.

Captivated by the possibilities presented by new weapons, although unable to exploit their potential, Maj. Gen. Benjamin F. Butler agreed to purchase twelve Gatlings and twelve thousand rounds of ammunition. Ordered in mid-summer 1863, at a cost of $12,000, the guns were delivered to Butler's Army of the James and used briefly in May 1864. Butler's order plus the purchase of a few Gatlings for use on naval vessels gave Gatling some business but did nothing to ignite interest in the weapon within the War Department.[7]

Perhaps because he did not really understand the workings of the Washington bureaucracy, Gatling had limited his attempts to gain official attention for his weapon to applications to various branches of the military. When in early 1864 the inventor finally asked President Lincoln to consider his weapon, he was perhaps a year too

A Bold Step Forward

late. Conscious of the increasing strength of the Union military position, concerned with the problems of the upcoming presidential election, and affected by repeated collisions with the adamantine Ripley, Lincoln had lost interest in new weapons. He gave Gatling no help.[8]

Despite his lack of commercial success, Gatling continued to improve the design of his machine gun. A new model produced in 1865 used a copper .58 caliber rimfire cartridge, a major advance in ammunition design. This version was a vast improvement over the gun patented in November 1862.[9] Gatling's work was rewarded when the new chief of ordnance, Brig. Gen. Alexander B. Dyer, agreed to give the Gatling gun an official test.

Brig. Gen. Alexander B. Dyer, chief of ordnance, 1864-1874. *Courtesy*: U.S. Military Academy Archives.

During his service at the Springfield Arsenal Dyer had become familiar with the new developments in small arms. In December 1864 he wrote to Secretary Stanton that the ". . . experience of the war has shown that breech-loading arms are greatly superior to muzzle loaders for infantry as well as for cavalry, and that measures should immediately be taken to substitute a suitable breech-loading musket in place of the rifle musket. . . ."[10] The new ordnance chief was also aware of the need for improvements in the methods of testing new weapons and the necessity ". . . for improving munitions of war if we are to keep pace in these with other nations. . . ."[11] He specifically asked for a ". . . suitable ground for the proof and experimental firing of ordnance and small arms."[12]

While they demonstrated his appreciation of the importance of recent developments in technology, General Dyer's support of the breech-loading rifle and his request for an adequate proving ground meant little unless the funds needed to implement his ideas were available. At the end of the Civil War, Congress rapidly reduced appropriations, and the proving ground was not purchased. Despite the fact that several multishot breechloaders were commercially available, congressional concern for economy forced the army to use a single-shot breechloader made by altering the muzzle-loading rifles that jammed the arsenals and armories in 1865.[13] In the post-Civil War era money—or more precisely the lack of it—would determine the pace of progress in arming the American army.

In January 1865 a greatly improved Gatling gun was put through a series of tests at the Washington Arsenal. According to the description by Lieut. Isaac W. Maclay, the ordnance officer in charge of the tests, the four-barrel, .58 caliber gun weighed 224 pounds, its carriage 202 pounds, and the limber an additional 200 pounds. Maclay fired the contents of a twenty-round tin feed case at a 10-foot by 10-foot target at ranges of 100, 300, and 500 yards. The results were impressive: At the shorter distances all twenty rounds hit the target, while at 500 yards nineteen rounds struck the target. Additional trials included a rapid-fire exercise during which twenty shots were fired in only eight seconds. A total of three hundred cartridges were fired during the entire test, and Maclay noted that the only mishap occurred on the 220th shot when the number two barrel burst.

A Bold Step Forward

Gatling gun, model 1865. *Courtesy*: Smithsonian Institution.

At the end of the strictly factual portion of his report Lieutenant Maclay enumerated what he perceived as faults in the construction of the gun. He believed that the rifling of the Gatling was too shallow and had too rapid a twist; that while the weight of the gun carriage could be reduced, the gun frame and trunnions needed reinforcement; and that despite the Gatling's accurate performance its rear sight was not made for the gun. None of these comments pointed to a major defect in the pattern or construction of the gun; Gatling's efforts in refining the design of his invention had begun to pay dividends. On the positive side Maclay noted that the Gatling could fire rapidly and accurately, that it could be loaded while firing thus permitting continuous firing, and that the 1865 version of the Gatling gun did not leak gas at the breech.[14] By itself the report could not justify government procurement of the Gatling gun; together with General Dyer's interest in new weapons, however, the results of the tests did insure that Gatling's invention would receive further official consideration.

Within a month of Maclay's test an official party that included Brigadier General Dyer and the famous ex-commander of the Second Corps, Maj. Gen. Winfield Scott Hancock, witnessed a demonstration of the new machine gun. Although he still suffered from the effects of the wound that he had received at Gettysburg, Hancock had been given the task of forming the First Army Corps of Veteran Volunteers. This unit was to be made up of veterans who had served at least two years and who had been persuaded to reenlist by the combination of Hancock's reputation and substantial financial rewards.[15] Impressed by the capabilities of the Gatling gun, Hancock sent Dyer a written request that twelve Gatlings be purchased for his new corps.[16] Dyer endorsed the request and in addition asked the secretary of war to authorize the purchase of ". . . two experimental Battery Guns [Gatlings] of one inch calibre for flank defense."[17] Besides representing a dramatic change from Ripley's attitude of positively refusing to consider the purchase of novel weapons, the ordnance chief's endorsement gave the first indication of a new role for the Gatling—as part of the secondary armament of coastal fortifications. "Flank defense" referred to the close defense of American coastal forts from attacks by foot troops.[18]

Secretary Stanton asked if there were not enough Gatlings in the Department of Virginia and with the Army of the James to fill Hancock's requisition.[19] To answer Stanton's question, General Dyer directed Lieutenant Maclay to conduct a second series of tests using a Gatling taken from the arms store at Fortress Monroe, Virginia. Maclay tested the gun and in early March 1865 forwarded a brief report to the Ordnance Office. The report was limited to a description of the gun and its operation and noted that this version of the gun used small steel chambers rather than the copper cartridges and that a considerable amount of gas escaped from the breech of this earlier model during firing.[20] His report ended War Department interest in the earlier version of the Gatling gun.

In the spring of 1865 the Civil War was rapidly drawing to a close, and only nine of the infantry regiments of the projected First Army Corps of Veteran Volunteers were formed. Consequently the Gatling gun unit that General Hancock had envisioned never took

A Bold Step Forward

Billinghurst and Requa battery gun, cal. .50. *Courtesy*: George M. Chinn, *The Machine Gun* (Washington, D.C.: GPO, 1951).

shape, and the weapon seemed to be headed for the oblivion that had claimed its predecessors.[21] However, several factors in the equation for success had changed. The chief of ordnance was personally interested in the weapon, and he had defined a role for machine guns in the secondary armament of coastal fortifications, a mission that was one of the principal peacetime duties of the land forces.

During the Civil War the War Department was offered at least nine devices that might reasonably be classified as machine guns.[22] Two of the multibarrel guns, the Billinghurst and Requa rifle battery and the Vandenburgh volley gun, are worthy of special note. Built in late 1861 by the Billinghurst Company of Rochester, New York, the first model of the rifle battery had twenty-five barrels mounted side by side on a metal platform, which in turn was fixed to the axle of a light, two-wheeled carriage. Initially the gun used light steel casings, which were loaded with loose powder and a bullet and then inserted in a steel clip. The loaded clip was placed behind the row of barrels and then levered forward so that the steel cartridges entered the barrels of the gun. The rifle battery was fired by a single percussion cap which ignited a powder train running to a hole in the base of each cartridge.

Although it was crude when compared to the Gatling or Ager guns, the gun could attain a rate of fire of 100 to 175 rounds per minute. Since the gun used a heavy powder charge, its shots carried to a distance of 1,200 to 1,300 yards. However, multibarrel construction meant that the gun and its carriage weighed 1,382 pounds and required a two-horse team. While the mechanism of the gun was simple, use of a powder train prevented firing the gun in damp or rainy weather.[23]

First brought to the attention of the Ordnance Department in January 1863, the Billinghurst and Requa gun had already received substantial publicity and favorable endorsements from Lieut. W. Mitchell, USN, Col. Richard Delafield, Corps of Engineers, and Governor Edwin D. Morgan of New York. Maj. Gen. Benjamin Butler and his successor in New Orleans, Maj. Gen. Nathaniel Banks, were persuaded to order some of the new guns; but Banks' guns never arrived, and Butler's forces apparently did not use the two that they received. The Billinghurst Company's claim to Butler for $2,532 to pay for the guns was disallowed because the purchase of the weapons had not been made in accordance with established Ordnance Department procedures.[24] Nonpayment was a hazard that salesmen of early machine guns faced in their attempts to secure the financial rewards that often came with a government contract.

Public demonstrations of the new gun and other efforts to advertise its capabilities also reached more experienced soldiers. Brig. Gen. William F. Barry, the inspector of artillery, witnessed a demonstration in 1863, but unlike the two political generals he was not greatly impressed. Barry denied that the Billinghurst gun could be used as an artillery piece but conceded that it might be "extremely serviceable" in a defensive role, particularly when emplaced in field works or fortifications.[25] Barry had in fact placed the gun in the role that was a principal use of artillery during the Civil War. However, the capabilities of the Billinghurst gun could not compare with the versatility of standard field artillery weapons such as the model 1857 Napoleon gun-howitzer.[26]

A Bold Step Forward

After repeated applications the Billinghurst and Requa rifle battery was finally granted an official test in August 1864. Carried out at Washington Arsenal by Lieut. Howard Stockton, the test was confined to a trial for accuracy against a 7-foot by 25-foot target at a distance of 640 yards. The results were bleak, for of the three hundred shots fired only twenty-six hit the target. The test report, which contained a description of the gun and its equipment as well as an account of the trials and their results, concluded with a bland comment about the simplicity and reliability of the mechanism of the gun. By revealing the inaccuracy of the gun, the trials accomplished their purpose; further Ordnance Department attention was unnecessary.[27]

The Vandenburgh volley gun, invented by Oliver Vandenburgh, a general in the New York State Militia, was first offered to the British government, which ignored it. Vandenburgh then turned to the United States government as a potential customer. After four months of negotiation the Ordnance Department agreed to test three models of Vandenburgh's "new kind of artillery," on the condition that the inventor bear the considerable cost of shipping

Vandenburgh volley gun, cal. .50, with eighty-five barrels. *Courtesy*: George M. Chinn, *The Machine Gun* (Washington, D.C.: GPO, 1951).

the weapons from England to the United States. Tests were conducted in April and again in August 1864 with uniformly poor results. The three versions of the Vandenburgh gun submitted to the War Department had 85, 121, and 151 barrels and weighed 500, 730, and 930 pounds respectively. Loading was accomplished by inserting powder and bullets into individual chambers located in the weapon's massive breech. The breech was then screwed into the rear of the gun so that each chamber was aligned with a barrel. Ignition of a central powder charge in the breech produced jets of flame, which in turn fired charges in the individual chambers.[28] The test supervisor, Capt. James G. Benton, reported that the largest gun had a maximum range of 1,200 to 1,300 yards; when fired at a 7-foot by 24-foot target at a distance of 660 yards, however, only 18 of the 1,057 test shots struck the target. Benton contrasted this poor showing with the record of a 12-pounder, gun-howitzer, which fired three shells at the same range and scored fifty-six hits on the target. Equally damaging was the comment that it took a single workman nine hours to clean the Vandenburgh gun properly. Since the gun carriage had broken during firing, Benton concluded that this machine gun was of such "delicate and complicated construction" that it would not stand the strain of continuous firing. Based on the finding that the Vandenburgh volley gun was hopelessly inaccurate, that it required excessive time to clean, and that it was too delicate to stand the rigors of combat, Captain Benton recommended against its adoption.[29] At the conclusion of the August series of tests, the test supervisor termed the volley gun "a very worthless weapon."[30]

Ordnance Department experiments with the Billinghurst and Requa and Vandenburgh machine guns illustrate the change that Ripley's dismissal had made in the official attitude toward newly developed arms. Persistence in their contacts with the technical branch of the War Department now made it possible for inventors to obtain consideration for their creations even when these devices turned out to be as militarily worthless as these two guns proved to be. Ripley's retirement was undoubtedly the major factor in unclogging the system for test and evaluation of new weapons, but another factor was that by 1864 the recently expanded Ordnance Department had adjusted to the demands of the war and could afford to detail at

A Bold Step Forward

least junior officers to test new weapons.³¹ Wartime experience and the superior performance of breech-loading rifles and the various new types of cannon that were being produced no doubt served to stimulate Ordnance Department interest in new weapons.

The history of the Vandenburgh, Billinghurst, and Requa machine guns illuminates a very real defect in the army system for evaluating proposals for new weapons: There was no provision for a preliminary screening of these proposals. The proposal was either rejected when it reached the office of the chief of ordnance or the device was subjected to a full-scale test and evaluation. There was no intermediate stage in the process that would allow technical experts to examine the weapon for obvious defects sufficient to justify its rejection without full-scale tests. Thus considerable effort was wasted in testing such weapons as the Vandenburgh, and Billinghurst and Requa guns; the propensity for fouling of the former and the vulnerability of the latter to damp weather were defects that could have been easily detected by an experienced ordnance officer. The poor performance of the two guns also indicates the low level of competition that the Gatling gun faced in 1864 and 1865. It is quite obvious today and must have been obvious to the Ordnance Department in 1865 that the design of the Gatling gun was far in advance of all other machine guns.

Late in April 1865 the heads of the War Department staff bureaus received an order to cut expenditures to the lowest possible level ". . . in view of an immediate reduction of forces in the field and garrison and the speedy termination of hostilities. . . ."³² The chief of ordnance was directed to end procurement of weapons and ammunition as quickly as possible. The level of Ordnance Department spending dropped rapidly; amounting to $43,112,531 in 1865, expenditures sank to $16,551,677 a year later and by 1870 declined to $2,442,345.³³ Although they faced the certain prospect of a continued decline in the amount of money available for the purchase of new weapons, ordnance officials decided to continue to test the Gatling gun.

Following the successful trials of Gatling's weapon in early 1865, General Dyer suggested that the inventor develop a gun with a 1-inch bore. Dyer also ordered Capt. Stephen Vincent Benet, the officer who would eventually replace him as chief of ordnance, to develop a buckshot cartridge for a 1-inch Gatling gun. Early in 1866 a prototype 1-inch smooth-bore Gatling was delivered to the Frankford Arsenal for testing with the buckshot cartridge.[34] The Frankford trials had mixed results. The Gatling-buckshot combination produced an awesome, seemingly continuous stream of projectiles at point-blank range. But when the 35-foot by 15-foot target was removed to a distance of 200 yards, only 33 percent of the buckshot hit the target and of these approximately one-quarter failed to penetrate its 1-inch boards. Increasing the range by an additional 50 yards halved the number of hits and raised the amount of shot hitting but failing to penetrate the target to 50 percent. These tests demonstrated that the performance of Benet's buckshot cartridge and the smooth-bore Gatling did not equal that of 12-pounder canister ammunition, a round that artillery officers considered effective to an extreme range of 350 yards.[35]

General Dyer's idea for a buckshot cartridge was an ingenious attempt to use an artillery concept, canister ammunition, in an early version of a radically different type of weapon. The specific cause of the poor performance of the buckshot cartridge was that the relatively small bore of the Gatling gun restricted the size of the shot that could be used. This meant that the individual pellets lacked the mass necessary to give them the desired range and penetration. The attempt to increase Gatling firepower by using an artillery approach, a bigger bore gun and a canister round, took a direction opposite from the solution eventually adopted—that of using rifle ammunition and increasing the rate of fire of the machine gun. Since early machine guns resembled artillery weapons in many respects, the tendency to attempt to use artillery concepts with these new arms was natural.

The next series of tests, conducted under the direction of Capt. Thomas G. Baylor, Ordnance Corps, at the Washington Arsenal in June and July 1866, took the form of a direct competition between a rifled, 1-inch Gatling and a smooth-bore, 24-pounder howitzer used for the flank defense of fortifications. Exceptionally thorough in concept and execution, the competition demonstrated that the Ordnance Department was seriously interested in the military potential of Gatling's machine gun.[36]

A Bold Step Forward   45

Although the results of the previous tests of the buckshot cartridge had not been encouraging, Baylor used the round in a one and one-half minute timed-fire exercise. He calculated that the Gatling discharged between twelve hundred and sixteen hundred projectiles, whereas the four rounds that the howitzer could fire in the same period produced 192 individual shot when canister ammunition was used and about seven hundred projectiles if shrapnel shells were fired. Having compared the volume of projectiles that the two weapons could produce, Baylor moved to the usual series of test firings over distances that varied from 100 to 1,200 yards. The Gatling was fired at 48-foot by 6-foot target using buckshot at ranges up to 200 yards and solid bullets at more distant targets; it scored over 60 percent hits at 100 yards and 25 percent hits at 1,200 yards. More accurate than the Gatling at close range, the performance of the howitzer—which had switched to shrapnel ammunition—became less impressive as the range increased. Partially the result of the unreliable fuses used with shrapnel ammunition, the diminishing accuracy of the howitzer underscored the advantage of the Gatling at longer ranges. The overall performance of the Gatling not only surpassed that of the flank-defense howitzer, but the versatility and reliability of the machine gun at all ranges clearly demonstrated its superiority for use in defending permanent works or field fortifications against infantry attacks.

Concerned with evaluating the durability as well as the performance of the Gatling, Captain Baylor subjected the gun to a simple test of its ability to withstand careless treatment. The test model of the gun was wiped free of all oil, thoroughly wetted and then exposed to the weather for two and a half days; it was then taken directly to the range. Loaded, aimed, and cranked by a single soldier, the gun fired at a rate of slightly more than a round per second for a ninety-second period. This performance pleased Benton, and he concluded that the Gatling's machinery ". . . is simple and strong and . . . not . . . likely to get out of order."[37] Mechanical reliability and durability, always a central concern of the Ordnance Department, was especially important in a test that pitted the complex Gatling against the simple and durable muzzle-loading howitzer.

In his report Captain Baylor echoed earlier assessments of the power of the machine gun as a defensive weapon and expressed his opinion that the ". . . moral effect of the 'Gatling' Gun would be very great in repelling an assault as there is not a second of time between each discharge, leaving no time for the assailants to advance between the discharges."[38] Baylor had identified the continuous nature of machine-gun firepower—a key difference between the capabilities of this new weapon and those of the conventional artillery and infantry arms of the period. The results of the tests and Captain Baylor's evaluation proved to be the final link in the chain of evidence that convinced General Dyer that the Gatling was worth buying.

On August 24, 1866, the conservative, cost-conscious Ordnance Department contracted for fifty 1-inch and fifty .50 caliber model 1866 Gatling guns. The 1-inch guns cost $2,000 apiece and the .50 caliber version was priced at $1,500 a copy. Certainly Baylor's tests had justified purchase of some Gatlings on an experimental basis, but the procurement of a hundred guns—particularly when federal arsenals were filled with more conventional artillery pieces—was a bold move. No major European power had evinced more than a passing interest in machine guns; yet, General Dyer had committed his bureau to a contract that would eventually cost the government $162,485.[39]

There are several possible reasons for the size of the Gatling contract. Captain Baylor's tests had demonstrated that the model 1866 Gatling gun was an excellent antipersonnel weapon. In fact the design of the weapon was so good that no machine gun would equal, let alone surpass, its performance until Hiram Maxim patented the first truly automatic machine gun in 1884. Viewed in terms of weapons design, the Ordnance Department contract appears justified.

An extremely large order may have been required to persuade a manufacturer to tool up to produce the Gatling gun. Shortly after the hundred-gun contract had been signed, production of the Gatling was transferred from the Cooper Fire Arms Manufacturing Company of Philadelphia to the Colt Armory in Hartford, Connecticut. With this move the Gatling gun and its inventor secured the backing of a large, established arms maker with ample manufacturing capacity and considerable influence in government circles; at the same time the War Department obtained additional assurance that the terms of its contract would be fulfilled. The Colt Company gained the immediate financial boost of a large government contract at a time when surplus weapons were flooding the domestic arms market, and it assumed control of the best model of a promising new type of weapon. Able to point to a sizable contract with the American army, salesmen began to make small but significant sales of the gun abroad.[40]

In April 1865 Secretary Stanton had ordered General Dyer to ". . . stop all purchases of arms. . . ." Sixteen months later the drastic and continuing decline in the amount of money available for the purchase of arms may have forced ordnance officials to make a large purchase of a promising new weapon, the Gatling gun, while they still had the money. At the same time experience with the extremely high level of expenditures of the Civil War may have loosened some of the normal peacetime reluctance of ordnance officials to spend large amounts of money on new weapons.

NOTES

1. Paul Wahl and Donald R. Toppel, *The Gatling Gun* (New York, 1971), pp. 13-17; W.H.B. Smith, *Small Arms of the World*, 8th ed. (Harrisburg, Pa., 1966), pp. 100-102.

2. National Archives, Record Group (hereafter cited as NA, RG) 156, "Letters, Endorsements, Reports Sent to the Secretary of War 1812-89," vol. 14, p. 31.

3. Wahl and Toppel, *Gatling*, p. 18.

4. Ibid.

5. NA, RG 156, "Register of Letters Received Relating to Inventions 1812-70," entry 312, p. 97.

6. Wahl and Toppel, *Gatling*, p. 19.

7. NA, RG 156, "Letters, Endorsements, and Reports Sent to the Secretary of War 1812-89," vol. 15, p. 163; McWhinney, Rindge and Co., July 2, 1863, NA, RG 156, "Registers of Applications for Orders from Manufacturers and Suppliers of Ordnance and Ordnance Stores 1862-76," vol. 1, p. 3; Wahl and Toppel, *Gatling*, pp. 19-20, 24-25.

8. Wahl and Toppel, *Gatling*, p. 22; Robert V. Bruce, *Lincoln and the Tools of War* (New York, 1956), p. 290. Several writers have cited

Gatling's identification as a Confederate sympathizer as a possible reason for official indifference to his weapon. The *Official Records* contain two references to Gatling that identify him as a member of the Order of American Knights, an organization of Confederate sympathizers. Since neither of the letters appears to have gone farther than the District of Indiana in the Northern Department, there is reason to doubt that officials in Washington knew of Gatling's alleged Southern sympathies. Wahl and Toppel, *Gatling*, pp. 22-24; George M. Chinn, *The Machine Gun* (Washington, D.C., 1951), pp. 50-51; U.S. War Department, *The War of Rebellion: A Compilation of the Official Records of the Union and Confederate Armies*, ser. 2, vol. VII, pp. 298, 342 (hereafter cited as *OR*).

9. Chinn, *Machine Gun*, p. 51.
10. Dyer to Stanton, December 5, 1864, *OR*, ser. 3, vol. IV, pp. 971-72.
11. Dyer to Stanton, October 22, 1864, *OR*, ser. 3, vol. IV, p. 803.
12. Ibid.
13. Dyer to Stanton, October 20, 1865, *OR*, ser. 3, vol. V, pp. 142-43; Russell F. Weigley, *History of the United States Army* (New York, 1967), p. 238; Fred Albert Shannon, *The Organization and Administration of the Union Army, 1861-1865* (Gloucester, Mass., 1965), vol. I, p. 142. There were a million Springfield rifle-muskets and a half-million foreign or captured guns in storage in arsenals and depots at the end of the war.
14. NA, RG 156, "Reports of Experiments 1826-71," vol. 98, entry 70.
15. Shannon, *Organization*, vol. II, p. 90; Weigley, *History*, p. 215; Bruce, *Lincoln*, pp. 290-91.
16. NA, RG 156, "Register of Letters Received, Chief of Ordnance," vol. 1 (1865), February 15, 1865, entry 68.
17. NA, RG 156, "Letters, Endorsements, and Reports Sent to the Secretary of War 1812-89," vol. 15, p. 268.
18. *Farrow's Military Encyclopedia*, 1885 ed., s.v. "Flank-Defense."
19. NA, RG 156, "Registers of Letters Received Relating to Improvements and Inventions 1812-70," vol. 1 (1865), section in the rear of the volume devoted to the secretary of war, entry 87, February 18, 1865.
20. NA, RG 156, "Reports of Experiments 1826-71," vol. 98, entry 72.
21. Weigley, *History*, p. 215; NA, RG 156, "Statement of Purchases of Ordnance 1861-67," entry for Gatling guns.
22. In 1885 *Farrow's Military Encyclopedia* defined a machine gun as a ". . . gun designed to deliver against animate objects a strong, rapid, continuous and accurate fire of small projectiles at all ranges suited to infantry; to be served by the fewest possible number of men, and also to give a fire that may, in many cases, be as effective as the discharge of canister from artillery." In 1901 Joseph S. Herron defined the machine gun as a

A Bold Step Forward

weapon ". . . that is loaded and fired by machinery, that is, by a mechanism operated with a crank or handle, or by automatic utilization of the energy of recoil or a part of the energy of the powder gases." *Farrow's Military Encyclopedia*, 1885 ed., s.v. "Machine-Gun."; J.S. Herron, U.S. War Department, Adjutant General's Office, "Machine Guns," *Notes of Military Interest For 1901* (Washington, D.C., 1902), p. 120. The nine weapons and the dates on which they were first offered to the War Department are: the Union repeating gun (December 1861), a "battery of rifles" (February 1862), the Raphael repeater (August 1862), the Gatling gun (December 1862), the Billinghurst and Requa rifle battery (January 1863), the Vandenburgh volley gun (February 1864), the McCarty gun (April 1864), "diverging cannon" (March 1865), and Kellogg's gun (March 1865).

23. The gun was later adapted to use copper cartridges. Chinn, *Machine Gun*, pp. 35-36; NA, RG 156, "Reports of Experiments 1826-71," vol. 98, entry 53, pp. 6, 9-10, and entry 64.

24. NA, RG 156, "Reports of Experiments 1826-71, vol. 98," entry 53, pp. 1, 4-5, 8-9; NA, RG 156, "Letters, Endorsements, Reports to the Secretary of War 1812-89," vol. 15, pp. 156, 174, 296.

25. NA, RG 156, "Reports of Experiments 1826-71," vol. 98, entry 53, pp. 9-10.

26. Common field artillery weapons included the 6-pounder gun, the 3-inch Ordnance rifle, the 10- and 20-pounder Parrot rifles, and the 12-pounder Napoleon gun-howitzer. The rifled weapons used a wide variety of shells, shot, canister, and grapeshot. The smooth-bore 6 and 12 pounders used the same general types of ammunition, but they were particularly effective as antipersonnel weapons when using grapeshot or canister at ranges of 350 yards or less. Early machine guns were usually compared with this particular combination of weapon and ammunition. Jack Coggins, *Arms and Equipment of the Civil War* (Garden City, N.Y., 1962), pp. 64-67, 76-81.

27. NA, RG 156, "Reports of Experiments 1826-71," vol. 98, entry 64.

28. Chinn, *Machine Gun*, pp. 43-46; NA, RG 156, "Letters, Endorsements, and Reports Sent to the Secretary of War 1812-89," vol. 14, pp. 494, 505, 514; U.S., Ordnance Department, *Collection of Ordnance Reports*, vol. III (Washington, D.C., 1890), pp. 277-78; Coggins, *Arms*, p.44.

29. NA, RG 156, "Reports of Experiments 1826-71," vol. 98, entry 60.

30. Ibid., entry 63.

31. Bruce, *Lincoln*, pp. 32-33.

32. General Order 77, War Department, Adjutant General's Office, April 28, 1865, *OR*, ser. 3, vol. IV, p. 1280.

33. Ibid.,; U.S. War Department, *Annual Report of the Secretary of War, 1865*, vol. II (Washington, D.C.), p. 994; *Annual Report of the Secretary of War, 1866*, vol. I, p. 178; *Annual Report of the Secretary of War, 1870*, vol. I, p. 287.

34. Wahl and Toppel, *Gatling*, p. 28; NA, RG 156, "Reports of Experiments 1826-71," vol. 98, entry 76.

35. NA, RG 156, "Reports of Experiments 1826-71," vol. 98, entry 77; Coggins, *Arms*, p. 67.

36. NA, RG 156, "Reports of Experiments 1826-71," vol. 98, entry 78.

37. Ibid.

38. Ibid.

39. NA, RG 156, "Registers of Contracts and Orders for Ordnance and Ordnance Equipment 1861-97," vol. 3, p. 2; U.S., Congress, House, *Executive Document 99*, 40th Cong., 2d sess., 1868, pp. 986-87; *Army and Navy Journal*, December 22, 1866, p. 279.

40. Wahl and Toppel, *Gatling*, p. 37.

III

INERTIA TAKES OVER, 1866-1880

Auspicious circumstances surrounded the initial army investment in the Gatling gun. The inaugural purchase of one hundred Gatlings assured an adequate supply of the weapons for service tests by troop units. Unlike his predecessors, Chief of Ordnance Alexander B. Dyer was personally interested in the new weapon, a fact that would encourage his subordinates to devote time and attention to the Gatling. Most important was the gun itself. The model 1866 Gatling, while still beset with numerous flaws, was superior in design and capabilities to any of its predecessors. Had it been employed in an imaginative and innovative fashion, the Gatling gun might well have become a standard item in the armament of army field forces. But as the army moved into and through the decade of the 1870s, it became apparent that the military potential of the Gatling gun was destined to go unfulfilled. The army did not develop tactical doctrine and an organization for using the weapon, and the guns were often consigned to grease-covered oblivion in ordnance storehouses. Shortcomings in the Gatling, cost-conscious conservatism within the army, and lack of imagination contributed to the failure to take advantage of the military potential of the Gatling gun; this failure highlighted the absence of an intellectual and bureaucratic apparatus within the military that could make an organized response to change. In the shrunken, post-Civil War army change came piecemeal or not at all.

The purchase of a large number of Gatling guns in 1866 did not end Ordnance Department experimentation with the weapon. In November 1866 Capt. Stephen Vincent Benet fired one hundred rounds of a newly developed center-fire cartridge from a Gatling.

The young ordnance officer reported that no misfires or jams occurred and commented that ". . . centre fire cartridges, add one hundred percent to the value and efficiency of the [Gatling] gun."[1] Developed by an English colonel, E. M. Boxer, the center-fire primer was much less susceptible to accidental detonation than the exposed rim-fire primer. Unlike rim-fire primers, Boxer's primers could be replaced, so that the cartridge case was reusable. In 1870 Col. Hiram Berdan, a weapons expert and the Civil War commander of Berdan's Sharpshooters, devised a technique for forming a cartridge casing from a single disc of brass, thereby greatly increasing the uniformity and reliability of ammunition while reducing its cost.[2] The combination of the Berdan case and Boxer primer provided machine-gun designers and their military customers with cheap, reliable, and uniform ammunition. These developments in ammunition design greatly enhanced the reliability and hence the military value of machine guns.[3]

Manufacture and delivery of the first production-model machine gun was rapid. Ordnance officials accepted the first one on April 20, 1867, less than nine months after the contract was signed. The last of the one hundred Gatling guns were accepted on August 23, 1867. Considering that production was transferred to Colt after the contract had been signed, that new production facilities had to be built, and that each weapon was examined and tested by ordnance officials prior to acceptance, completion of the entire contract in a day less than a year was remarkable.[4]

The rapid delivery of the Gatlings was matched by the speed with which ordnance officials issued the new weapons. In July 1867 the *Army and Navy Journal* reported that five Gatling guns had already been sent to frontier posts and expressed the hope that it would shortly be able to report on their performance in combat.[5]

Procured in large numbers after a short series of tests, the model 1866 Gatling was not free of mechanical defects. In October 1867 Lieut. John G. Butler, the ordnance officer at Fort Leavenworth, Kansas, reported a potentially dangerous defect in the design of the .50 caliber Gatling. If the gun was cranked at the highest possible speed, the timing of its firing cycle changed. When this change took place, bullets frequently struck a crossbar at the front of the frame of the gun and produced fragments which ricocheted into the gun crew. Fortunately, this defect was easily corrected by redesigning the crossbar so that it no longer lay in the path of the bullets.[6]

Another fault in the design of the frame of the Gatling placed a serious limitation upon the effective use of the weapon. In the .50 caliber model, limited traversing capability was provided by a handwheel and threaded axle arrangement attached to the rear of the gun. But rapid and radical changes in the direction of the gun's fire could be accomplished only by shifting the trail of the gun carriage. The trunnions of the 1-inch Gatling rested on the cheek-pieces of the gun carriage in conventional artillery fashion; consequently this model could be traversed only by the method of shifting its trail. Lack of traverse was to be compensated for by using buckshot ammunition, a solution that was only partially satisfactory, since buckshot had been shown to have serious range limitations.[7] Clearly the usefulness of both the 1-inch and the .50 caliber Gatling guns was limited by the difficulty encountered in traversing the fire of the gun.

The problem was not identified quickly because the performance expectations of Ordnance Department officials and line officers were influenced by experience with contemporary artillery weapons, which lacked a traversing mechanism.[8] This fault was eliminated by improvements in the design of the later versions of Gatling's weapon, which gradually replaced the 1866 models. A problem quickly identified by the commanders of units using the weapon was the great weight and lack of mobility of the first Gatling. Because of the intrinsically heavy multibarrel design, Gatling never entirely solved this problem.

The initial issue of the guns occurred before the Ordnance Department had time to choose standard carriages, limbers, and caissons for the guns. A board of officers convened in December 1867 and quickly selected a carriage and caisson designed at the Watervliet Arsenal for the .50 caliber Gatling and a 6-pounder gun carriage and caisson altered to accommodate the heavier 1-inch Gatling. These models, recommended by the experts at Watervliet, the arsenal that served as the army gun carriage factory, had several advantages. Patterns for the carriages were available, and immediate production meant early distribution of the completed outfits to field units. Construction in a government facility would insure close control of both the quality of the product and its cost; it would also help to justify the continued existence of a federal arsenal.[9]

Less than a year after it had accepted its initial shipment of Gatlings, the Ordnance Department received its first report on the gun from the field. Maj. Alfred Gibbs, the commander of the Seventh Cavalry Regiment stationed at Fort Leavenworth, condemned the carriages, caissons, and limbers of the four .50 caliber guns issued to his regiment. According to Gibbs these pieces of equipment were ". . . vastly too heavy for the weight they were intended to carry."[10] He advocated mounting the gun and its ammunition boxes on the chassis of the standard field ambulance. Drawn by a team of four horses, this arrangement would carry the machine gun ". . . anywhere that the cavalry could go."[11] Specific in his criticism of the running gear issued with the Gatling, Gibbs failed to comment upon the performance of the gun beyond noting the problem with its timing. The cavalry commander also failed to give any information concerning how the guns were used or what type of unit should be organized to use them. These omissions limited the usefulness of his report to the Ordnance Department and to the rest of the army.

General Dyer forwarded Gibbs' report to Col. Peter V. Hagner, the commander of the Watervliet Arsenal, for comment. In his reply, Hagner conceded that for normal use the carriages could have been made lighter. According to Hagner, both the experts at Watervliet and the board of officers reviewing the design had been influenced by the need for exceptionally durable equipment, by a desire to make the parts used interchangeable with similar items used in other pieces of equipment, and by a set of requirements laid down by Gatling. These requirements included making the carriage heavy enough so that the recoil of the gun would not disturb its aim, a goal that could have been met by locking the wheels of the gun carriage during firing, and mounting the machine gun high enough so that it could be cranked while its operator was standing, a position which was less fatiguing, if more exposed. The inventor also advocated carrying a large supply—ninety-five hundred rounds—of ammunition with each gun, and he specified that the carriage and caisson should be drawn by separate two-horse teams.[12] Hagner exaggerated the importance of Gatling's ideas when he termed them "requirements," but they did lend weight to the staff decision to select the heavier gun carriage, a decision in which Colonel Hagner had participated. His reply to Gibbs' criticism ended Ordnance and War Department interest in Major Gibbs' report.

In reality Major Gibbs had little chance of effecting a change in the carriages of the machine guns assigned to his unit. The design of the equipment was already established, and the continued decline in ordnance funds rendered replacement unlikely until each item wore out or became totally obsolete. But Gibbs' report and Hagner's reply do illustrate the difference between the primary concerns of field commanders and the considerations that shaped the design of the equipment that the commanders were told to use. The cavalry commander was interested in performance; the machine gun had to be capable of staying with the cavalry if it was to be employed when the unit made contact with the enemy. If the weapon could not keep up, it would be worse than useless on campaign, since men would have to be left with the gun to guard it after it had dropped out of the cavalry column. On the other hand, Colonel Hagner was concerned with the durability of the equipment and the interchangeablility of its parts, factors that affected maintenance and service life, issues of considerable importance to the Ordnance Department. The fact that in designing its carriage to be as durable and long-lived as possible the technical experts had rendered the Gatling virtually useless as a field weapon does not seem to have affected Colonel Hagner or his superiors.

The conflicting views of Gibbs and Hagner illustrated a longstanding military problem. The combat arms had no official method of influencing the design or redesign of the equipment that they used. While individual officers or boards made up of officers from the combat branches might recommend that certain items of equipment be adopted, the chief of ordnance and the technical experts of the Ordnance Department made the final selection of equipment. In such circumstances bureaucratic considerations such as cost, durability, and the availability of appropriations were at least as important as the requirements of the field forces in determining the type of equipment to be purchased.

Mechanical defects and a lack of mobility were problems that, while they severely limited the usefulness of the Gatling in field operations, could be overcome by changes in the design of the gun and its supporting equipment. Defining the role that the weapon was to play in combat and devising the doctrine and organization necessary for the execution of this role were problems of greater complexity and great importance. General Dyer had identified a position for the Gatling in the secondary armament of fortifications. Other officers had posited use in guarding defiles, bridges, causeways, and fords—areas in which enemy movement would be canalized—and in protecting the flanks of infantry formations.[13] The nature of these roles, which had been filled by conventional artillery pieces using canister or grapeshot, reflected the prevailing opinion that machine guns were a sort of specialized, antipersonnel artillery weapon. Army capacity to devise more specific and important roles for its machine guns rested largely upon individual initiative.

In the 1860s and 1870s tactical doctrine was not the product of a systematic effort by staff agencies and schools to discover the best methods for using various weapons, to codify these techniques in manuals, and to publish these manuals for the information and guidance of the army. This does not mean that tactics were particularly simple or could be mastered with little effort. However, since the War Department and the headquarters of the army lacked an operational planning staff or a permanent agency that was primarily responsible for monitoring, supervising, or stimulating the development of doctrine, the creation of tactical doctrine was left to interested and dedicated individuals.[14]

The procedure for advancing new tactical doctrine or changes in accepted concepts was fairly well defined. The author of the new or improved technique first wrote a paper that described in exact detail the proposed change or addition to accepted doctrine. The paper, together with a request for approval and adoption of the proposal it contained, was sent through official channels to the Adjutant General's Office; it was then forwarded to the commanding general of the army. As it made its way up the chain of command, the paper would acquire a number of official endorsements. Frequently, commanders would critique the proposal; often critical, sometimes laudatory, these endorsements commonly contained facts or opinions that helped the commanding general to evaluate the proposal. If the commanding general decided that the paper had merit, he would ask the secretary of war to appoint an official board to study the matter. After examining the proposal and comparing it with current doctrine bearing upon the same subject, the board would submit its comments and recommendations in a written report. If the board recommended adoption of the new idea, the secretary of war usually instructed the adjutant general to publish orders announcing the adoption of the new doctrine and directing appropriate implementation.

The entire process of introducing new doctrine was involved, slow, and sometimes expensive. No less than the process for bringing a new weapon to the official attention of the War Department, the procedure for changing doctrine depended almost entirely upon the initiative and perseverance of the individual who originated the proposal. Since the key to success was the support of the commanding general, it was almost essential to be known by him or to have the support of men whom he knew. In the absence of a staff capable of evaluating a proposal according to its tactical merits, the commanding general was obliged to base his action upon the author's reputation. If the proposal was not well received by the commanding general, it would find its final resting place in the voluminous correspondence files of the Adjutant General's Office.[15]

The army had developed a means of evaluating proposals for new or improved tactical theories even though that procedure may appear to have been designed to discourage rather than to foster innovation. Essentially passive, the system could only evaluate concepts, and the army did little to encourage its members to develop such ideas. Where could one get the original idea for a new tactical theory concerning machine guns? Four possible sources of inspiration appear to have been open to army officers and interested civilians. These were : (1) combat or campaign experience with a machine gun, (2) experience gained by employing machine guns in tactical exercises or maneuvers, (3) the transfer of doctrinal and organizational concepts used in the field artillery, and (4) the doctrine and organizations developed by foreign armies. In practice one might expect a proposal for new tactical doctrine to reflect ideas derived from a combination of these sources.

In 1867 the American army was entering a prolonged period of sporadic warfare with hostile Indians on various parts of the frontier. The possibility of developing tactical doctrine for machine guns based upon their use in battle against Indians depended upon a number of factors. Were Gatling guns available when and where warfare broke out on the frontier? Were they employed, and was their employment successful or unsuccessful? Most important, was one of the officers who witnessed the use of the weapons capable of drawing positive inferences from what he had seen, able to organize and write down the concepts he drew from these inferences, and determined enough to persevere in the lengthy process of placing his theories before the proper authorities? While it doubtless gave thinking officers ideas about the power and proper use of machine guns, the Indian warfare of the 1870s and 1880s never produced the favorable conjunction of factors necessary for the development of a theory for using machine guns.

Field exercises also failed to indicate new ways of employing machine guns. Assigned the tasks of policing the frontier, garrisoning the South, and guarding the coasts, the army had by 1869 been dispersed among 255 separate posts. Divided among posts that were often scattered across several states or territories, infantry and cavalry regiments rarely assembled in their entirety. Tactical exercises at regimental level were, therefore, infrequent.[16]

During the last three decades of the nineteenth century artillery doctrine provided the basis for most ideas about the use of machine guns in the field. So long as the machine gun was heavy enough to require a wheeled carriage, the idea that it was a species of light artillery prevailed. Schooled in the use of rifle and bayonet, infantry officers left the employment of heavy supporting weapons to the artillery.

Although the army considered the Gatling an experimental item, by the end of 1868 the gun had been given two roles: as a light artillery piece when used in the field and as an antipersonnel weapon for the close defense of permanent fortifications.[17] As enunciated by General Dyer in 1864, the role of the Gatling in the defense of coastal fortifications was established by an investigation of their armament in early 1867. A board of officers under Col. William Maynadier reviewed the state of the coastal defenses and made a series of recommendations for the modernization of their armament. Favorably endorsed by General Grant, the report of the Maynadier Board recommended that ". . . the Gatlin [sic] Gun or a gun of Similar character may be advantageously adopted in place of the present flank defense howitzer."[18] Secretary Stanton's approval of the report constituted the authority to incorporate machine guns in the defenses of the seacoast forts. The static role of the Gatling in the seacoast forts did nothing to advance the development of machine-gun doctrine, but it did insure that the Ordnance Department would continue to test new machine guns as they appeared.

After a flurry of enthusiasm for the Gatling, military interest in the weapon began to decline. Reductions in manpower and funds prevented arming existing artillery units with Gatlings or forming new units to use the weapon. Moreover, frontier warfare called for highly mobile cavalry, not slow-moving artillery units. In these circumstances extensive support for the weapon would be required if the Gatling was to gain more than a peripheral place in the armament of the land forces. Such support did not materialize, partly because the energies of General Dyer, the man most likely to be a strong advocate of the gun, were absorbed in a struggle to defend his personal reputation. Accused by a congressional select joint committee of engaging in various corrupt and criminal practices, Dyer was able to vindicate himself only after a six-month investigation of his conduct by a court inquiry. On May 15, 1869, army headquarters published a general order containing the findings of the court, which ended an affair that had occupied Dyer's attention for a year, leaving him little time for such novel subjects as machine guns.[19]

In 1869 a board of artillery officers headed by Col. William A. Barry did produce a draft field artillery manual that mentioned the Gatling. Other than prescribing the amount of ammunition to accompany the 1-inch and .50 caliber guns, the board did little more than confirm the general view that the Gatling was primarily a defensive weapon.[20] The manual failed to clarify the ambiguous relationship between the artillery and the still experimental Gatling gun.

As American enthusiasm for the machine gun declined, tension between Prussia and France stimulated the interest of Napoleon III in modernizing the armament of the French army. Facing an opponent whose well-equipped army had recently achieved a brilliant, if bloody, triumph over the Austrians at Königgrätz, the French emperor found that both his infantry and artillery needed new arms. Napoleon III favored the infantry and spent 113 million francs on a new rifle, the *chassepot*, but he could not obtain 13 million to spend on his artillery.[21] Prussia took the opposite course and equipped its artillery with new Krupp breech-loading guns made of steel. Under the supervision of a brillliant inspector general, Gustav E. von Hindersin, the training and tactics of the Prussian artillery achieved new standards of precision.[22] When the Franco-Prussian War began, the Prussian artillery had far more guns—11,300 to 3,000—than the French, and it had better ammunition. French shells were time-fused and set to explode at ranges of 1,200 and 2,800 meters, while Prussian shells were equipped with percussion fuses, which detonated on impact and were usable at all ranges.[23] A major factor in the Prussian victories in 1870-1871, the superiority of the Prussian artillery had a decisive effect upon the first large-scale use of machine guns in combat.

The French army had been experimenting with a machine gun, the multibarrel Montigny *mitrailleuse*, since 1860. Finally adopted in 1869, the gun fired *chassepot* cartridges at a rate of about 370 rounds per minute. Together the gun, carriage, limber, and twenty-one hundred rounds of ammunition weighed approximately two tons.[24] Production at Meudon arsenal was carried on under security conditions so extreme that only those officers and men who were to operate the *mitrailleuses* were allowed to see them. The principal result of such secrecy was that neither the gunners who were to operate the *mitrailleuse* nor the commanders who were to employ it gained enough experience with the weapon to be able to use it effectively.

Given the lack of practical experience with the gun, the short time between its adoption and use in combat, the gun's physical characteristics, transportation and logistical requirements, and the probability that only the French artillery had the experience necessary to move, support, and operate the gun, classification of the *mitrailleuse* as an artillery weapon appears not only logical but necessary.²⁵ The decisive failure of the French army was that it attempted to use its machine guns as long-range counterbattery weapons rather than in the close-range support of the defensive positions of the French infantry.²⁶

On August 4, 1870, in one of the initial engagements of the war, a *mitrailleuse* battery attempted to engage Prussian artillery shelling French positions on the high ground of Château-Geisberg. The battery occupied an exposed position on a knoll marked by a stand of poplar trees. In the exchange that followed, a Prussian artillery shell exploded on a French caisson and mortally wounded Gen. Charles A. Douay; the French machine guns were withdrawn. Experience quickly demonstrated that the *mitrailleuse* was ineffectual against artillery at ranges beyond 500 yards and that it was a failure as a counterbattery weapon.²⁷

Correct in their judgment that the *mitrailleuse* was a failure as a long-range artillery piece, French authorities missed the implications of an incident during the Battle of Gravelotte-St. Privat when a *mitrailleuse* battery concealed in the infantry lines repulsed a Prussian attack and inflicted severe casualties.²⁸ The French deemed the *mitrailleuse* a failure and failed to perceive its value as an infantry support weapon. Severely prejudiced against machine guns by its experience with the *mitrailleuse*, the French army did not adopt a standard machine gun until 1899. Large purchases of machine guns were not made until the subject threatened to become a political issue in 1907.²⁹

About the same time that the French army adopted the *mitrailleuse*, the Prussian army conducted an investigation of machine guns and concluded that ". . . the very narrow sphere within which their effect was restricted did not at all compensate for the *personnel* and materiel required in serving them."³⁰ Beginning the war with France without any machine guns, the Prussian forces did employ an experimental battery of machine guns belonging to the Bavarian army. A multibarrel weapon like the *mitrailleuse*, the gun had some success on the battlefield, but the Prussian staff rated its overall performance poor. Coupled with observation of the French army's disastrous experience with the *mitrailleuse*, this judgment reinforced the prejudice against machine guns that already existed in the higher echelons of the Prussian army. After the Franco-Prussian War, German military writers generally ignored or condemned the use of machine guns in field service, and the German army did not become actively interested in the weapon until 1900.[31]

In evaluating the Franco-Prussian War, historian Michael Howard notes,

> ... in an age when technological change was transforming the nature of war in a manner as unpredictable as that of our times, the events of 1870 for long provided the only examples which experts could study of the problems which principally perplexed them; the effect of modern weapons on tactics. . . .[32]

The experiences of the war arrested French and German interest in machine guns for more than a quarter of a century; in these circumstances, it is not surprising that American observers drew few lessons from what they saw of machine-gun employment in the war.[33] Military prejudice resulting from the improper employment of an outdated machine gun blinded the principal continental military powers to the potential of a revolutionary weapon. Such was not the case in two actively expanding imperial powers.

Russia had been among the first countries to express interest in Gatling's invention, and by the late 1860s, the Imperial Army owned a number of Gatlings. Originally the Russians substituted Gatling gun batteries for field guns, but the disastrous consequences of similar French practices apparently convinced the Russian staff that this was unwise. Rather than discard the Gatling completely, the Russians organized a few machine-gun units under the control of their artillery directorate. These units performed effectively in the Russo-Turkish War.[34] However, the Russian army failed to develop its machine-gun doctrine further, and in 1900 the Russian military still considered the machine gun to be an artillery weapon.

Great Britain began experimenting with machine guns in the late 1860s, and in September 1870 British authorities decided to adopt the Gatling gun. The guns were assigned to the Royal Artillery, but this branch, strongly influenced by the events of the Franco-Prussian War, treated the Gatlings with hostility. In 1876 a correspondent writing to the *Army and Navy Journal* from England described the dilemma that the British faced in trying to develop an organizational role for a gun which, while it had the logistical and personnel requirements of artillery, was not an artillery weapon. According to the article the British army had concluded that Gatlings would be employed with the infantry.[35]

British colonial troops soon began to test this concept. Gatlings were issued to a British colonial force during the Ashanti War of 1873-1874, but the carriages were not suited to the terrain and the guns were not employed in combat. During the Zulu War of 1879 Gatlings were used against the mass attacks of the Zulu warriors; impressed with the effectiveness of the machine guns, two British officers, Lord Chelmsford (Frederick Thesiger) and Lieut. F. M. Goold-Adams, Royal Artillery, developed theories on how the weapons should be employed. Chelmsford claimed the machine gun should be employed by his branch, the infantry; Goold-Adams proposed attaching one Gatling gun to each battery of field artillery for defensive purposes. Both Chelmsford and Goold-Adams saw the Gatling as a defensive weapon, but they did stipulate that its fire could be used to support the final stages of an infantry attack.[36]

Despite the effectiveness of the machine gun and growing support for its use, the British artillery continued to ignore the weapon. The *London Broad Arrow* observed:

> Hitherto the Royal Artillery have fought shy of the [Gatling] gun because it is not a gun, but a collection of rifle barrels. Infantry have not the wherewithal to accommodate Gatlings—i.e., horses, drivers, etc. . . . ; while the *role* of cavalry scarcely admits of the addition of Gatlings *en permanence*.[37]

Hampered by a technology that had not yet produced a relatively lightweight machine gun and by rigid concepts of the roles of combat arms, the British army in the 1870s did not develop a doctrine and organization for the use of the machine gun.[38]

In 1867 the U.S. Army had classified the Gatling gun as an experimental light artillery weapon, a status that gave the military the time and organizational flexibility necessary to determine the specific role that the weapon would play. But the role of the machine gun could not be left semidefined forever, and in the 1870s military authorities made a number of attempts to determine exactly where the Gatling gun fitted in the armament of the field forces. Official interest in the Gatling centered around use of the gun in permanent works. On the last day of May 1873 Secretary of War William W. Belknap appointed a board of officers to investigate again the use of large caliber (1-inch) Gatling guns for the flank defense of coastal works.[39] The board was composed of engineer, ordnance, and artillery officers. Although the selection of new or improved weapons was within the purview of the Ordnance Department, the practice of including representatives of other concerned technical services as well as officers from the using arm was not unusual at this time; it resulted in a better evaluation of the weapon under consideration and tended to reduce subsequent objections to the work of the board either by other technicians or by the users themselves. In accordance with custom the board took its name from its president, Maj. Quincy Gillmore, Corps of Engineers.

Under the direction of Major Gillmore, an engineer and distinguished artillerist who had personally directed the siege of Charleston during the Civil War, two different approaches to the task of evaluating the Gatling were adopted. Both the 1-inch and a .42 caliber Gatling were tested in direct competition with an 8-inch siege howitzer and a 12-pounder Napoleon. The board also conducted a thorough review of the results of previous tests of the Gatling gun. Since the review began first, the board was able to incorporate several procedures from earlier trials into its test program. This unusual dual approach testifies to the imagination, professional competence, and thorough approach of the Gillmore Board.[40]

Trials for accuracy were conducted at ranges varying from 1,000 to 1,150 yards against ten 6-foot by 50-foot targets arranged to ". . . represent a column of infantry, by companies at full distance, approaching or retiring from the battery. . . ."[41] Test firing again demonstrated that as an antipersonnel weapon the Gatling was superior to either of its competitors. Copying an English test, the Gatling was fired in competition with riflemen using the standard .45 caliber Springfield rifle; at ranges of 150 yards and beyond the machine gun outshot groups of trained marksmen. According to the calculations of the board, one Gatling was the equal of fifty-two riflemen firing individually or seventy men firing against time. These figures presented a powerful argument for the use of Gatling guns with the infantry and cavalry; however, since the board was not empowered to comment upon such subjects, its report was restricted to a flat statement of its findings. The tests again demonstrated that beyond 200 yards buckshot fired from a 1-inch Gatling was ineffective; this ended Ordnance Department interest in large-caliber Gatling guns.[42] The Gillmore Board recommended purchase of Gatling guns of the same caliber as ". . . the service small-arm, so that the ammunition will be interchangeable between the two."[43]

The records of earlier trials that the board reviewed included navy experiments and reports of two series of tests of Gatlings conducted by the British army at Shoeburyness, England. Since the second of these series was conducted in November 1871, the British officers directing the test were aware of both the poor performance of the *mitrailleuse* batteries in the Franco-Prussian War and the Prussian prejudice against machine guns. After diagnosing faulty employment as the basic reason for the failure of the *mitrailleuse* and noting that the Gatling was seldom used in the war, the British test committee decided that machine guns were especially useful as defensive weapons. The Englishmen concluded that the Franco-Prussian War had demonstrated that machine guns were not useful as offensive weapons except when enemy artillery was inferior.[44] Instructive in both form and conclusions, the British army reports were the most current documents considered by the Gillmore Board.

Thorough and impartial in its work, the Gillmore Board conducted a model investigation; its report formed the most detailed and clearest exposition of the capabilities of the Gatling gun that the American army had yet produced. The advantages of the gun as an antipersonnel weapon were delineated in a lengthy paragraph, which covered its usefulness in increasing infantry firepower at a critical point in a battle and in such operations as defending entrenchments and defiles, covering the embarkation or debarkation of troops, and protecting field artillery batteries. But having mentioned several uses for Gatling guns in field operations, the board restricted its recommendations to the armament of the coastal forts—the subject that its orders specifically delineated. Although a board of officers might uncover evidence pointing to a different—and even more important—use for a new weapon, it was bound to confine its recommendations to the subject it had been directed to investigate. Other recommendations could be ignored by the reviewing authorities, as they were not covered by the orders authorizing the inquiry.

The report of the Gillmore Board did not go beyond recommending the adoption of a rifle-caliber Gatling gun for use as an antipersonnel weapon in the coastal forts. But the new chief of ordnance, Brig. Gen. Stephen Vincent Benet, requested adoption of the .45 caliber Gatling as an auxiliary arm for all branches of the service and called for a final determination of how the army would use the Gatling.[45]

Brig. Gen. Stephen Vincent Benet, chief of ordnance, 1874-1891. *Courtesy*: U.S. Military Academy Archives.

Prompted by the Gillmore Board report, Secretary Belknap convened a board of engineers to study the use of Gatling guns in permanent fortifications. The president of the board, Col. Zealous B. Tower, called for the installation of one Gatling on each flank of the casemated forts. This was an expensive proposition requiring purchase of 221 Gatling guns; in fact, the Tower Board stated that 209 guns should be emplaced immediately to cover the approaches to thirty-three of the nation's coastal works. General Benet asked for $292,000 to buy the guns. The chief of ordnance also claimed that as of March 1874 the Gatling gun had been adopted as ". . . an auxiliary arm, not only for the flank defense of fortifications, but for all branches of the service."[46] Neither congressional nor military action on these recommendations matched the enthusiastic spirit with why they were made; Congress appropriated only enough money for fifty additional Gatlings, and future events demonstrated that the position of the Gatling had not yet been settled.[47]

In the same year that large-scale use of the Gatling gun in the fixed portions of the nation's defenses was recommended, a new version of the weapon was rejected by the most mobile arm of the service. Setting to work at the Watervliet Arsenal, the Board on Cavalry Equipments examined a wide variety of items including a lightweight Gatling designed for pack transportation. The members of the board judged the weapon to be unsatisfactory primarily because it took too long to unpack and assemble. The board also criticized the tripod mount of the gun, noting that with this mount the Gatling could not be shifted to a new position as easily as with a carriage mount; lacking mobility, the tripod-mounted Gatling might, on occasion, be exposed to capture. The Cavalry Equipments Board suggested that the Gatling be mounted upon a lightweight carriage drawn by a single horse. This rig would give the Gatling gun the mobility it needed for operations with cavalry units.[48] In 1874 the army accepted the lightweight carriage that Major Gibbs had recommended six years earlier.[49]

The army's lack of progress in refining the equipment associated with the Gatling complemented its inability to define the combat role of the weapon. In 1874 the *Army and Navy Journal* carried an unsigned letter whose writer claimed considerable experience with the Gatling and expressed the opinion that it was an infantry weapon.[50] In 1881 a board of artillery officers recommended that "... the calibre .45 machine gun [Gatling] ... be united with batteries of eight guns."[51] This advice was ignored, and three years later the historian of the American artillery, William E. Birkhimer, noted that the army had still not defined the combat role of the machine gun.[52] The American army had initially viewed the machine gun as a type of artillery, but the events of the Franco-Prussian War appeared to demonstrate that machine guns could not be used as conventional artillery weapons. Faced with this dilemma and with little opportunity to gain additional information about the weapon, most American military theorists ignored the weapon until 1899.[53]

NOTES

1. National Archives, Record Group (hereafter, NA, RG) 156, "Reports of Experiments 1826-71," vol. 98, entry 79.

2. William R. Crites, "The Development of Infantry Tactical Doctrine in the United States Army, 1865-1898," (MA thesis, Duke University, 1968), pp. 49-50; Joseph W. Shileds, *From Flintlock to M1* (New York, 1954), pp. 95-97.

3. The final advance in cartridge design was made in 1881 when Major Rubin, a Swiss ordnance officer, designed a case that did not have a protruding rim around its base. The "rimless" cartridge eliminated the problems in the functioning of the gun's mechanism that were caused by rimmed cases. Crites, "Infantry Doctrine," pp. 53-54. The Berdan process was particularly important, as it produced a cartridge case that could stand the stresses involved in firing and extraction without rupturing or tearing and leaving part of the case in the chamber to jam the gun.

4. U.S., Congress, House, *Executive Document 99*, 40th Cong., 2d sess., 1868, pp. 986-87.

5. *Army and Navy Journal* (hereafter cited as *A-N Jou.*), July 13, 1867, p. 741.

6. Paul Wahl and Donald R. Toppel, *The Gatling Gun* (New York, 1971), p. 32; NA, RG 156, "Reports of Experiments 1826-71, vol. 98, entries 84 and 85.

7. Wahl and Toppel, *Gatling*, pp. 33-35.

8. The lack of traverse in the 1-inch Gatling was never corrected.

9. NA, RG 156, "Reports and Correspondence of Ordnance Boards 1827-70," Box 81, "Recommendations of the Ordnance Board," February

1868; see recommendation 74, p. 50, and recommendation 80, p. 52; U.S., Ordnance Department, *Ordnance Memoranda No. 9* (Washington, D.C., 1868), p. 17.

10. NA, RG 156, "Reports of Experiments 1826-71," vol. 98, entry 89.
11. Ibid.
12. NA, RG 156, "Reports of Experiments 1826-71," vol. 98, entry 90.
13. NA, RG 156, "Reports of Experiments 1826-71," vol. 98, entry 78.
14. See Crites, "Infantry Doctrine," chap. 1, particularly pp. 12-15.
15. Ibid., pp. 13-14.
16. Russell F. Weigley, *History of the United States Army* (New York, 1967), pp. 267, 290.
17. William E. Birkhimer, *Historical Sketch of the Organization, Administration, Materiel, and Tactics of the Artillery, United States Army* (Washington, D.C., 1884), p. 297.
18. "Proceedings of a Board of Officers convened in virtue of Special Orders No. 29, War Department AGO," January 18, 1867, NA, RG 156, "Reports and Correspondence of Ordnance Boards 1827-70," Box 81.
19. Dyer to John M. Schofield, July 20, 1868, U.S., War Department, *Proceedings of a Court of Inquiry . . . to Examine into the Accusations against Brig. and Bvt. Major General A. B. Dyer, Chief of Ordnance*, vol. II, p. 478-86, 610.
20. The 1-inch Gatling was to have 2,592 rounds per gun, a load that weighed 1,655 pounds; the .50 caliber weapon would have 10,200 rounds, or 1,059.5 pounds of ammunition per gun. The high weight of the 1-inch Gatling cartridge presented a serious obstacle for field use of the gun. NA, RG 94, Microcopy M-619, Roll 681, frames 44, 62, 65, 93; Roll 682, frames 10-11.
21. Michael Howard, *The Franco-Prussian War: The German Invasion of France, 1870-1871* (New York, 1961), pp. 35-36.
22. Howard classifies the ". . . effectiveness of Prussian artillery [as] . . . the greatest tactical surprise of the Franco-Prussian war." Howard, *Franco-Prussian War*, pp. 5-6. For information on General von Hindersin see Prince Kraft Zu Hohenlohe-Ingelfingen, *Letters on Artillery* (London, 1898), chap. 11.
23. Howard, *Franco-Prussian War*, pp. 66, 118.
24. G. S. Hutchison, *Machine Guns: Their History and Tactical Employment* (London, 1938), pp. 9-10. Battlefield experience proved that the effective range of the *mitrailleuse* was limited to approximately 500 yards. Hutchison, *Machine Guns*, pp. 11-15; Bernard and Fawn Brodie, *From Crossbow to H-Bomb* (Bloomington, Ind., 1973), pp. 144-45.
25. Brodie, *From Crossbow*, pp. 144-45; Howard, *Franco-Prussian War*, p. 36; Crites, "Infantry Doctrine," p. 47.

26. The fact that *mitrailleuse* batteries replaced one-third of the artillery batteries in the French army and thus further diminished the number of field guns in the artillery may partially account for their use in a counter-battery role. Hutchison, *Machine Guns*, pp. 26-27.

27. Ibid., p. 13.

28. Ibid., pp. 17-18.

29. Ibid., pp. 100-101; J. S. Herron, "Machine Guns," *Notes of Military Interest For 1901*, U.S., War Department, Adjutant General's Office (Washington, D.C., 1902), pp. 132-35.

30. *A-N Jou.*, June 1, 1872, p. 605.

31. *A-N Jou.*, November 5, 1870, p. 181; C.H.B. Pridham, *Superiority of Fire* (London, 19;45), p. 29; Hutchison, *Machine Guns*, pp. 29-30; Herron, *Mil. Notes 1901*, pp. 135-37.

32. Howard, *Franco-Prussian War*, p. xi.

33. The United States' highest ranking observer, Maj. Gen. Philip H. Sheridan, noted the use of *mitrailleuse*, but he was apparently unimpressed by the weapon. Philip H. Sheridan, *Personal Memoirs*, vol. II (New York, 1888), pp. 371, 375, 447, 451-52.

34. *A-N Jou.*, December 27, 1873, p. 315; October 21, 1876, p. 174; January 13, 1877, p. 363; Wahl and Toppel, *Gatling*, p. 83.

35. Hutchison, *Machine Guns*, pp. 30-31; *A-N Jou.*, July 8, 1871, pp. 752-53; December 30, 1871, p. 323. April 29, 1876, p. 619; Pridham, *Superiority*, p. 31.

36. Hutchison, *Machine Guns*, pp. 30-31; *A-N Jou.*, July 8, 1871, pp. 752-53; December 30, 1871, p. 323. April 29, 1876, p. 619; Pridham, *Superiority*, p. 31.

36. *A-N Jou.*, February 28, 1874, p. 459; Hutchison, *Machine Guns*, p. 39; F.M. Goold-Adams, "On The Question Whether Any Development Of The Material Of Field Artillery Is Necessitated By The General Adoption Of Entrenchments On The Field of Battle; And If So, On The Direction Such Developments Should Take," U.S., War Department, Ordnance Office, *Ordnance Notes*, 119 (November 3, 1879), pp. 201-2 (hereafter cited as *Ord. Notes*).

37. *A-N Jou.*, May 3, 1879, p. 701.

38. Hutchison, *Machine Guns*, pp. 46-47; *A-N Jou.*, March 26, 1881, p. 711. In the late 1870s the Royal Navy developed shipboard roles for the Gatling gun as an antipersonnel weapon similar to the swivel gun on eighteenth-century warships and as an antitorpedo boat weapon. In both cases the key appears to have been the mounting; properly mounted a machine gun could deliver a high volume of fire across a wide area. It could also track small, high-speed craft operating close to warships, a function that the guns in the main battery could not perform.

39. U.S., Ordnance Department, *Ordnance Memoranda No. 17* (Washington, D.C., 1874), p. 5.
40. Ibid., p. 17.
41. This would be an assault column of regimental strength. Ibid., pp. 9-10.
42. Ibid., pp. 8-10, 33-34.
43. Ibid., pp. 45-46.
44. Ibid., pp. 26-29. This conclusion appears to have been widespread after the Franco-Prussian War. It helps to explain why the success of machine guns employed in a defensive role against primitive peoples did not arouse more interest in the weapon among military experts in the period from 1880 to 1900.
45. Ibid., pp. 45-47.
46. *Annual Report of the Chief of Ordnance, 1875*, pp. 44-47; Birkhimer, *Historical Sketch*, p. 294.
47. *A-N Jou.*, July 18, 1874, p. 769.
48. "Extract from the proceedings of the Board on Cavalry Equipments," March 28, 1874, NA, RG 156, doc. 1622 (Encl.) (1874).
49. NA, RG 156, "Reports of Experiments 1826-71," vol. 98, entry 89.
50. *A-N Jou.*, February 21, 1874, p. 443.
51. *A-N Jou.*, September 10, 1881, p. 115.
52. Birkhimer, *Historical Sketch*, p. 295.
53. A survey of manuals produced by American civilian and military writers prior to 1899 reveals that without exception the machine gun was treated as a special type of artillery piece. In 1896 the Artillery School convened a board of officers to review Samuel M. Mills' machine-gun manual. There is no indication that the board received or reviewed any papers or other material containing information or ideas on the tactical employment of machine guns. "Proceedings of a Board to revise and bring up to date 'The Description and Service of Machine Guns' by Mills," NA, RG 94, doc. 34840/A filed with 34225.

IV

IN PURSUIT OF PERFECTION, 1881-1897

During the 1870s and until the turn of the century army interest in the machine gun centered in the Bureau of Ordnance. Although restricted by a shortage of funds, officers in the Ordnance Department kept abreast of the development of new and improved weaponry by reviewing literature from a variety of sources and by periodic testing of promising new arms. Information concerning new equipment was disseminated within the Ordnance Department and to the army by a variety of departmental publications. Brig. Gen. Stephen Vincent Benet, chief of ordnance from 1874 to 1891, shared General Dyer's interest in machine guns. Benet supported the work of Battery F, Second Artillery, a light artillery battery that from 1878 to 1881 actively experimented with various types of machine guns and machine-gun tactics. The practical result of this work was the publication in 1886 of a body of advanced organizational and tactical theory for machine guns; the author, Maj. Edward B. Williston, had commanded Battery F during the experiments with machine guns. The trials that Battery F conducted represented the only systematic attempt by the army to investigate the tactical capabilities of the machine gun prior to the early 1900s.

Ordnance Department operations were hindered by the fact that funds available to it decreased greatly in the 1870s and 1880s. Following the Civil War, total army expenditures shrank from $284 million in 1866 to $32 million in 1878 and then rose slowly to a pre-Spanish-American War high of $55 million in 1894.[1] The combination of low spending levels and the rapid pace of weapons development placed a premium upon Ordnance Department test and evaluation activities. Not only must the test officers insure that their evaluation of the weapon or device was reliable, but they had to resist pressure from the combat branches of the army who wanted new weapons.

Rapid advances in armament design meant that the combat arms needed new weapons, and ordnance test activities were watched closely for indications of the way in which the few available dollars were to be spent. As a consequence of such scrutiny, both the Ordnance Department system for the test and evaluation of new weapons and the decisions it influenced came under attack. These attacks, usually by line officers, centered around the contention that in the selection of weapons and equipment the Ordnance Department did not pay adequate attention to the opinions and desires of the officers responsible for using the equipment. According to Maj. Gen. Winfield Scott Hancock the Bureau of Ordnance operated as "practically a close [sic] corporation" in armament matters.[2] Hancock's complaint that line officers played no part in the process of selecting new weapons and equipment was not entirely true, for line officers were often included in test and evaluation boards and were sometimes in the majority on these panels.[3] However, the general thrust of the criticism was correct; in a controversy between a line officer and a technical expert, the War Department normally adopted the position of the ordnance official. There were several reasons for Ordnance Department domination of the weapons selection process.

First, the Bureau of Ordnance represented a body of expert technical opinion unified by the workings of the departmental chain of command. The chief of ordnance and his staff could be expected to understand the broader issues, particularly fiscal matters, which had to be considered in making procurement decisions, and such considerations—weighty ones when dealing with the Secretary of War—would be part of their judgment.

Another factor was the position of the Ordnance Office within the War Department. Close association with the commanding general and the secretary of war operated in favor of the technician and against the combat arms officer, who was often separated from the seat of decision by thousands of miles and a lengthy chain of command. The combat arms, unlike the staff bureaus, were not organized; they had no chief residing in Washington who could represent their interests. For this reason the line officer was handicapped in any struggle with the Ordnance Department. Rarely was there a unified body of opinion among line officers on armament matters. These points explain why the Ordnance Department was all-powerful in weapons selection; moreover, in the last two decades of the nineteenth century the Ordnance Department increased the percentage of ordnance officers serving on the boards that evaluated new weapons.

As the test and evaluation of new weapons became increasingly important in the 1870s and 1880s, the Ordnance Department began to standardize these operations. Before and during the Civil War tests had been conducted by one or more officers designated by the chief of ordnance and appointed by the secretary of war. After the Civil War, test and evaluation were taken over by permanent boards. The Board of Heavy Ordnance, appointed in 1872, was followed two years later by a Board of Ordnance charged with testing heavy rifled guns. In 1876 the latter body was redesignated the Ordnance Board and given the permanent mission of testing, proving, examining, and reporting on ordnance materiel. It was also to submit opinions on technical questions relating to artillery and to outline the experiments needed to answer these questions.[4] Despite the scope of its mission, the Ordnance Board did not conduct all test and evaluation activities.

Created in 1888 as a result of renewed military and congressional interest in the development of new weapons, the Board of Ordnance and Fortification was not under the direct control of the chief of ordnance. Instead, the new body was headed by the commanding general of the army and included an artilleryman and an engineer as well as an ordnance officer; it reported directly to the secretary of war. Congress charged the Board of Ordnance and Fortification with making ". . . all needful and proper purchases, investigations, experiments, and tests, to ascertain with a view to their utilization by the Government, the most effective guns, . . . small arms, cartridges, projectiles, fuzes, explosives, torpedoes, armor-plates, and other implements and engines of war. . . ."[5] By legislative fiat the Ordnance Department had acquired a new associate. Both the Ordnance Board and the Board of Ordnance and Fortification at various times tested new and improved machine guns offered to the Ordnance Department.

The first major competitor of the Gatling gun was a two-barrel weapon patented in 1874 by William Gardner. Operated by a hand crank, the Gardner machine gun did not possess the Gatling's high rate of fire, but test records indicate that it was reliable in operation and cheaper and lighter than the Gatling. After testing several models of the Gardner gun, the Ordnance Board recommended that the weapon be tried by a troop unit, and two guns were shipped to Battery F, Second Artillery. After a prolonged series of trials in the rugged Texas terrain, the gun was judged inferior to the Gatling in overall performance.[6] Although the relatively lightweight one- and two-barrel versions of the Gardner gun represented the closest approach to a practical infantry machine gun before the development of the Maxim gun, the Ordnance Department chose to continue purchasing the reliable and well-established Gatling.

The next major competitor for the Gatling gun—and the weapon that would eventually replace it—was the Maxim automatic machine gun, patented in 1884. Two years after the initial Maxim patent a French chemist, Paul Vielle, succeeded in perfecting a non-corrosive smokeless powder.[7] A major advance in weapons technology, smokeless-powder ammunition gave its user major tactical and technical advantages.[8] By drastically reducing the smoke produced during firing, smokeless-powder ammunition greatly improved the soldier's opportunity to aim and eliminated the dense clouds of black-powder smoke, which made the "fog of war" a reality. Using the new ammunition, an individual rifleman or machine-gun team could fire from a camouflaged position without revealing their location with a cloud of smoke.

Smokeless powder was of special value to the machine-gun designer. It is a clean-burning propellant, which leaves the mechanism and bore of the machine gun relatively free from the residue that quickly fouls weapons firing black-powder ammunition. Black powder burns quickly and generates a short power impulse with a high chamber pressure; smokeless powder continues to burn after reaching maximum pressure and produces a prolonged power impulse with a relatively low chamber pressure but a higher residual pressure in the bore. A prolonged power impulse and high residual bore pressure were useful characteristics for inventors seeking to develop automatic machine guns powered by recoil forces or by expanding powder gases.[9] A prolonged pressure impulse also meant greater thrust for the bullet with lower maximum pressure in the gun. This led to the development of lighter machine guns with substantially longer ranges than comparable black-powder weapons. During the same period in which Vielle made his discovery, a Swiss officer, Major Rubin, produced a copper-jacketed, lead-core bullet suited to the high velocities produced by smokeless powder. In addition to its increased range and penetrating power, the decreased size and weight of Rubin's bullet reduced the weight of ammunition.[10] The production of smokeless powder and invention of the small-caliber, high-velocity bullet marked the end of the series of advances in small-arms ammunition that began in 1788. Without these advances the development of the machine gun would have been impossible.

The development of smokeless powder and other new explosives increased the power of small arms and artillery; it also made a major contribution to the process of moving the machine gun from its vague status as a novel piece of artillery to a position as an important infantry weapon. As the power of its shells and propellant charges increased and as other improvements, particularly the hydropneumatic recoil mechanism, were invented, the artillery shifted from a short-range, direct-fire role to a long-range, indirect-fire weapon. In the process the machine gun assumed the role of providing close-range fire support for the infantry.

Before 1884 all machine guns depended on an external power source—usually the muscle power of the operator. In the spring of 1884 Hiram Maxim, an American engineer living in England, produced the first self-powered or automatic machine gun. Actuated by recoil, the gun attained a rate of fire of over six hundred rounds per minute.[11]

In the spring of 1885 Maxim demonstrated his invention before a group that included the Prince of Wales, the Duke of Cambridge, and Lord Garnet Wolseley. A member of Wolseley's party, Lieut. Gen. Sir Andrew Clarke, advised Maxim to simplify his gun to increase its appeal to the military. Maxim followed Clarke's suggestions, and by 1886 the basic form of the Maxim machine gun was fully developed. During the next fifteen years it enjoyed substantial commercial success.[12]

The Ordnance Board tested the Maxim in 1888 and judged the gun to be ". . . light, compact, and not complicated in construction, considering the many functions it has to perform."[13] Impressed with the performance of the Maxim, the board recommended that the government buy one of the weapons for further tests; however, its owners withdrew the gun from testing. Despite a report that a substantial number of Maxims that the Austrian government had purchased had proved to be defective, the army tested the gun in 1890 and again in 1895.[14]

Early Ordnance Department tests of machine guns were mainly concerned with evaluating the operational capabilities of a particular weapon; later trials reflected increased interest in the mechanical reliability and durability of the weapon. Durability was a particular concern for the automatic machine gun with its complex and delicate mechanism. Ordnance Department tests were a major impediment to the rapid adoption of an automatic machine gun by the American army. The records of the tests of the Maxim in 1890 and 1895 indicate that the weapon jammed when "Two handfuls of coarse seashore sand [were] thrown into [its mechanism]. . . ."[15] After immersion in a solution of corrosive ammonium chloride for ten minutes followed by exposure to the open air for two days, the Maxim failed to fire because the finely machined rear bearing surfaces of its action were rusted together.[16] Relatively lightweight and capable of sustained automatic fire while operated by a single soldier, the Maxim gun lacked the reliability and endurance of the Gatling. The delicate mechanism of the gun was vulnerable to dirt and corrosion, but these tests were not a realistic reflection of the level of maintenance that the gun would receive in field operations. Neither the trials in 1890 nor those in 1895 resulted in a favorable recommendation for the Maxim gun.

In 1890 a famous American designer of sporting arms, John M. Browning, patented a machine gun powered by the expanding powder gases produced when a cartridge was fired. Army and navy boards tested the 39-pound Browning gun and found it to be simple and easy to operate. While the navy bought a number of Browning guns, the Ordnance Department was not satisfied with the weapon's performance.[17] Additional tests a year later revealed that the Browning jammed frequently. When the air-cooled gun was fired continuously, its barrel overheated and accuracy declined drastically; after about five thousand rounds had passed through it, the barrel was worn out. Again, the gun was rejected.[18] Browning's patent of a gas-operated machine gun in 1890 marked the end of the basic development of the machine gun. Subsequent modifications in the design of the weapon reflected advances in metallurgy as well as new ideas about how it should be employed.[19]

Aware of the competition that new machine guns posed for his invention, Gatling continued to improve his gun. He devoted particular attention to its size, weight, and transport, and in the 1870s Gatling guns designed for a variety of uses, such as pack transport, appeared. Changes in the Gatling also followed changes in the caliber of the standard service rifle. Shortly after the end of the Civil War the army adopted .50 caliber ammunition; in 1873 it switched to .45 caliber small arms, and then in 1892 chose a new rifle, the .30 caliber Krag-Jorgensen. In nineteen years the bore diameter of the service rifle—and, therefore, the caliber of the Gatling gun—changed twice.[20] According to Gatling, replacing equipment rendered useless by changes in rifle caliber cost his company $500,000. At least thirteen new models of the Gatling gun appeared between 1870 and 1900. Frequent model changes meant short production runs and outmoded machinery, factors that helped to keep the cost of the Gatling gun high.[21]

The high price of the gun and the low level of appropriations for arms caused the Ordnance Department to buy Gatlings in small lots.[22] Most of the guns were sent to arsenals and to the forts in the nation's coast defenses; in 1894 the eighty-four Gatlings assigned to troop units were distributed among forty-nine army posts.[23] Despite its high cost, the Gatling remained the standard army machine gun until 1903. Made in Connecticut, the home state of Senator Joseph R. Hawley, chairman of the Senate Committee on Military Affairs, the Gatling had a considerable commercial edge over the British-made Maxim machine gun, its major competitor after 1885.[24] This advantage was formally recognized in the Fortifications Appropriations Act of 1888, which specified that ". . . all guns and materials purchased under the authority of this section shall be of American production and furnished by citizens of the United States."[25] The fact that it was made in America probably insured that the Gatling would be the standard army machine gun until it was conclusively demonstrated to be obsolete. With modernization of its machine guns stymied by the primacy of the Gatling, army doctrine remained undeveloped.

As the result of both its own test activities and continued interest in European developments in weaponry, the Ordnance Department collected a considerable fund of technical information and, to a lesser degree, tactical concepts concerning the machine gun. Such information was included in an Ordnance Department program that disseminated information of technical and professional interest to members of the Ordnance Corps and, when appropriate, to the army as a whole. Articles intended only for members of the Ordnance Corps were distributed by a series of *Notes On the Construction of Ordnance*. Initially these articles were largely translations of foreign work, but as the Ordnance Department gained members with scientific and technical expertise, a substantial number of the *Notes On the Construction of Ordnance* contained the work of American ordnance officers and civilian experts. Changes in the subject matter of the articles reflected the shift of Ordnance Department interest from theoretical matters to practical concerns such as the properties of smokeless powder and the design of rapid-fire fieldpieces.[26]

Information of interest mainly to ordnance officers was published in *Ordnance Notes*, which were sent to members of the Ordnance Corps with an information copy mailed to each army post. Matters of wider professional interest were covered in numbered *Ordnance Memoranda* sent to all persons and libraries with an interest in the subject covered. Both *Ordnance Notes* and *Ordnance Memoranda* communicated information and the official Ordnance Department position on a variety of subjects, including machine guns, to a wide audience within the army.[27]

Distribution of Gatling guns to frontier posts gave army units an opportunity to gain experience with the weapon during the campaigns against hostile Indians that marked frontier life in the 1870s. Normally kept in post ordnance storehouses, machine guns were issued to units at the request of their commanding officers. When a unit no longer needed them, the weapons were returned to the ordnance store.[28] Such an arrangement was convenient for the using units, whose commanders avoided permanent accountability for the weapons and the chore of maintaining them. The Ordnance Department retained control of the Gatlings, so that they could be shifted from post to post as required, but it restricted use of the guns for training exercises or experiments.

In 1878 the chief of ordnance directed that batteries containing both Gatling guns and conventional artillery pieces be assembled at five arsenals and the National Armory in Washington, D.C. This equipment was to be held ready for issue to regular units. Probably prompted by the riots and labor troubles of 1877, the measure appears to have provided for the armament of army units dispatched to restore order in large metropolitan areas; of the arsenals storing the mixed batteries, the one in Indianapolis was closest to the frontier.[29] The order further reduced the number of guns available for use on the frontier.[30]

Between 1874 and 1878 Gatling guns were fired at hostile Indians on six occasions. Employed under conditions ranging from the parched plains of the Anadarko Agency in Indian Territory to the deck of a steamer on the Columbia River, Gatlings generally performed satisfactorily when they could be brought to bear upon the elusive hostiles.[31] During the Red River War, Lieut. Col. Thomas H. Neill, Sixth Cavalry, used Gatling fire to prevent hostile Cheyenne Indians from entrenching themselves within rifle range of his position near Darlington Agency. In 1877 the pursuit of Chief Joseph's Nez Percé band was punctuated by a fierce fight in which forces under Maj. Gen. Oliver Otis Howard used the fire of two Gatlings to repulse repeated Nez Percé attacks that were pressed home with a determination and vigor unusual in Indian warfare. But burdened by its Gatlings and a mountain howitzer, Howard's force was unable to keep up with the Nez Percé as they continued their long trek toward Canada.[32] Slower than their adversaries, army regulars could ill afford the additional loss of mobility imposed by the Gatling guns.

The most famous instance of nonuse of Gatling guns in Indian warfare occurred during the Sioux Campaign of 1876. Brig. Gen.

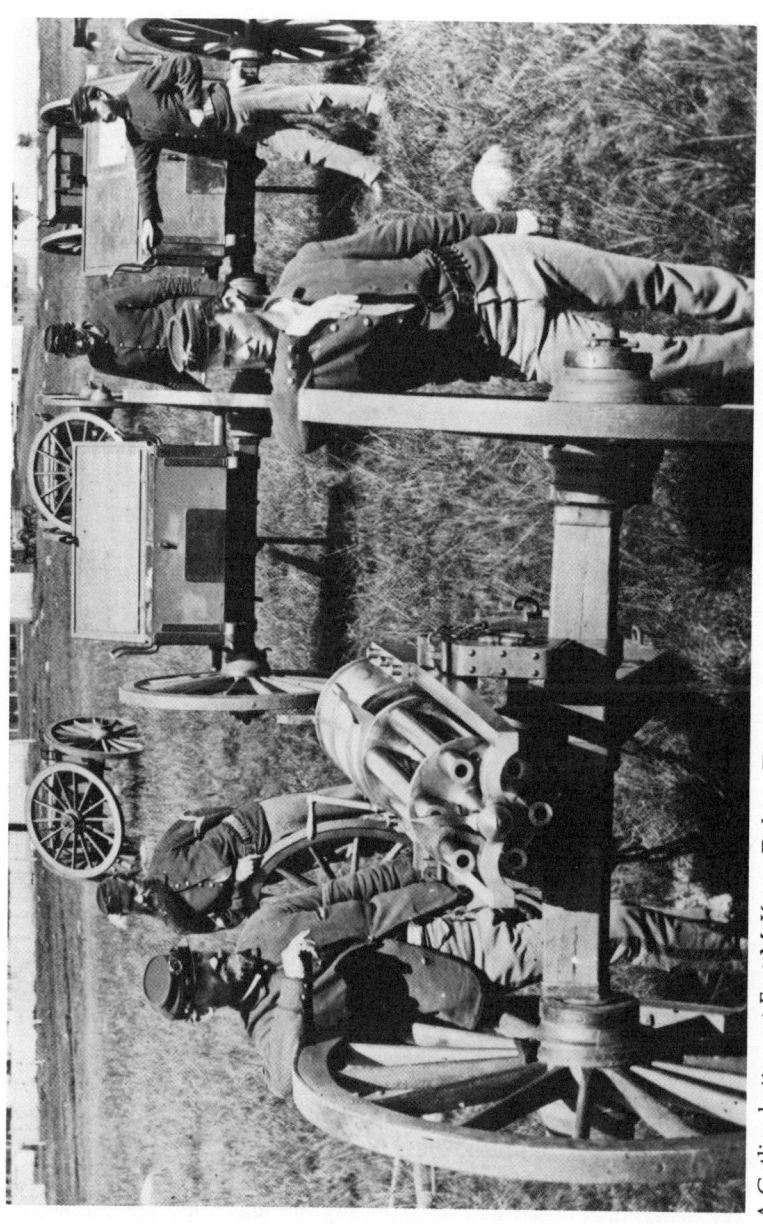

A Gatling battery at Fort McKean, Dakota Territory. *Courtesy:* National Park Service, Department of the Interior.

Alfred H. Terry, commander of a column operating against the Indians, formed an ad hoc detachment of four Gatlings manned by a thirty-two man detail from the Twentieth Infantry; the unit had enough firepower to break the back of any Indian attack that had been encountered.[33] Terry offered the Gatlings to Lieut. Col. George Armstrong Custer for use in the reconnaissance that Custer was to lead into the valley of the Little Big Horn River. Aware of the limited mobility of the .50 caliber Gatling reported by Major Alfred Gibbs of the Seventh Cavalry, almost a decade earlier, Custer ". . . declined the offer of Gatling guns, because they might hamper our movements through such a rugged country."[34] The key to defeating the Indians lay in overcoming the vast difference in the mobility of the two sides in order to bring the disciplined firepower of the regulars to bear upon the hostiles. Anything that slowed the cavalry columns or restricted their ability to negotiate difficult terrain was counterproductive no matter how much firepower it represented.[35]

Historian Fairfax Downey hypothesizes that with one more squadron and three ". . . machine guns spitting 1200 shots a minute at a massed foe—and the Battle of the Little Big Horn might have been a different story."[36] Accepted reconstructions of the battle, however, suggest a different picture. After splitting his command into four parts, Custer and 215 men rode into the broken terrain that lay across the Little Big Horn River from a gigantic Sioux camp. Caught in ground that favored the individual skirmishing tactics of the Indians, Custer and his men were overwhelmed in a confused fight that probably lasted little more than an hour.[37] Assuming that the Gatlings could have kept pace with Custer's or Maj. Marcus A. Reno's commands during their precipitate advance and subsequent attempts to withdraw to defensible terrain, the conclusion that the unwieldy .50 caliber guns with their limited traverse and semitrained teams and crews could have been employed effectively against the fleeting targets presented to them is debatable.

After the Custer massacre the columns that gingerly probed for the Sioux frequently included Gatlings and conventional artillery. The commander of one of these forces, Col. Nelson A. Miles, again raised the complaint that Gatlings lacked mobility in rough country. Miles also noted that at long ranges it was impossible to adjust

Gatling fire because the strike of the small-caliber bullets could not be seen. He asked that the eight .50 caliber Gatlings and an outmoded Rodman gun assigned to his command be replaced by a small-bore Krupp fieldpiece.[38]

Col. Henry Hunt, former chief of artillery for the Army of the Potomac, voiced a more balanced appraisal of Gatling's machine gun. Optimistic concerning the usefulness of the gun in combat, Hunt admitted that use of the Gatlings in Indian warfare had not produced "very creditable results." In his opinion the poor performance of the Gatlings resulted from the lack of trained gunners and the poor quality of the horses drawing the guns.[39]

The fact that it was operated by untrained crews and drawn by poor-quality horses certainly reduced the chance that the Gatling gun would see large-scale use on the frontier. The tendency of the gun to jam due to fouling and a defective design, which limited the traverse of the gun barrels, further reduced the usefulness of the weapon, but the key deficiency was its lack of mobility.[40] The role of the Gatling gun in frontier warfare depended upon Ordnance Department reaction to Major Gibbs' early request for a lightweight carriage to give the gun the mobility it needed to keep up with cavalry columns. The failure to respond to Gibbs' criticism with an effective program to reduce the weight and increase the mobility of the Gatling gun and its supporting equipment effectively precluded extensive use of the machine gun in Indian warfare.

The reasons for the inability of the machine gun to make significant headway within army organization and doctrine in the period prior to 1898 were varied and complex. But the history of the period reveals that military activities were governed by one overriding consideration—money, or more precisely the lack of it. Shortage of funds severely hampered efforts to modernize army weaponry and organization.

The size of the post-Civil War army peaked in 1866 with 57,072 officers and men entered on the rolls; by 1877 the nation's land forces had dwindled to a low of 24,140, and army strength remained below 29,000 until the Spanish-American War. The field artillery, which had limited utility in frontier warfare and was expensive to maintain, was neglected. In 1873 General Sherman noted that only one of the twelve batteries assigned to each artillery regiment was equipped and trained as a field battery. The other eleven batteries were armed and trained as infantry, some to man the coastal forts. Ten years after this report a second battery in each regiment was equipped as a light artillery battery, but even with this addition the army had only ten batteries of field artillery to support twenty-five infantry and ten cavalry regiments.[41]

Congress resisted War Department efforts to increase the size of the field artillery; no more batteries were added until 1898. Short of funds, the army allowed the equipment and efficiency of the existing batteries to deteriorate. After a survey of field artillery units in 1885, the inspector general labeled their condition unsatisfactory. Three years later he noted that some batteries were still equipped with guns of Civil War vintage.[42] During the Cuban campaign of 1898 the performance of the American artillery indicated that the condition of the field batteries had not improved greatly. With its mobile element almost extinct, the artillery branch did not have the resources to explore the potential of the machine gun.

By the mid-1870s the work of the Gillmore and Tower boards had firmly established the position of the machine gun as part of the secondary armament of the coastal forts. When coastal defense became a subject of considerable interest to Congress in the late 1880s, the army concentrated its attention upon the construction and primary armament of these forts. In the mid-1890s the War Department finally reviewed the state of the secondary armament of these works.

In 1896 a board of engineer officers decided that machine guns would be used for the "near defense" of coastal batteries and for covering the harbor mine fields with fire. "Near defense," the term that replaced "flank defense," meant using machine guns ". . . to oppose landing parties, giving them a mount upon movable carriages light enough for easy and ready transfer to any desired point of defense."[43]

Reassessment of the requirements of the coastal forts revealed that a total of 480 machine guns were required to complete the secondary armament of the seacoast works.[44] Realizing that he must use army resources before asking for money to buy additional guns, the chief of ordnance, Brig. Gen. Daniel W. Flagler, decided to call in the ninety machine guns assigned to posts in the interior. Flagler reasoned that the disappearance of the frontier and the final

In Pursuit of Perfection 85

pacification of the western tribes in the early 1890s had ended the need for machine guns at those posts. Instead of asking the secretary of war to issue an order recalling the guns, Flagler decided to conduct a survey to determine how many guns could be spared. Given the "bird-in-hand" philosophy common to most troop commanders, the results of the survey were not surprising. Field commanders claimed that the guns were needed for outfitting expeditions, training, and "in case of emergency." Conditioned by a thirty-year period of diminishing resources, these officers were reluctant to part with any weapon, even one that was never used; according to the survey, only sixteen Gatlings were available for use in the coastal forts.[45] The placement of additional machine guns in the seacoast works proceeded at the slow pace allowed by annual appropriations.

While American interest in the Gatling gun flagged, British forces began to develop an organization and doctrine for employing machine guns. First used in 1873-1874, machine guns were a normal component of British expeditionary forces as the century drew to a close. In 1898 a battery of six Maxim guns took part in the climactic conclusion of the conquest of the Sudan at Omdurman. In a battle witnessed by numerous foreign military attachés, the Maxim battery killed an estimated three-quarters of the 20,000 dervishes who fell to British arms.[46]

By 1900 the British army had integrated the machine gun in a limited fashion into the organization of their infantry; British machine-gun doctrine was the most advanced in the world. Developed for the special circumstances of colonial warfare—where the enemy normally lacked modern artillery—and restricted by the limitations imposed by horse-drawn transport and logistics, British doctrine held that the machine gun was a "weapon of opportunity" used for special purposes and for strengthening a defensive position.[47] A member of the British army in 1900 later observed that the term "weapon of opportunity" was so often used as a final explanation of how the machine gun was to be employed that it prevented the development of a more precise definition of the role of the gun.

Development of British machine-gun doctrine and organization ceased in 1900; in 1914 British units went to France with the machine-gun organization and tactics developed at the turn of the century. According to Maj. Gen. Ernest D. Swinton the lack of further development was an indirect result of the Boer War. Discovered to have certain mechanical defects, such as a tendency to jam, the machine gun was rejected as a major infantry weapon; the attention of the British army centered upon intensive marksmanship training, another method of increasing infantry firepower.[48]

Although the major opportunity for the American army to gain combat experience with the machine gun ended with the defeat of the plains tribes in the late 1870s, an experiment begun late in the decade allowed the army to gain some field experience with the weapon. In June 1878 Maj. Gen. E.O.C. Ord, commander of the Department of Texas, assigned a detachment of two .45 caliber Gatlings and twelve mounted soldiers to Battery F, Second Artillery. Soon thereafter the battery commander, Capt. Edward B. Williston, an experienced artilleryman who had held the Civil War rank of brevet colonel, signed receipts for four more Gatlings. During the spring and summer of 1879 Williston experimented with various organizational schemes and tested the equipment itself. He recommended that the War Department establish six-gun batteries of Gatlings with special ammunition carts in lieu of gun caissons. Enthusiastically endorsed by General Ord, Williston's plan was rejected by Lieut. Gen. Philip Sheridan. Sheridan favored using pack mules for carrying ammunition; General Sherman backed his subordinate, and the plan was shelved.[49]

Williston did not give up. After a six-month wait he sent a letter containing a detailed expression of his views as well as a rebuttal of Sherman's opinion that Gatling ammunition could be carried in infantry ammunition wagons or by pack mules. Williston pointed out that the standard Gatling caisson held only 3,920 cartridges, an amount that could be fired in less than ten minutes; the ammunition cart that he proposed would hold ten thousand rounds and would require a team of two horses instead of the five pack mules needed to carry an equivalent amount of ammunition. Williston also noted that while pack mules had to be kept under cover in combat, the ammunition cart that he advocated would move with the gun.[50]

General Ord again endorsed Williston's proposals and forwarded them to Sheridan with a request that he give them careful consideration. Sheridan continued to maintain that the ammunition cart would not be useful in Indian warfare, although he heartily recommended the cart for use in "civilized warfare." The secretary of war dismissed Williston's proposal with the glib remark that ". . . there does not appear to be any action necessary in this matter, there being no war between civilized peoples."[51] Here the action ended; not only were there no wars between "civilized peoples," but even the Indian wars were ending.

Late in 1881 Battery F was transferred to Fort Leavenworth, Kansas. Equipped with two Gatlings, two Hotchkiss revolving cannon, two Lowell battery guns, and a Gardner gun, the battery had a complement of fifty horses and thirty-one men. After arriving at Leavenworth, Captain Williston requisitioned three additional Gatlings and turned in the Lowell and Gardner guns.[52] Williston continued to experiment with machine guns until he was promoted to major and transferred to Washington, D.C., in 1885. From the capital, he was sent to the Watervliet Arsenal for tests of an ammunition cart built according to the plan that the War Department had refused in 1879. After extensive tests the cart was rejected.[53]

Promotion and assignment to staff duty did not end Williston's interest in machine guns. In June 1886 the *Journal of the Military Service Institution of the United States* carried a long article detailing his theories concerning the proper organization for the tactical use of machine-gun units. Williston categorized the machine gun as a special type of weapon separate from and not competitive with conventional field artillery weapons. In discussing tactics, the author concentrated upon the defensive value of the machine guns and their utility for covering the landing and embarkation of troops.[54] The second idea was probably rooted in Williston's Civil War experiences, for such operations had been common in both the eastern and western theaters of the war.

To strengthen his argument Major Williston cited successful use of machine guns in the Franco-Prussian War and in the Sudan as well as statements by Generals Sherman, Benet, and Hunt favoring the gun. He believed that machine guns could provide the firepower needed to bolster the morale and augment the fire of the undisciplined volunteer units, which traditionally made up the bulk of the wartime American army. To do this, machine-gun units were to be organized as part of a Machine Gun Service activated in the event of war. The Machine Gun Service would be an elite corps, headed by a brigadier general, and would be staffed with select infantry, cavalry, and artillery officers. A peacetime school would train National Guard machine-gun units. The basic component of the Machine Gun Service was to be a mounted battery of twelve guns. Highly mobile, the flexible organization could be divided into two six-gun batteries or six two-gun platoons. A battery would be assigned to each infantry and cavalry division; army corps would retain reserves of two additional batteries; and additional reserves of two batteries per corps would be held at army level.[55] Williston's proposal for distribution of machine-gun units resembled the artillery organization developed by the Union army. He did not specify whether he intended to use the reserve batteries as a reserve of firepower for influencing the course of the battle or in the Civil War mode as a reserve of fresh units to replace those used up in battle.

Williston's proposal for a separate machine-gun service was never acted upon. The concept of placing machine guns in batteries and then distributing these batteries at division, corps, and army level conformed to accepted artillery practice and to the conventional view that the machine gun was an artillery weapon. But the idea of a separate wartime service created by drawing handpicked officers from the combat arms was not practical. Plagued by a shortage of officers, commanders would not support a scheme that would deprive them of the best of their junior officers at the outbreak of war. The proposal to establish a machine-gun school made sense, but only as a part of a larger school such as the one at Fort Leavenworth. National Guard machine-gun batteries could be created only if Congress appropriated the money to buy the guns and the states agreed to fund the units on a continuing basis; neither of these actions was likely. Given the low level of military budgets and manpower, creation of a machine-gun service was feasible only in wartime. But the same constraints, cost and lack of manpower, prevented the peacetime preparation necessary to make the scheme work.

The machine gun was no longer a novelty in 1886, and to many military men its lackluster record indicated limited utility. Major Williston was aware of this attitude and devoted several pages to a discussion of four obstacles that hindered the introduction of the machine gun into army units. They were: general ignorance of the capabilities of the weapon and the consequent failure of most army officers to comprehend its value; widespread opinion that the machine gun was useful only as a defensive weapon; utilization of Gatling guns to ornament posts or careful storage to prevent their deterioration, which prevented practical work and experimentation with the weapons; and the large number of models of machine guns, which had led to a diffusion of experimental effort.[56]

None of the officers whose critiques were published at the end of Williston's article accepted all of his ideas. Lieut. Col. Adelbert R. Buffington, an ordnance officer who had worked with the Gatling, endorsed the technical portions of the article and gave particular support to the use of a pasteboard box for packing ammunition.[57] Bvt. Maj. Gen. Wesley Merritt, a senior cavalry officer, found the proposal for a machine gun service one that Williston ". . . could hardly hope to see carried out." Merritt concluded that artillery would seriously limit the tactical usefulness of machine guns. Bvt. Maj. Gen. Henry J. Hunt disagreed with Williston's organizational concepts; Hunt advocated adding a Gatling gun to each artillery battery to increase the defensive capabilities of the battery.[58] These reactions clearly indicate that in 1886 the American military remained unconvinced of the military worth of the machine gun.

Major Williston held that the central reason for the failure of the American military to accept the machine gun was a lack of experience, particularly combat experience, with the weapon. To remedy this, he advocated searching ". . . for information on the subject among the nations of Europe."[59] In 1886 such a search would have produced little support for his ideas and would probably have contributed considerable information and opinion that could be used to refute them. Far ahead of contemporary military thought in his ideas about machine guns, Major Williston could not change the position of the weapon in the army by himself.

The machine gun, classified as an auxiliary artillery weapon, slowly faded into the limbo that a weapon with such an ambiguous role could be expected to occupy during peacetime when economy and not military necessity dictated policy. By 1889 target practice with the Gatling was often canceled because the posts where the guns were located had no ammunition for practice firing of the weapons.⁶⁰ Two years later the general shortage of ammunition was so acute that the chief of ordnance proposed that all target practice with Gatlings be suspended because operation of the weapon was ". . . so simple that in my judgement little, if any, actual firing is necessary to teach the soldier to operate it properly."⁶¹ The War Department did cut the amount of ammunition authorized for target practice. In addition to a yearly allowance of twenty thousand rounds to the Light Artillery School at Fort Riley, Kansas, only four of the fifty-five posts that had Gatlings were allocated ammunition for target practice. The two thousand rounds that they received could be used only if the chief of ordnance approved the expenditure. By 1890 post commanders generally stored their machine guns or placed them in a location where the carefully shined brass and freshly painted carriage of the Gatling gun added a martial note to the appearance of the post.⁶² In neither case were the guns used or crews trained; machine-gun doctrine was similarly neglected.

As outlined in *Farrow's Military Encyclopedia* in 1895, the army continued to view Gatling guns as a special sort of defensive artillery piece to be retained for use at division level.⁶³ Yet the artillery remained unable to find a place for the machine gun. In the preface to his *Handbook for Light Artillery*, Alexander B. Dyer, the son of the Civil War chief of ordnance, gave the following evaluation of the machine gun: "While I do not consider that machine-guns are proper weapons for the light artillerist, I feel that occasions may arise when knowledge regarding them may prove of service; hence the chapter pertaining to them."⁶⁴ Although he outlined the organization of a light artillery battery that could be applied to machine guns, Dyer's chapter on machine guns was confined to a discussion of the mechanisms of various models of the weapon.⁶⁵ His work marked the end of a thirty-year period during which the United States Army had adopted the machine gun and then had failed to develop either a doctrine or an organization to use it.

NOTES

1. U.S., Department of Commerce, Bureau of the Census, *Historical Statistics of the United States, Colonial Times to 1957* (Washington, D.C., 1960), p. 718.

2. Maj. Gen. Winfield Scott Hancock, October 19, 1876, U.S., Congress, House, *Report of a Sub-Committee of the Committee On Military Affairs Relating to the Reorganization of the Army*, House Misc. Doc. 56, 45th Cong., 2d sess., 1878, pp. 7-8.

3. During the Civil War, and to a lesser extent in the 1870s, test and evaluation boards contained substantial numbers of line officers; in 1873 the Gillmore Board was headed by an engineer and contained an artillery and an ordnance officer. In 1881 a board appointed to select a new rifle was made up of two infantry officers and one officer each from the cavalry, artillery, and ordnance. U.S., Ordnance Department, *Ordnance Memoranda No. 17* (Washington, D.C., 1874), pp. 45-47; Sidney B. Brinckerhoff and Pierce Chamberlain, "The Army's Search for a Repeating Rifle: 1873-1903," *Military Affairs* XXXII (Spring 1968): 23-24.

4. Joyce D. Ciarrochi, Jesse T. Midkiff, and Garry D. Ryan, comps., *Preliminary Inventory of the Textual Record of the Office of the Chief of Ordnance (Record Group 156)*, pt. 1, mimeographed, (Washington, D.C., 1964), pp. 28-29.

5. Fortifications Appropriations Act, U.S., *Statutes at Large*, vol. 25, sec. 6, pp. 490-91.

6. The Gardner gun and its carriage weighed a total of 502 pounds versus 839 pounds for the Gatling and carriage. U.S. War Department, *Annual Report of the Chief of Ordnance, 1880* (Washington, D.C., 1880), pp. 387-90; Ordnance Office to Ordnance Board, July 25, 1884, National Archives, Record Group 156 (hereafter cited as NA, RG 156), "Letters, Telegrams, and Endorsements Sent to Ordnance Officers and Military Storekeepers 1839-89," vol. 68, pp. 24-25; *Annual Report of the Chief of Ordnance, 1885*, p. 674.

7. W. Y. Carman, *A History of Firearms From Earliest Times to 1914* (London, 1955), pp. 163-64.

8. By 1889 the armies of all major powers had adopted small-caliber rifles using smokeless powder. Joseph W. Shields, *From Flintlock to M1* (New York, 1954), pp. 139, 144.

9. George M. Chinn, *The Machine Gun* (Washington, D.C., 1951), pp. 141-42.

10. W.H.B. Smith, *Small Arms of the World*, 8th ed. (Harrisburg, Pa., 1966), pp. 78-79, 109; Bernard and Fawn Brodie, *From Crossbow to H-Bomb* (Bloomington, Ind., 1973), p. 143; Fairfax Downey, *Sound of the Guns* (New York, 1956), p. 179; Shields, *Flintlock*, pp. 141-44.

11. Chinn, *Machine Gun*, pp. 129-33; Smith, *Small Arms*, pp. 107-8.

12. Chinn, *Machine Gun*, p. 131; F. V. Longstaff and A. Hilliard Atteridge, *The Book of the Machine Gun* (London, 1917), pp. 25-26. The Maxim was adopted by the British, Russian, and German armies before

1901 and by the American army in 1903. J. S. Herron, "Machine Guns," *Notes of Military Interest for 1901*, U.S., War Department, Adjutant General's Office (Washington, D.C., 1902), pp. 135, 138, 146.

13. *Annual Report of the Chief of Ordnance, 1888*, p. 71.

14. Ibid., pp. 66-71; *Army and Navy Journal* (hereafter cited as *A-N Jou.*), February 11, 1888, p. 572; March 3, 1888, p. 630; January 25, 1890, p. 428; *Annual Report of the Chief of Ordnance, 1896*, pp. 239-48.

15. *Annual Report of the Chief of Ordnance, 1890*, p. 456.

16. Report of test of Maxim-Nordenfelt Automatic Machine Gun, cal. .303, November 18, 1895, NA, RG 156, "Letters and Endorsements Sent Jan. 1895-Mar. 1901," entries 138, 162, p. 16.

17. *Annual Report of the Chief of Ordnance, 1895*, pp. 80-83; U.S., War Department, *Annual Report of the War Department, 1904* (Washington, D.C. 1904), vol. X, p. 112; Chinn, *Machine Gun*, pp. 160-68.

18. Chinn, *Machine Gun*, p. 164; Proceedings of a Board of Officers Appointed to test the Colt Automatic Machine Gun, August 11, 1896, NA, RG 156, doc. 8900/Incl. 13.

19. In addition to the Gardner, Maxim, and Browning guns the Ordnance Department also tested the Lowell battery gun (1878), the Taylor battery gun (1878), the Nordenfelt machine gun (1881), the Robertson machine gun (1895), and the Skoda machine gun (1895) in the period from 1878 to 1898. U.S., Ordnance Department, *Index to the Reports of the Chief of Ordnance, 1864 to 1912* (Washington, D.C., 1913), pp. 86-88.

20. From 1892 to 1957 army small arms used .30 caliber ammunition. (Standard rifle ammunition was redesigned in 1903 and 1906, but the caliber did not change.) Russell F. Weigley, *History of the United States Army* (New York, 1967), pp. 268, 290; Chinn, *Machine Gun*, p. 54; Smith, *Small Arms*, pp. 621, 626.

21. *A-N Jou.*, February 7, 1891, p. 400. The manufacturers of the Gatling realized a substantial return on their product. In 1869, seventy Gatlings were sold to the Russian government for $1,500 each, a price that was more than double the production cost of the gun. Five years later the company secretary stated that it was company policy to keep prices for the guns high; cost and price figures for this period support this statement. Paul Wahl and Donald R. Toppel, *The Gatling Gun* (New York, 1971), p. 39, 70-71.

22. Procurement of small numbers of Gatlings and frequent model changes combined to saddle the army with a variety of types of Gatlings. Following the initial purchase of fifty 1-inch and fifty .50 caliber model 1866 guns, only two purchases of comparable size are recorded—fifty-six .45 caliber model 1874 guns, and forty-four .45 caliber model 1875 guns.

In Pursuit of Perfection 93

Nevertheless, the 159 guns procured between 1874 and 1877 indicate that interest in the Gatling was high ten years after their initial purchase. But following the 1870s the number of guns purchased declined; between 1890 and 1895 only thirty-one Gatlings were bought. The price of $1,000 per gun remained high. U.S., Ordnance Department, *Description of Gatling Guns Cal. .45 with Rules and Regulations for Their Inspection* (Washington, D.C., 1878), pp. 17-18; *Annual Report of the Chief of Ordnance, 1895*, p. 24; W. B. Alliston to Secretary of War, May 28, 1890, NA, RG 156, doc. 2931 (1890).

23. Adjutant General's Office Brief, subject: Requirements of Machine Guns in Fortifications, February 29, 1896, NA, RG 156, doc. 9544, encl. 12 (1896).

24. Joseph R. Hawley to Secretary of War, May 8, 1890, NA, RG 156, doc. 2894 (1890).

25. Fortification Appropriations Act, U.S., *Statutes at Large*, vol. 25, sec. 6, pp. 490-91.

26. Of the eighty-five *Notes On the Construction of Ordnance* published between July 20, 1882, and October 2, 1902, thirty-six articles were of American origin and forty-nine of foreign origin; French (twenty-four) and Italian (ten) publications were particularly well represented. U.S., Ordnance Department, *Notes On the Construction of Ordnance*, nos. 1-85 (July 20, 1882-October 2, 1902).

27. U.S., Ordnance Department, *Rules and Regulations for the Government of the Ordnance Department* (Washington, D.C., 1877), p. 10.

28. Gatlings were issued eleven times between 1873 and 1876. NA, RG 156, "Quarterly Summary Statements of Ordnance and Ordnance Stores in the Hands of Troops 1872-1876," vol. I, pp. 157-58; vol. II, pp. 95, 143, 146, 149-50, 152-53, 155.

29. The other four arsenals were: the Allegheny Arsenal, the Rock Island Arsenal, the Washington Arsenal, and the Watertown Arsenal. NA, RG 156, "Letters, Telegrams, and Endorsements Sent to Ordnance Officers and Military Storekeepers 1839-89," vol. 51, pp. 336-38.

30. By 1878, 269 Gatlings—51 1-inch, 59 .50 caliber and 159 .45 caliber—had been purchased. U.S., Ordnance Department, *Description of Gatling Guns*, pp. 17-18.

31. Reports of the performance of the Gatling mentioned problems caused by jamming due to grit in the mechanism of the gun as well as an inability to adjust the fire of the gun. The carriage of the gun and its ammunition feed also were the subjects of adverse commentary.

32. Lieut. Col. Thomas H. Neill, April 7, 1875, *Annual Report of the Secretary of War, 1875*, vol. I, pp. 86-87; Fairfax Downey, *Indian-Fighting Army* (New York, 1941), pp. 236-39.

33. *A-N Jou.*, June 3, 1876, p. 689; *Annual Report of the Secretary of War, 1876*, vol. I, p. 459.

34. Lieut. Francis M. Gibson, Seventh Cavalry, to Katherine Gibson, July 4, 1876, Katherine Gibson Fougera, *With Custer's Cavalry* (Caldwell, Idaho, 1940), p. 267.

35. The mobility of the Gatling was further reduced by the practice of making up teams of condemned cavalry horses to draw the guns. Handled by infantrymen whose duties did not normally include driving and caring for gun teams, these substandard horses were given either a gun-carriage-limber combination weighing 1,834 pounds or a caisson-limber-ammunition combination weighing 1,920 pounds to draw. Downey, *Sound*, p. 176; NA, RG 156, "Reports of Experiments 1826-71," vol. 98, entries 70 and 98.

36. Downey, *Indian*, p. 198.

37. Robert M. Utley, *Frontier Regulars* (New York, 1973), pp. 259-60.

38. Col. Nelson A. Miles to Acting Adjutant General, Department of Dakota, September 16, 1876, NA, RG 156, doc. 4257 (1878) encl. 1; *A-N Jou.*, February 10, 1877, p. 431.

39. Col. Henry Hunt to Representative Levi Maish, February 11, 1878, U.S., Congress, House, *Report of a Sub-Committee of the Committee On Military Affairs Relating to the Reorganization of the Army*, House Misc. Doc. 56, 45th Cong., 2d sess., 1878, pp. 95-96.

40. The problem of jamming was reported as early as mid-1874. Lieut. Col. J. W. Davidson to Acting Chief of Ordnance, June 21, 1874, NA, RG 156, doc. 3130 (1874).

41. U.S., Department of Commerce, Bureau of Census, *Historical Statistics*, pp. 736-37; Edward Ranson, "The Endicott Board of 1885-86 and the Coast Defenses," *Military Affairs* XXXI (Summer 1967), p. 79.

42. Ranson, "Endicott Board," p. 80 and fn. 41.

43. NA, RG 156, "General Correspondence, 1894-1913," doc. 9544, encl. 33 (1896), 2d endorsement, May 20, 1896.

44. Chief of Ordnance to Senator W. C. Squire, February 12, 1896, NA, RG 156, doc. 12307.

45. Adjutant General's Office Brief, subject: Requirements of Machine Guns in Fortifications, February 29, 1896, NA, RG 156, doc. 9544, encl. 12 (1896).

46. G. S. Hutchison, *Machine Guns: Their History and Tactical Employment* (London, 1938), pp. 67-70; Chinn, *Machine Gun*, p. 142; C.H.B. Pridham, *Superiority of Fire* (London, 1945), pp. 41-42; Smith, *Small Arms*, pp. 109-10.

47. In 1900, machine guns were distributed in the British army as follows:

    Infantry brigade (4 battalions)—two 2-gun sections.

Mounted infantry battalion (2 companies)—one 2-gun section.
Cavalry brigade (3 regiments)—one 3-gun section.
Herron, *Mil. Notes, 1901*, pp. 138-39; Hutchison, *Machine Guns*, pp. 59-60.

48. Ernest D. Swinton, *Eyewitness* (Garden City, N.Y., 1933), pp. 7-8.

49. Battery F was designated as a light artillery battery by War Department General Order 246, November 17, 1880, NA, RG 94, Microcopy M-727, Roll 14, Return of the Second Regiment of Artillery, Record of Events for June, August and December 1878 and November 1880; NA, RG 156, "Letters Received 1812-94," doc. 1756 (1879), 3d., 6th, and 7th endorsements.

50. Capt. E. B. Williston to Assistant Adjutant General, Department of Texas, July 3, 1879, NA, RG 156, doc. 1756A (1879).

51. First through fourth endorsements to Capt. E. B. Williston to Assistant Adjutant General, Department of Texas, July 3, 1879, NA, RG 156, doc. 1756A (1879).

52. Bvt. Maj. Gen. John Pope to Col. R. Williams, November 19, 1881, NA, RG 94, Microcopy M-689, Roll 54, Frames 148-50; Capt. E. B. Williston to Chief of Ordnance, March 17, 1882, NA, RG 156, doc. 1120 (1882).

53. S. V. Benet to Secretary of War, November 17, 1885, Ordnance Department, *Collection*, vol. III, p. 190.

54. Edward B. Williston, "Machine Guns and the Supply of Small-Arm Ammunition on the Battle-Field," *Journal of the Military Service Institution of the United States*, VII (June 1886), pp. 121-23, 132.

55. Ibid., pp. 122-25, 133-40.
56. Ibid., pp. 125-26, 128.
57. Ibid., p. 161.
58. Ibid., pp. 162-65.
59. Ibid., p. 121.

60. Maj. H. C. Cook to Assistant Adjutant General, Department of the Missouri, November 13, 1889, NA, RG 156, doc. 3397 (1891).

61. Fourth endorsement, Ordnance Office, October 5, 1891, NA, RG 156, "Press Copies of Letters, Endorsements, and Telegrams Sent" ("Miscellaneous Letter"), October 1885-July 1894, June 1897-February 1903, vol. 252, pp. 464-65.

62. Ibid.; Adjutant General to Commanding General, Department of the Missouri, November 13, 1889, NA, RG 156, doc. 3397 (1891).

63. Edward S. Farrow, *Farrow's Military Encyclopedia*, vol. I (New York, 1895), p. 752.

64. Alexander B. Dyer, *Handbook for Light Artillery* (New York, 1896), p. iii.

65. Ibid., pp. 261-64, 316-61.

V
COMBAT AND ITS RESULTS, 1898-1901

The Spanish-American War brought the first important demonstrations of the effectiveness of the machine gun. In 1898 and 1899 a young infantry lieutenant, John Henry Parker, attempted to thrust the machine gun into a central position in army doctrine and organization. Although this effort failed, employment of machine guns by units in the field began the process that eventually resulted in the partial integration of the machine gun in army doctrine and organization.

Entering the army during a period when there was more time available than there was work to do, Lieutenant Parker was given the job of training a crew to man the Gatling gun assigned to his post. Here he discovered opportunity where others had found drudgery.[1] The young infantryman became an "expert" on machine guns and developed a tactical theory for their employment in battle. Detailed to the Infantry and Cavalry School at Fort Leavenworth in 1897, Parker presented a paper explaining his ideas to the commandant of the Fort Leavenworth Schools, Brig. Gen. Hamilton S. Hawkins.[2] In it Parker described a cart that he had designed and that he claimed would enable a machine gun to ". . . be carried by its crew with a firing line of infantry *on the offensive*, over almost any kind of ground . . ."[3] Parker identified lack of tactical mobility as a key obstacle to the large-scale use of machine guns and offered his carriage as a solution to the problem. Having theoretically freed the machine gun from its immobility, the innovative infantryman explained how to make the best use of its firepower.

To Parker the machine gun was a mechanical substitute for the firepower of a large reserve of riflemen—a *"MASSED RIFLE IN*

RESERVE." Committed at the decisive moment during an attack, the gun would insure penetration of the enemy line; during withdrawal operations or in a defensive position, machine guns would force the enemy to maintain his distance or accept heavy losses if he chose to attack. Parker admitted that the weapon was vulnerable to artillery fire, but he failed to consider the effect upon tactics should both sides possess and use machine guns. Impressed with the student officer's work, Hawkins forwarded Parker's paper to the War Department where, probably because of its esoteric nature, it was ignored.[4] Parker rejoined the Thirteenth Infantry Regiment and moved with it to Tampa, Florida, in May 1898.

Undeterred by lack of War Department interest in his work, Lieutenant Parker decided to form a unit to test his theories

Lieut. John Henry Parker. *Courtesy*: Parker, *History of the Gatling Gun Detachment of the Fifth Army Corps at Santiago*.

concerning the use of machine guns in combat.[5] In Tampa he took his plan to the commander of his regiment, Lieut. Col. Alfred T. Smith; Smith rejected it immediately. Following the advice of two fellow officers, Parker submitted a typewritten copy of his plan to Col. Arthur MacArthur, the senior officer on the staff of the expedition commander, Brig. Gen. James F. Wade. According to Parker's plan his organization would possess

(a) The fire-action of good infantry.
(b) The mobility of cavalry.
Its qualities, therefore, must be rapidity and accuracy, both of fire and movement.
Its employment on the defensive is obvious. On the offensive it is expected to be useful with advance guards, rear guards, outposts, raids, and in battle. The last use, novel as it is, will be most important of all.

* * *

The *moral effect* of its presence will be very great; . . . [firing] (over the charging line) in many cases. Last, but very important, the occupation of a captured line by this organization at once will supply a powerful, concentrated, and controlled fire, either to repulse a counter-charge or to fire on a discomfited, retiring enemy.

* * *

There is one vital limitation upon the proposed organization; viz., it must not be pitted against artillery.[6]

MacArthur approved the proposal and arranged an appointment with Wade, but Maj. Gen. William Shafter assumed command of the expedition and General Wade left for Chickamauga before Parker could see him.

At this point John T. Thompson, the ordnance officer at Tampa, offered to act as Parker's advocate with the staff.[7] He told Parker that a shipment of fifteen .30 caliber Gatling guns that General Shafter had asked for had arrived in Tampa.[8] Shortly thereafter Lieutenant Parker was appointed an assistant ordnance officer, and on May 27, 1898, Fifth Corps authorized the formation of the Provisional Gatling Gun Detachment. Parker began to train his men, but the Gatling Gun Detachment was not included when the expedition received orders to sail. Once again Thompson provided a solution; Parker was given responsibility for ammunition security, and his detachment formed an unauthorized escort. With Thompson's assistance Parker succeeded in getting his men and guns aboard the transport *Cherokee.*

Parker's initial plan specified a detachment of one officer, six noncommisisoned officers (NCOs) and thirty-seven enlisted men equipped with three Gatlings. On June 3, 1898, the detachment had four guns but only two NCOs and ten enlisted men. Between the first and second sailing of the Fifth Corps, Parker secured an appointment with General Shafter and persuaded him to authorize the addition of twenty men to the unit. Parker knew the men he wanted; orders designating the additional men were issued immediately. Evidently impressed by the earnest young infantry officer and the merit of his plan, Shafter placed the Gatling Gun Detachment in the first element of the Fifth Corp's landing order.[9]

At Tampa, Parker exhibited a number of characteristics that marked his career: initiative, ingenuity, ambition, and the ability to present his ideas concisely, forcefully, and persuasively. His ability to convince first Thompson and then Shafter of the worth of his proposal was crucial to the success of his project. Parker benefited from the lack of efficient staff control of the expedition and the loose chain of command in Tampa. Both he and Thompson exploited the resulting confusion by working largely in the gaps between the authority of various commanders, first to separate Parker from the control of his regiment and then to obtain authorization and transport for his detachment. Both staff and command did assist in the formation of a unit designed to employ a weapon in which they were interested, but John Henry Parker must receive the lion's share of the credit for the creation of the Gatling Gun Detachment.

Parker's detachment did not participate in the opening battle of the Cuban campaign at Las Guasimas, but an American machine gun unit was present. Several wealthy members of the First Volunteer Cavalry had given the regiment a detachment of two Colt model 1895 machine guns, and one of them, Sgt. William Tiffany, commanded the unit. After landing at Daiquiri, Tiffany secured two mules to carry the guns, but the Colts were only marginally effective.[10]

After the victory at Las Guasimas the Fifth Corps readied itself for an assault on the Spanish defenses around Santiago. Little can be said of the plans for the attack except that they disregarded the lessons of the Civil War.[11] Poor reconnaissance and failure to use local information on the nature of the battlefield added to the dangers of an overly complex plan of attack. Having forgotten that artillery was largely ineffective against intrenched infantry and that enemy counterbattery fire could be devastating in response, Shafter failed to realize that their magazine rifles and smokeless powder ammunition gave the Spaniards the enormous advantage of almost invisible firepower. Battlefield wire communication was available, but the Americans did not use it properly; consequently tactical control devolved upon the senior officers who actually led the attack. At 6:30 A.M. on July 1, 1898, the battle began with a secondary attack on the village of El Caney. From 8:30 A.M. until 1:00 P.M. the main American force, Brig. Gen. Samuel S. Sumner's cavalry division and Brig. Gen. Jacob F. Kent's infantry division, struggled to get into position for the principal assault. Since only one small road led to the Spanish positions, both divisions were forced to move over half a mile in column, ford the Aguadores River, and then deploy—all while within range of the Spanish rifles and artillery. After suffering heavy casualties during the movement to their attack positions, the troops had to cross the shallow San Juan River and approximately 500 yards of open ground before reaching the Spanish positions along the crests of San Juan and Kettle Hills. At 1:00 P.M. Sumner ordered his troops to advance against Kettle Hill. As the advance began, the Gatling detachment opened fire in support of Kent's attack on the trenches and blockhouses on San Juan Hill.[12]

Shafter's initial orders to the Gatling detachment were to protect Capt. George S. Grimes' light artillery battery on El Pozo Hill. Here Parker's unit came under Spanish counterbattery fire and was ordered to the rear. At 9:00 A.M. he returned to El Pozo and received orders to "Find the Seventy-first New York Volunteers and go in with them, if you can. If this is not practicable, find the best position you can and use your guns to the best advantage."[13] Parker located the Seventy-first New York Volunteers lying beside a trail and went forward to reconnoiter the ground on the far side of the Aguadores ford. Upon his return he met Col. George M. Derby, a member of Shafter's staff, who advised him to wait until the infantry was fully deployed before moving the Gatlings across the Aguadores and into firing position.

At approximately 1:00 P.M. Parker received this message: "General Shafter directs that you give one of your guns to Lieutenant Miley [John D. Miley, Shafter's aide], take the others forward beyond the ford where the dynamite gun is, and go into action at the best point you can find."[14] Three Gatlings were moved to a position about 600 yards from the Spanish trenches on San Juan Hill. After the Gatlings had fired on the Spanish positions for almost nine minutes, the leading elements of the American attack reached a position 150 yards from the enemy defenses, and Parker ordered his guns to cease firing. As soon as the position was taken, Parker moved his guns to the crest of San Juan Hill.[15]

That evening Parker's detachment moved to positions occupied by Theodore Roosevelt's First Volunteer Cavalry Regiment. The Gatlings participated in the repulse of a Spanish sally and silenced an unprotected 160 mm (6.3-inch) rifled gun at a range of about 2,000 yards. On the morning of July 2, 1898, Parker received reinforcement, the two Colt machine guns commanded by Sergeant Tiffany. The next night these guns were placed in the trenches along with three of the Gatlings.[16] On July 4 a Sims-Dudley pneumatic dynamite gun also came under his control, and for the next week Parker commanded his Gatling detachment, the Colt guns, and the dynamite gun. His commander was Theodore Roosevelt, now colonel of the First Volunteer Cavalry, and the Gatling detachment became a *de facto* part of the "Rough Riders." The future president and the young machine-gun enthusiast soon became good friends.[17] Roosevelt was optimistic about the military potential of machine guns, but the reactions of regular army officers were mixed.

The most enthusiastic reports of the performance of the Gatling guns were by the captains and lieutenants who actually led the charge up San Juan Hill. Lieut. Dwight W. Ryther, Sixth Infantry, stated that the ". . . Gatling-gun fire prepared the way for the

Working a Gatling gun while almost hidden in the deep grass in front of Santiago. *Courtesy:* The National Archives.

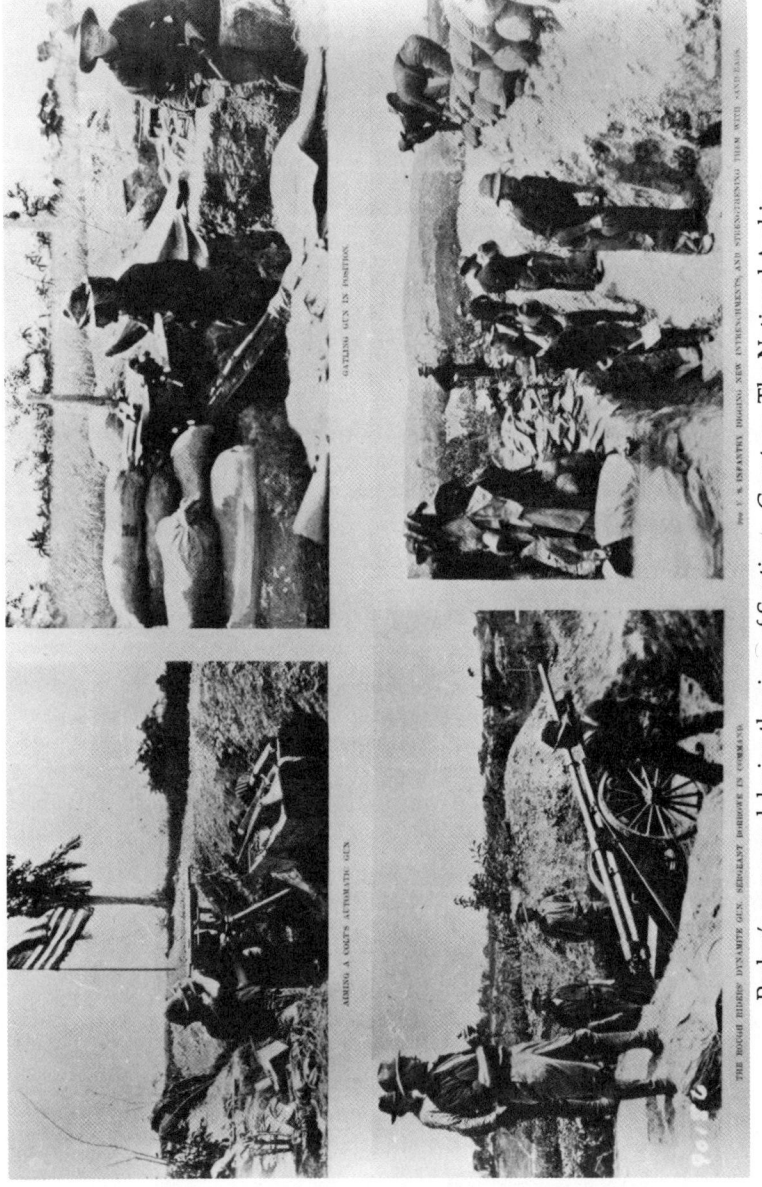

Parker's command during the siege of Santiago. *Courtesy:* The National Archives.

assault of the hill very effectively."[18] Capt. Lyman W.V. Kennon, Sixth Infantry, gave a more detailed analysis:

> From here could be seen the effect of the fire of our Gatling gun which had the range accurately and was sweeping along the trenches of the enemy with the utmost precision. It greatly demoralized the enemy, some of whom could be seen running from their places.[19]

A member of Parker's regiment, Capt. James B. Goe, rendered the most glowing report of all.

> The battery of the Gatling guns under Lieutenant Parker, Thirteenth Infantry, was opening fire on the enemy's trenches from a position on our right and rear. This fire had a magical effect, and the Spaniards were seen getting out of their works with a rush and disappearing toward Santiago. If it had not been for the timely aid given by Lieutenant Parker's guns, our loss would have been terrible during the remainder of the attack.[20]

While these reports illustrated the value of machine-gun fire in the support of an infantry assault, they did not consider further use of the weapon. Maj. Philip Reade of the Inspector General's Corps addressed this subject.

> The work of the Gatling-gun battery, and the Colt's automatic machine gun on the firing line before Santiago demonstrated the value of such fire, and this type of gun should not be omitted from future schemes of organization.[21]

Parker was the only other officer who mentioned the future use of machine guns in his report.

As might be expected, the coverage given the operations of the Gatling Gun Detachment in the reports of senior officers diminished as the rank of the officers increased. Two regimental commanders, Colonel Roosevelt and Lieut. Col. Henry C. Egbert, Sixth Infantry, commented on the effectiveness of the Gatling Gun Detachment. General Hawkins, commander of the First Brigade of Kent's division, observed the effect of the Gatling guns, but his official report did not mention them.

General Wheeler credited the Gatling guns with having "done good work." Shafter stated simply that Parker and the Gatling Gun Detachment rendered "most efficient service."[22] The brevity of the comments contained in the after-action reports is not surprising, for all of them were relatively brief. As the rank of the reporting officer increased, the scope of the narrative broadened; hence the amount of space devoted to any phase of the attack on July 1 or the siege that followed necessarily decreased. Strictly an account of events, the reports did not present an analysis of the battle. All of these factors tended to obscure the significance of the actions of the Gatling Gun Detachment on and after July 1, 1898. The Santiago campaign provided the American army with the opportunity to test machine guns in combat against an army equipped with modern weapons. Parker's brief use of machine guns provided a partial demonstration of their power, but their effectiveness had yet to be recognized.

Shortly after his return to the United States, Parker sent a letter outlining his proposal for an experimental "Tactical Unit of Machine Guns" through official channels to the War Department. He called for the formation of a 106-man company, which he would command, to be equipped with nine model 1895 Gatling guns. After recommending that the unit be stationed at Fort Meyer, Virginia, presumably because it would be close to the War Department and Congress, Parker asked that the officer selected to command the unit ". . . be given ample latitude and suitable rank."[23] He then stated his belief that a bill authorizing a machine-gun corps for the army would be introduced at the next session of Congress and added that a draft of such a bill had been given to Gen. Joseph Wheeler. Referred to the chief of artillery for comment, Parker's proposal met the conventional position that ". . . machine guns are artillery weapons, and the duty of organizing and equipping a machine gun battery . . . should . . . be entrusted to a battery of artillery."[24] Perhaps reminded of his experience with Gatling guns in 1876, Major General Miles concurred with this opinion, and Parker's proposal for an experimental machine-gun detachment was dropped.[25]

Despite War Department indifference to his ideas, Lieutenant Parker continued his efforts to promote the machine gun. In the spring of 1899 he sent a series of letters to the War Department stating his desire to raise, train, and command a regiment of black soldiers, which would be wholly or partially equipped with machine guns. Again he failed to interest the War Department in his idea.[26]

Parker also used books and articles to develop and explain his ideas. His first book, *History of the Gatling Gun Detachment Fifth Army Corps, At Santiago, With a Few Unvarnished Truths Concerning That Expedition*, appeared in late 1898. Parker did not intend to present a complete and detailed exposition of his theories concerning the proper use of the machine gun; rather he ". . . hoped to place before the intelligent American public some correct ideas of the new arm which was tried thoroughly at Santiago for the first time in the history of the world."[27] Thus the volume is mainly a colorful description of the experiences of Lieutenant Parker and the Gatling Gun Detachment.

Instead of discussing his tactical and organizational concepts in a single chapter, Parker used his narrative to illustrate the various facets of his theory.[28] His estimates of the value of the machine gun as a defensive and offensive weapon and of the effect of its fire on the morale of enemy and friendly troops were amply supported by his story. Experience had changed one tenet of his theory. Carefully inserted in the plan that he had presented at Tampa was the statement, "There is one vital limitation upon the proposed organization; viz., it must not be pitted against artillery."[29] Experience in combat led Parker to conclude that machine guns could silence enemy artillery pieces so long as they were within range of the machine guns.[30] Here he contradicted the dogma, from the Franco-Prussian War, that artillery was inherently superior to machine guns. The development of artillery as a long-range, indirect-fire weapon diminished the importance of Parker's discovery. In the future direct combat between machine guns and artillery pieces would be a rarity.

Parker's narrative was skillful and well written, but his argument had a major weakness: It lacked substantial and detailed factual support. The narrowness of his factual base forced Lieutenant Parker to use minor events to justify his hypotheses. The events of the Santiago campaign were too brief to provide enough evidence to force the army to change its attitude toward machine guns.

Throughout his book Parker was extremely critical of the efforts and failures of various branches of the army in the Cuban campaign. Many of his criticisms—such as those of the Ordnance, Quartermaster, and Medical departments—were justified. But their tone, and distribution to the general public at a time when the conduct of the campaign was under investigation and the reputation of the army was clouded, did little to enhance Parker's reputation in the eyes of his superiors. Shortly after his first book was published, Parker authored an article in the January 1899 issue of the *Journal of the Military Service Institution of the United States*; this article caused a controversy that furthered neither his career nor acceptance of his theories by the military authorities. In discussing the Cuban campaign, Parker turned his strongest fire upon the artillery. He believed

> ... that the artillery arm of the service had been moved back upon the battle-field to ranges not less than 1500 yards. ... The problem of supporting an infantry charge by some sort of fire immediately became the great tactical problem of the battlefield.
>
> * * *
>
> [The solution of this problem, then, was] ... that some form of machine gun must be adopted to take the place of artillery from 1500 yards down.[31]

The facts, as Parker saw them, were not revealed with similar clarity to fellow officers. To sustain his claim that the machine gun was important enough to be organized as ". . . a separate, independent, arm of the service," Parker had to demonstrate that artillery—particularly light artillery—could no longer operate in or close to the infantry firing line.[32] The actions of two batteries of light artillery located in the firing line on San Juan Hill on July 2, 1898, provided the evidence that he needed.

During the night following the battle for San Juan Hill, two batteries of light artillery moved into front-line positions only 500 yards from the Spanish trenches and in full view of the enemy. The artillerymen attempted to dig gun pits, but since the ground was extremely rocky, the pits were only a foot deep by dawn. In a postdawn exchange with the Spaniards the gun crews were driven to cover, and eventually the batteries were withdrawn.³³ Parker described the incident in the following manner:

> The one fact demonstrated more clearly than all others is that machine guns can live in positions utterly untenable for any kind of artillery. This was shown by the withdrawal of the combined batteries of Best and Parkhurst on the morning of July 2d, from ground held successfully by the Gatlings all the previous afternoon under well-directed artillery fire from the enemy, and against two countercharges. . . . *The artillery, having had several hours to dig gun-pits; fired only three rounds, and was compelled to seek safety in precipitate and disorderly flight.* The machine guns had not only remained on the same ground all the previous afternoon, but held their place on the infantry's most advanced line until the surrender, and never even thought of retiring. When they opened up they made themselves felt at once; they put out of action the battery that had driven Best and Parkhurst away, and kept it out of action until the surrender, in addition to giving substantial aid in holding down the enemy's trench fire.³⁴

The account supported Parker's contention that field artillery could no longer serve in the front lines.

When the article appeared, Capt. Charles D. Parkhurst, the commander of one of the batteries, initiated official action to force Parker to retract his statement concerning the "precipitate and disorderly flight" of the two batteries. Parkhurst's claim that the withdrawal was made under orders and was not a "flight" was sustained, and General Miles ordered Parker to publish a retraction. Parker obeyed, but the controversy was kept alive by the fact that his book contained substantially the same allegations plus additional material that was judged "improper and unmilitary."³⁵ Continued publication of the book was considered to be conduct unbecoming an officer and punishable by a court martial, but as the judge advocate general noted, a court martial would entail investigation and evaluation of the handling of the artillery at Santiago and would have the effect of "booming" Parker's book. Accordingly, he recommended that the entire matter be suppressed. Since no one wanted a renewed investigation of the Santiago campaign, Lieutenant Parker's punishment was limited to a written reprimand from the major general commanding the army.³⁶

Publication brought Parker's theories publicity, but it also gained him a reputation as an ambitious, iconoclastic officer with little regard for the established forms and courtesies of the service.[37]

In 1899 Lieutenant Parker published a detailed exposition of his views concerning the proper organization for and tactical use of machine guns in his second book, *Tactical Organization and Uses of Machine Guns in the Field*. He devoted an entire chapter to a review of the history of the machine gun in an attempt to demonstrate that ". . . the machine gun has come to stay. It is no longer an experiment."[38]

The young officer rejected both the traditional concept of employing machine guns in light artillery batteries and the British idea of incorporating machine-gun sections into the infantry, cavalry, and artillery. His reasons for not organizing machine guns as light artillery were: (1) the capabilities and therefore, the missions and tactics of the two weapons are fundamentally different; (2) use of machine guns as light artillery would lead to a reduction in the number of light artillery batteries authorized; and (3) the artillery had a history of hostility toward machine guns.

Parker's argument against incorporating machine guns in cavalry and infantry units rested on his contention that machine guns would interfere with the primary mission of the cavalry, which was reconnaissance, and the ". . . *one raison d'être of the infantryman which is . . . to get within bayonet range of his foe.*"[39] Instead, ". . . *machine guns should constitute a separate corps, distinct in personnel, in training, and in the line of promotion.*"[40]

The structure of the machine-gun corps was based on Parker's belief that each machine gun should form the nucleus of a separate gun section—a tactical unit capable of independent action.[41] Three gun sections formed a company, which would normally operate with a regiment of three battalions. This, Parker believed, was the ". . . largest number of guns which could be got into action effectively at any one time and place *on the offensive.* . . ."[42] Three machine-gun companies formed a battalion, which would support a brigade of three regiments; the battalion was the largest unit in the machine-gun corps. One additional battalion would be controlled by the corps commander; army corps with three divisions of infantry and one of cavalry would contain thirteen machine-gun battalions.[43]

Special machine-gun staff officers would be members of the staff of brigades and larger units. The machine-gun corps would be headed by a brigadier general, chief of the Machine Gun Corps—a position that Parker undoubtedly coveted. As part of a field army with an infantry strength of 100,000 men the machine-gun corps would number 6,059 officers and men.[44] Compared to the World War I ratio of about one member of a machine-gun unit for each five riflemen in a division, the size of the machine-gun service Parker proposed does not seem excessive.[45] In an army accustomed to a peacetime strength of perhaps 29,000 officers and men his figures must have seemed visionary.

The primary objection to Lieutenant Parker's theory was not the size of the organization that he proposed but the fact that it would be a separate branch of the service. At a time when the army was attempting to expand the size and number of its combat units, creation of an autonomous machine-gun service would almost certainly reduce the amount of money and manpower allocated to the existing combat branches. Parker's proposal posed the greatest threat to the artillery, and the members of this branch were adamantly opposed to a separate machine-gun service.

Parker's concept had a number of other defects. His basic premise that machine guns could operate individually was not supported by experience with the mechanical reliability of the weapon.[46] Independent action did not fit conventional principals of tactical and organizational control. The organizational scheme required a large number of officers, and assigning a specially trained officer to each gun was a luxury that an army chronically short of officers could ill afford. These deficiencies gave the army ample reason to reject the separate machine-gun corps.

The description of the machine-gun service led to a lengthy discussion of the employment of machine guns. Most of the tactical theory was not new, but a system that gave machine guns a prominent role in all tactical situations and particularly in offensive operations was a decided novelty. Drawing upon examples from the American Civil War, the Austro-Prussian War, and the Franco-Prussian War, Parker sketched a picture of gigantic armies moving toward their adversary on a broad front. The army that possessed his machine-gun service could seize key terrain and use machine guns to defend it until the main body of the army could deploy along the position taken by its advance units. This idea, reminiscent of the action of Buford's cavalry on the first day of the Battle of Gettysburg, foreshadowed the modern concept of using either armored cavalry or airborne or heliborne troops to seize key terrain and hold it until relieved by the van of the army.

Moving to the use of machine guns in the attack, Parker outlined his concept of future assault tactics. After the advance guard had discovered the enemy position, friendly artillery would move to the front and use its fire to silence the enemy guns. Machine guns would be employed to protect the movement of the artillery and to secure its firing position. When the friendly gunners had gained the ascendancy, the infantry would begin to deploy at a distance of 2,000 to 1,500 yards from the enemy position. Machine-gun sections would accompany the infantry, pause to fire over the heads of the advancing troops, and then move ahead to a new position while another gun opened fire; this continuous fire upon the enemy position would suppress his return fire. When the attacking infantry had moved to within 600 to 800 yards of the opposing works, it would begin to take casualties from enemy rifle fire, and the attack would be in danger of stalling. At this critical juncture all available machine guns would be moved as far forward as possible. They would then deliver a continuous fire upon the enemy position, suppressing his rifle fire and allowing the infantry to continue its assault. At the final instant before the infantry skirmish line reached the enemy position, the machine-gun fires would stop or be shifted to fall on a point to the rear of the enemy lines. As soon as the works were taken, machine-gun units would move forward to secure the newly occupied position against counterattack.[47] Parker's scheme was admittedly an idealized scenario and failed to consider how enemy machine guns might affect the outcome of such an assault.

Lieutenant Parker closed his book with a discussion of the effect of the machine gun upon the traditional arms. He correctly predicted that artillery would become a long-range weapon of "demolition," although this development was not brought about by the influence of the machine gun but by technical improvements in artillery materiel and techniques.[48] Perhaps influenced by the

American tradition of using cavalry as mounted riflemen, Parker made the incredible prediction that the ". . . conditions of cavalry service, as now understood, will not be materially modified by the introduction of machine guns."[49] Parker believed that the machine gun would replace rather than augment the rifle firepower of the infantry. He predicted ". . . the return of the bayonet as one of the most important weapons of infantry."[50] This belief paralleled ideas then gaining favor in the French army, but there is no evidence that Parker was influenced by French tactical thought. Quite clearly Parker's tactical theories suffered, as did others of the time, from the hiatus in European warfare after 1871. Lacking concrete evidence of the manner in which modern weapons would affect the nature of combat, Parker could only speculate about the shape of future warfare—a pastime that was open to all military writers.

Having undermined the rationale for his machine-gun organization, Parker's critics could dismiss his tactical theories, since they were linked to his concept of a separate machine-gun service operating with great freedom of action. However, some of his ideas were sound. The concept of the machine gun as a weapon of offensive combat and the principle of replacing the firepower of massed infantry with that of machine guns were important elements of the machine-gun tactics developed during World War I.

Reaction to Parker's second book varied. Theodore Roosevelt wrote, "I have just received your handbook and I think it invaluable."[51] The *Army and Navy Journal* published a review attributed to the *London Army and Navy Gazette*, which more accurately reflected the reception of the book by the military. According to the *Gazette* Parker failed to justify his tactical and organizational theories adequately, which laid him ". . . open to the charge of having proved too much, [which in the reporter's opinion] . . . is exactly what he has done."[52] The *Gazette* reporter softened his criticism with the remark that Lieutenant Parker ". . . has given us an immense amount of really sound teaching in what he has said about their [machine guns'] employment."[53]

John Henry Parker's initial attempts to bring about a radical change in the army's concept of the role of the machine gun in warfare failed. The army did not adopt his system of organization or accept his tactical theories, and in 1901 the machine gun was still classed as an artillery weapon.⁵⁴ Part of the reason for Parker's failure lay in the flaws in his theories, the animosity that his first book created, and the advanced nature of his ideas.

Parker's failure was also a function of his lack of success in using recognized channels to obtain official approval for his theories. The procedures for gaining acceptance of new tactical theories had not changed substantially since the 1870s.⁵⁵ Initially Lieutenant Parker worked within the established system. In December 1897 he submitted a paper describing his ideas for the use of machine guns through channels to the Adjutant General's Office. Parker did not have any supporters in this office or at higher levels, and his plan did not reach the commanding general.⁵⁶

Lieutenant Parker's second effort to promote the machine gun occurred during and after the Spanish-American War and ended with the publication of his second book. Although he succeeded in demonstrating the potential of the machine gun at Santiago, his later attempts to publicize the machine gun were marred by the controversy that stemmed from his tactless account of the battle for Santiago. During this attempt to gain approval of his theories Parker worked both within and outside military channels; his books represented a concerted effort to arouse interest in machine guns and in his tactical theories. But in 1898 and 1899 the attention of both the public and the military was focused upon the need for a general reform of the army; consequently Parker's work attracted little attention.

Parker did gain the support of Theodore Roosevelt and General Shafter, but neither of these men was in a position to further Parker's ideas within the War Department.⁵⁷ With the army defending itself from external attack and suffering from internal dissension, there was little chance that key officials—notably the commanding general—would support changes as radical as those Parker advocated. Parker evidently recognized the futility of further effort, for in 1899 he obtained a transfer to the Philippines. This move gave him the opportunity to obtain promotion and to use the machine gun in combat.

Paralysis of the army's system for innovation helped to frustrate Parker's efforts, but his failures were also a function of his personality. In a study of successful advocates of innovation in the

U.S. Navy, political scientist Vincent Davis has listed the following characteristics, which he found to be generally present in the career and personality of the successful innovator:

> 1. The . . . advocate . . . is usually a man in the broad middle ranks [major to colonel].
> 2. The . . . advocate is seldom the inventor of the innovation that he is promoting, but he usually possesses a uniquely advanced technological knowledge pertinent to the innovation that is not generally shared within the [army]. . . .
> 3. The . . . advocate is a passionate zealot.
> 4. The . . . advocate seldom pays any attention whatever to the way in which his crusading efforts may influence his personal career in the [army] . . . or elsewhere.[58]

As a member of the middle ranks of the officer corps, the innovator has served long enough to acquire "an organization-wide perspective," which enables him to fit his ideas into the doctrinal and organizational structure of his service.[59] Examination of Parker's theories demonstrates that while he had a good grasp of the impact of the machine gun upon tactics, he failed to understand the implications that it had for the army as a whole. His concepts, particularly the separate machine-gun service, aroused the resistance of the established combat arms. According to Parker the machine gun was a revolutionary weapon; the military resisted the threat it posed to the established order.

Parker did possess a considerable degree of expertise about the weapon he was promoting; however, this expertise did not give him the advantage that accrued to other advocates of innovaton. The machine gun could be understood by anyone who cared to read about it. If most military men knew little about the machine gun, their ignorance stemmed from a lack of interest in the weapon rather than its complexity. As part of promoting the machine gun, Parker advocated a new organization and new tactics. These were military topics on which most military men felt amply qualified to pass judgment.

Lieutenant Parker did advocate the machine gun with passionate zeal, so much so that his arguments earned him an official reprimand.[60] But in the last characteristic Davis identified, Lieutenant

Parker varied from the pattern set by successful advocates. Parker's main reason for promoting the machine gun probably was the hope that it would advance his career. In his unpublished biography of Parker, William H. Garrigus states that ". . . Parker decided that if he could develope [sic] the use and organization of the Gatling guns, his place in the army would be secure and he might attain advancement in rank."[61] Judged by Davis' standards, Parker lacked the characteristics of the successful advocate of innovation.

Although Parker's initial attempts to establish the machine gun as a weapon of major importance failed, use of the machine gun increased. After the Spanish-American War the United States was almost immediately involved in another, far more difficult conflict, the campaigns to crush the Philippine independence movement led by Emilio Aguinaldo and to pacify the Philippine archipelago. During these campaigns machine guns were employed in a variety of ways. For field use the guns were normally included in light artillery batteries; a typical organization was the platoon of artillery from F Battery, Fifth Artillery, commanded by Lieut. Charles P. Summerall. The platoon was composed of one 3.2-inch (81 mm) fieldpiece, a mountain gun, and a Gatling. During an action in the vicinity of Laguna de Bay, Luzon, this unit supported a battalion of the Thirty-ninth Infantry commanded by Maj. John Henry Parker. Placed in the infantry skirmish line, the guns gave the infantry supporting fire.[62] Machine guns were also part of the armament of bay and river gunboats.[63] During a campaign near the Bagbag River, Brig. Gen. Lloyd Wheaton used an armored train to carry supplies and artillery; the train was equipped with an artillery piece and three machine guns. In the fighting Wheaton's forces defeated insurgent forces armed with a Maxim machine gun.[64]

The experience that the army gained with machine guns in the Orient had, in the final analysis, more impact on their adoption by the army than Parker's demonstration at Santiago. In 1900 participation in the campaign against the Boxers gave the army another opportunity to evaluate the combat performance of the machine gun. Army units sent to China took two machine guns, one 6 mm (.236 caliber) Colt model 1895 gun and a .45 caliber model 1877 Gatling.[65] During an attack on Tientsin on July 13,

1900, the American army suffered its first serious defeat at the hands of an enemy using machine guns. The assault was stopped at the edge of a lake where the regiment was pinned under Boxer machine-gun and rifle fire from the walls of Tientsin. As the result of this action the War Department cabled Gen. Arthur MacArthur, the commander in the Philippines, to be ready to send an additional 5,000 troops to China; department officials also asked how many Colt machine guns could be spared from operations in the Philippines.[66] MacArthur replied that he could spare only two Colt guns and that the rest of his machine guns were employed in field operations. On July 14 Lieut. Col. Charles A. Coolidge, the new commander of the Ninth Infantry, rejected the Colt guns, and eleven days later Maj. Gen. Adna R. Chaffee, the commander of the China Relief Expedition, asked for three of the more reliable .45 caliber Gatlings.[67]

In August 1900 a Gatling gun detachment from the Sixth Cavalry helped to clear the walls around the gates of the Inner City of Peking and earned a commendation from Lieutenant Colonel Coolidge. After the capture of Peking the secretary of war directed that a legation guard composed of a regiment of infantry, four troops of cavalry with machine guns, and a light artillery battery be left in Peking.[68]

By the end of the Spanish-American War the army's need for modern weapons was evident. The following year the secretary of war, Elihu Root, called for the ". . . preparation of material of war, keeping pace with the progress of military science and adapted to the conditions to be anticipated when war shall arise."[69] Root's policy would eventually result in the adoption of a standard machine gun and the creation of several outstanding weapons, including the model 1903 Springfield rifle and the 3-inch (76 mm) model 1902 fieldpiece. In 1899, however, the Ordnance Department found that it did not have enough Gatling guns to satisfy the requirements of the forces in the Philippines. The navy, however, had a number of the model 1895 Colt guns chambered for the 6 mm cartridge used in the navy service rifle.[70]

Maj. Gen. Elwell S. Otis, the commander in the Philippines in 1899, asked the navy for some Colt guns and a substantial amount of ammunition; the initial shipment consisted of twelve guns and

300,000 cartridges.[71] The *Army and Navy Journal* commented caustically:

> Army officers are not altogether pleased that General Otis should have to apply to the Navy Department for rapid fire guns. The criticism about the Army Ordnance Department is that it spends too much time spliting [sic] hairs and in experiments that lead to no final result. With all of his excellent qualities General Flagler was slow to learn, and let us hope his successor will be less disposed to forget that the Ordnance Department exists for the Army, and not the Army for the Ordnance.[72]

Despite the need for a new and improved machine gun, the "hair splitting" continued; in 1900 the chief of ordnance, Brig. Gen. Adelbert R. Buffington, reported that the Ordnance Department did not have "sufficient reasons" for replacing the Gatling gun. According to Buffington opinion had not ". . . fully crystallized among military men as to what should be the part assigned to machine guns in the operations of war, nor what troops shall use them, nor what shall be their organization."[73] The ill-defined status of the machine gun was reflected in legislation that restructured the army and its artillery branch.

The weakness exposed by the Spanish-American War and the need for a large number of troops to pacify the Philippines compelled Congress to expand and restructure the army. On March 2, 1899, the legislators voted to maintain the regular army at its wartime strength of 65,000 men and to enlist up to 35,000 volunteers for service in the Philippines. This legislation satisfied the manpower requirements of the Philippine campaign but did not reorganize the army. The argument over changes in the size and structure of the military continued for two years. Initially controversy centered around proposed personnel increases. Senator Joseph R. Hawley called for an army of 98,763 officers and men, while Senator Francis M. Cockrell argued for a force of 60,000. With this disagreement unresolved the first proposal for army reorganization, H.R. 11022, was returned to committee and died there. The bill continued to classify the machine gun as an artillery weapon.[74]

In 1900 a new bill for army reorganization, S. 4300, appeared; by December it passed the Senate and was sent to the House. Now argument centered around the organization of the artillery. The Senate wished to retain the traditional regimental organization with its mixture of coast and field artillery batteries in each regiment. The House, on the other hand, desired to organize an Artillery Corps with two functional branches—coast artillery and field artillery. The coast artillery would be made up of separate companies, which would man the fixed coastal fortifications; the field artillery would consist of regiments designed for mobile warfare.[75]

After negotiation the House concept was adopted and included in the Army Reorganization Act of Febuary 2, 1901. Section Four of this act reads in part:

> That the Artillery Corps shall comprise two branches—the coast artillery and the field artillery. . . . the field artillery is defined as that portion accompanying an army in the field, and including field and light artillery proper, horse artillery, siege artillery, mountain artillery, and also machine-gun batteries: *Provided*, That this shall not be construed to limit the authority of the Secretary of War to order coast artillery to any duty which the public service demands *or to prevent the use of machine or other field guns by any other arm of the service under the direction of the Secretary of War.*[76]

Since this act formed the statutory basis for the structure of the army until mid-1916, Section Four—particularly its last portion—was crucial for the integration of the machine gun into the structure of the field forces. The section reflected the traditional concept of the machine gun as an artillery weapon, but it also reflected the lack of agreement within the army concerning the proper role for the machine gun. The discretionary feature of Section Four gave the army a legal "escape clause," which would permit the introduction of the machine gun into infantry and cavalry units.

NOTES

1. Parker graduated from the U.S. Military Academy with the class of 1892 (forty-ninth of sixty-two cadets graduated) and was commissioned in the infantry. Classmates included John McAuley Palmer (nineteenth of sixty-two) and Charles Pelot Summerall (twentieth of sixty-two). Parker

Combat and Its Results 119

served in a variety of staff positions including in the Judge Advocate General's Office in the Philippines as well as in the normal regimental assignments in the infantry. An extraordinarily brave officer, he was awarded the Silver Star Citation for gallantry in action at the Battle of San Juan Hill and later received the Distinguished Service Cross with three oak leaf clusters for acts of heroism in France during World War I. George W. Cullum, *Biographical Register of the Officers and Graduates of the U.S. Military Academy*, vols. IV, V, VIA, VII (Chicago, 1901-1930), entries for the class of 1892.

2. Students at this school received "practical instruction in minor tactics." The course was taught by five departments—tactics, strategy, engineering, law, and hygiene. Ira L. Reeves, *Military Education in the United States* (Burlington, Vt.: 1914), pp. 204-10.

3. Enclosure 1 to Parker to Secretary, Infantry and Cavalry School, December 28, 1897, National Archives, Record Group 156 (hereafter cited as NA, RG 156), doc. 25719 (1898), p. 6. Emphasis added.

4. Ibid.; William H. Garrigus, "Action Front! A Saga of the Service" (unpublished manuscript, a copy of which is located in the U.S. Military Academy Archives), chap. 3, p. 7 (hereafter cited as Garrigus MS).

5. The following account of Parker's activities at Tampa was drawn from John H. Parker, *History of the Gatling Gun Detachment Fifth Army Corps, At Santiago, With a Few Unvarnished Truths Concerning That Expedition* (Kansas City, Mo., 1898).

6. Ibid., pp. 26-28.

7. Thompson was a graduate of the U.S. Military Academy, class of 1882 (eleventh in a class of thirty-seven). Commissioned in the artillery, he transferred to the Ordnance Corps and served as an instructor in ordnance and gunnery at the U.S. Military Academy from 1896 to 1898. When Parker met him, Thompson was a first lieutenant; shortly thereafter he was commissioned a lieutenant colonel, U.S. Volunteers, and served as the ordnance officer for the Fifth Corps. During World War I Thompson was in charge of the design and manufacture of all army small arms. He was also the inventor of the famous Thompson submachine gun. Albert Nelson Marquis, ed, *Who's Who In America, 1930-1931*, vol. 16 (Chicago, 1930), p. 2181.

8. Thompson to General Flagler, May 12, 1898, NA, RG 156, doc. 26396 encl. 41.

9. Herbert H. Sargent, *The Campaign of Santiago de Cuba*, vol. II (Chicago, 1907), p. 16. The defensive capabilities of the Gatling were fairly well known in 1898. Shafter may have intended that the Gatlings land first in order to cover the rest of the expedition while it landed.

10. Theodore Roosevelt, *The Rough Riders* (New York, 1899), pp. 71, 85, 165.
11. Theodore Ropp, *War in the Modern World* (New York, 1962), pp. 180-84.
12. Sargent, *Campaign*, vol. II, pp. 83-117; Frank Friedel, *The Splendid Little War* (Boston, 1958), pp. 123-66.
13. U.S., War Department, *Annual Report of the War Department, 1898*, vol. I, pt. 2 (Washington, D.C., 1898), p. 458. This report was used as the basis for the account of Parker's actions during the Battle of San Juan Hill.
14. Ibid.
15. Ibid., pp. 457-59. The casualties of the Gatling Gun Detachment during the assault were one man killed and one wounded.
16. *Annual Report of the War Department, 1898*, vol. I, pt. 2, p. 459. Parker removed the wheels from three of the Gatling carriages to lower their height, leaving the fourth gun intact to serve as a mobile reserve. The two Colt guns were not used on July 1, 1898, since they and their ammunition had to be hand carried to the front. Parker, *Gatling*, pp. 160-64.
17. Parker administered Roosevelt's oath of commission as a colonel of U.S. Volunteers. Roosevelt wrote the preface for Parker's first book. The manuscript copy of the preface bearing Roosevelt's handwritten corrections is in the manuscript collection of the U.S. Military Academy Library.
18. *Annual Report of the War Department, 1898*, vol. I, pt. 2, Report of 2d. Lieut. D. W. Ryther, p. 298.
19. Ibid., Report of Capt. L.W.V. Kennon, p. 288.
20. Ibid., Report of Capt. J. B. Goe, p. 422.
21. Ibid., p. 618.
22. Ibid., Report of Lieut. Col. Henry C. Egbert, p. 356; Theodore Roosevelt, *The Letters of Theodore Roosevelt*, 6 vols., vol. II: *The Years of Preparation: 1898-1900*, ed. Elting E. Morison (Cambridge, Mass., 1951), letter to Leonard Wood, July 20, 1898, p. 857. (Hereafter cited as Roosevelt, *Letters*.) Joseph Wheeler, *The Santiago Campaign* (Philadelphia, 1899), pp. 77, 271; Charles Johnson Post, *The Little War Of Private Post* (Boston, 1960), p. 184; *Annual Report of the War Department, 1898*, vol. I, pt. 2, Report of Brig. Gen. H. S. Hawkins, p. 305; *Annual Report of the War Department, 1898*, vol. I, pt., 2, p. 154. Shafter's aide, Lieut. John D. Miley, considered the Gatlings to be ". . . one of the most important factors in the capture of the Spanish works." John D. Miley, *In Cuba With Shafter* (New York, 1899), pp. 113-14.

Combat and Its Results

23. Parker to Adjutant General's Office, Subject: Outline of Organization of Proposed Experimental Tactical Unit of Machine Guns, n.d., NA, RG 94, doc. 126518 (1898).
24. Ibid.
25. Acting Adjutant General to Parker, September 23, 1898, NA, RG 94, doc. 126518.
26. Parker to Adjutant General, March 3, 1899, NA, RG 94, doc. 209813; Roosevelt to Adjutant General, March 6, 1899, NA, RG 94, doc. 209813; NA, RG 94, Microcopy M-698, Roll 885, entry for Letters Received—Parker, John H., for 1899.
27. Parker, *Gatling*, p. 12.
28. Ibid., pp. 93-98, 159, 168.
29. Ibid., pp. 27-28.
30. Ibid., p. 168.
31. Ibid., pp. 93-94.
32. John H. Parker, "Uses of Machine Guns," *Journal of the Military Service Institution of the United States* XXIV (January 1899): 13.
33. Freidel, *Splendid*, pp. 176-77.
34. Parker, "Uses of Machine Guns," pp. 11-12. Emphasis added.
35. Capt. C. D. Parkhurst to Adjutant General's Office, January 16, 1899, NA, RG, 94, doc. 193056 (1899); Parker to Editor, *Journal of the Military Service Institution of the United States*, February 6, 1899, NA, RG
36. Brig. Gen. G. N. Lieber to Adjutant General, June 27, 1899, NA, RG 94, doc. 193056 (1899); "Extracts from Efficiency Reports in Case of John H. Parker, Captain 28th Infantry," September 13, 1906, Library of Congress, Theodore Roosevelt Papers, Series no. 1, Box 111.
37. The *Army and Navy Journal* commented diplomatically:

> Lieut. Parker's book is dashing. His soul was hot against the follies perpetrated by officers who were obstacles to orderly method, and he writes vigorously and with freedom. Primarily his book is an argument for Gatlings, but it is also the record of a bright writer and competent observer of a memorable fight.

Army and Navy Journal (hereafter cited as *A-N Jou.*), December 10, 1898, p. 344.
38. John H. Parker, *Tactical Organization and Uses of Machine Guns in the Field* (Kansas City, Mo., 1899), p. 45.
39. Ibid., pp. 61, 64, 66-67.
40. Ibid., p. 68. The connection between Williston's earlier theory of a

separate machine gun corps and Parker's Theory is not clear. Parker claimed that he had not heard of Williston's theory until after the Santiago campaign. Parker did credit Williston with developing the idea of a separate machine gun service, but he gave Gatling credit for originating the concept. Parker, "Uses of Machine Guns," p. 14.

41. Parker, *Tactical Organization*, p. 82. A gun section consisted of one specially trained officer and nine enlisted men. One machine gun would normally operate with each infantry battalion. Ibid., pp. 84-87.

42. Ibid., p. 87.

43. Ibid., p. 95. This would mean 351 machine guns per corps. This allotment of strength can be compared with the U.S. Army tables of organization of August 4 and November 1, 1918, where a three-division corps with two cavalry regiments had 688 heavy machine guns in its infantry and cavalry formations plus 96 machine guns in various corps troop organizations. U.S. Department of the Army, *United States Army in the World War, 1917-1919*, vol. I (Washington, D.C., 1948), pp. 295, 341.

44. Parker, *Tactical Organization*, p. 97.

45. This ratio is based upon the organization of the American infantry division as it existed on November 11, 1918. The total number of riflemen in the division was 12,288, and the total number of machine gunners was 2,616. The ratio does not include the men assigned to corps or army machine-gun units. U.S., War Department, Army War College, Historical Section, *Order of Battle of the United States Land Forces in the World War, American Expeditionary Forces—Divisions* (Washington, D.C., 1931), pp. 446-47.

46. The commandant of the School of Musketry later commented, "Jams and breakdowns to which the Maxim, along with other types of machine guns, is subject, have been noted. . . . This failing is well recognized wherever machine guns have been adopted, in the quite universal provision that these guns shall never be used singly. "Statement of the Commandant, School of Musketry, Concerning Machine Guns," U.S. Army, Military History Research Collection, Carlisle Barracks, Carlisle, Pa., Reference No. UF 5090-U6.

47. Parker, *Tactical Organization*, pp. 143-45, 152-57.

48. Ibid., pp. 190-91; see also H.C.B. Rogers, *Artillery Through the Ages* (London, 1971), pp. 93-136.

49. Parker, *Tactical Organization*, p. 192.

50. Ibid., p. 187.

51. Roosevelt to Parker, March 28, 1899, Library of Congress, Theodore Roosevelt Papers, Letterbook series 2, vol. 16, p. 219.

52. *A-N Jou.*, September 2, 1899, p. 13. General Robert Lee Bullard,

Combat and Its Results   123

Parker's commander in the Philippines, later stated that *"Parker's mind and conception had run far ahead of the advanced military minds of the world."* Garrigus MS, Introduction, p. 2.

53. *A-N Jou.*, September 2, 1899, p. 13.

54. Section 4 of the Army Reorganization Act of 1901 included machine-gun batteries as part of the field artillery. Army Reorganization Act, U.S, *Statutes at Large*, vol. 31, sec. 4, 749 (1901).

55. Crites, "Infantry Doctrine," pp. 13-14.

56. Garrigus MS, chap. 3, p. 7.

57. Roosevelt was governor of New York and Shafter was the commanding general of the Department of California, a post far removed from the center of power in Washington, D.C. Both men did help Parker secure an assignment to the Philippines. U.S., War Department, *Official Army Register for 1899* (Washington, D.C., 1899), p. 263, hereafter cited as *Army Register* with appropriate date. Roosevelt to Parker, September 4, 1899, Library of Congress, Theodore Roosevelt Papers, Letterbook series 2, vol. 19, p. 141.

58. Vincent Davis, *The Politics of Innovation: Patterns in Navy Cases*, Monograph Series in World Affairs, vol. 4 (Denver, Colo.: 1967), pp. 51-53.

59. Ibid., p. 52.

60. In a letter to Elihu Root, Roosevelt observed, "In private life he [Parker] talks altogether too much. . . ." Roosevelt, *Letters*, vol. II, p. 1056. Commenting on this fault, Parker wrote:

> General, I have tried to do my duty over here [in the Philippines]; and have tried especially to do it quietly, without notoriety. I have tried especially to keep out of the newspapers, desiring to show the army that I am not a seeker of cheap notoriety, as some of my friends (?) have charged.

Parker to Shafter, April 21, 1900, Library of Congress, Papers of Theodore Roosevelt, vol. 12, pp. 3668-71.

61. Garrigus MS, chap. 2, p. 4.

62. Garrigus MS, chap. 7, pp. 1-3; Parker to Adjutant, Thirty-ninth Infantry, January 4, 1900, Library of Congress, Papers of Theodore Roosevelt, vol. 9, pp. 2738-40; Report of Capt. H. J. Reilly, Lt. Bat. "F," 5th Arty, and a copy of detailed report of Lieut. C. P. Summerall, NA, RG 156, doc. 27682, encl. 43 and 44.

63. *Annual Report of the War Department, 1899*, vol. I, pt. 4, p. 222.

64. Uldarico S. Baclagon, *Philippine Campaigns* (Manila, 1952), pp. 97-103.

65. *Annual Report of the War Department, 1900*, vol. I, pt. 9, telegrams: Corbin to MacArthur, July 12, 1900, and MacArthur to Adjutant General,

July 13, 1900, p. 149. Other expeditionary forces also had machine guns; the largest number were with the British who had eight. The Germans had two and the Italians one machine gun. U.S., War Department, *Reports on Military Operations in South Africa and China* (Washington, D.C., 1901),p.532.

66. *Annual Report of the War Department, 1900*, vol. I, pt. 9, p. 20. The regiment suffered heavy casualties: the regimental commander and nineteen enlisted men killed, four officers and seventy-two enlisted wounded, one man missing. At the beginning of the engagement, the regiment totaled 15 officers and 418 enlisted men. Ibid., pp. 18, 21, Corbin to MacArthur, July 16, 1900, p. 150.

67. Ibid., MacArthur to Adjutant General, July 18, 1900, p. 153; Coolidge to Corbin, July 24, 1900, p. 159, Chaffee to Adjutant General, August 5, 1900, p. 167.

68. Ibid., pp. 66, 69, 76, Corbin to Chaffee, September 25, 1900, p. 196.

69. U.S., War Department, *Five Years of the War Department Following the War With Spain, 1899-1903, As Shown in the Annual Reports of the Secretary of War* (Washington, D.C., 1904), p. 61.

70. In 1899 the *Army and Navy Journal* reported nearly 500 Colt machine guns in service in the navy, but a report from Samoa indicated that the Colts were largely worthless. A later article stated that the guns jammed due to difficulties with the 6 mm cartridge. *A-N Jou.*, May 20, 1899, p. 898, and June 3, 1899, p. 946.

71. *A-N Jou.*, August 12, 1899, p. 1182.

72. Ibid.

73. *Annual Report of the War Department, 1900*, vol. III, p. 38.

74. Russell F. Weigley, *History of the United States Army* (New York, 1967), p. 308; U.S., Congress, Senate, *Statements of Objections of Five Members of the Committee on Military Affairs to Bill (H.R. 11022) for the Reorganization of the Army of the United States and for Other Purposes*, 55th Cong., 3d sess., 1899, pp. 1-2; U.S., Congress, House, "The Clerk reading an Amendment to the Army Reorganization Bill, H. Res. 11022," *Congressional Record*, 55th Cong., 3d sess., January 30, 1899, XXXII, pt. 2, p. 1258.

75. U.S., Congress, House, *Efficiency of the Military Establishment*, H. Rept. 2010 to Accompany S. 4300, 56th Cong., 2d sess., 1900, pp. 1-2. The House concept was favored by army artillery officers. U.S., Congress, Senate, Committee on Military Affairs, *Army Bill, Hearings Before the Committee on Military Affairs, Senate, on S.R. 4300*, 56th Cong., 2d sess., 1900, pp. 86-87.

76. Army Reorganization Act, *U.S., Statutes at Large*, vol. 31, sec. 4, 749 (1901). Emphasis added.

VI

FROM STEPCHILD INVENTION TO STANDARD EQUIPMENT, 1901-1906

While use of the machine gun in the Far East stimulated American interest in the weapon, combat experience with it was limited. Lacking data about its combat performance, army staff agencies found it difficult to decide how the machine gun should be used. Despite the creation of the General Staff in 1903, the War Department was slow to come to grips with doctrinal problems. The architects of the General Staff had meant their creation to be concerned primarily with large-scale problems such as manpower mobilization and planning for war. In its early years, however, the attention of the staff tended to focus either upon operational issues stemming from army involvement in the Philippines or Cuba, or upon familiar, if minute, questions of detail, which the regimental experience and common sense of the untrained staff officers enabled them to solve. The result was that substantial mid-range issues, such as the selection of new weapons and the creation of doctrine and organization for their employment, were addressed in a haphazard fashion. It is not surprising, therefore, that the initial link in the chain of events leading to the development of machine-gun doctrine and organization was forged by a staff bureau, the Ordnance Department.

Ordnance Department action came first because, according to the practice of the time, doctrine and organization were fitted to the requirements of a specific piece of equipment. The practice of developing doctrine tailored to a specific weapon rather than casting it in broad terms adaptable to a wide range of models of a particular type of weapon meant that development of doctrine and organization waited upon the conclusion of the search for a new machine gun—a search that began in 1899 and lasted until the end of 1903. It also raised the possibility that both doctrine and organization would have to be reworked each time the army chose a new machine gun.

The period from 1899 to 1904 was one of far-reaching structural reform in the army. The beneficial effects of the creation of the General Staff and the expansion and revision of army force structure are well known.[1] What is often overlooked is the disruptive effect of these changes upon the army at the time that they took place. Army leaders found themselves operating in totally new areas without the guidance of traditional precedents and procedures. Both staffs and commanders were largely unfamiliar with the new organizations and concepts with which they had to deal. Lacking a staff college, the army had neither trained staff officers nor the technical knowledge of how a staff should operate. Consequently army leaders as well as their staffs were forced to spend a great deal of their time solving organizational and administrative problems. In such circumstances only the most pressing or simplest problems were resolved.

In the Ordnance Department the situation was complicated by the pressing demands of the Philippine Insurrection and by the fact that between the spring of 1899 and the end of 1901 the office of the chief of ordnance changed hands twice.[2] Amidst an atmosphere of change, the Ordnance Department continued to pursue its cautious, time-honored methods of selecting weapons.

In the summer of 1899 the commander of the Springfield Armory appointed a board of officers ". . . to consider and report upon such inventions and devices as the commanding officer may submit to it."[3] Supplementary orders directed the board to test the Maxim solid-action, Vickers R. C. automatic, Hotchkiss, and Colt machine guns.[4] Because its orders did not specify the type of information the Ordnance Department needed, the Springfield Board merely reported the capabilities of each weapon. It did not assess the relative value of the machine guns, nor did it rank them in order of merit.

At the conclusion of the tests, the three remaining guns—the Vickers R. C. automatic gun had been withdrawn by its manufacturers—were recommended as "suitable" for army use.[5] Confronted with a choice among three "equals," Brig. Gen. Adelbert R.

From Stepchild Invention to Standard Equipment 127

Buffington adopted an interim policy of procuring and issuing nonstandard Colt machine guns while continuing to produce the .30 caliber model 1895 Gatling gun.⁶ The test system had failed to give the ordnance chief the information he needed to choose a new machine gun. In 1900 the system for weapon selection was incomplete; it tested arms but did not produce a comparative assessment of their utility.

Although purchase of nonstandard Colt guns was authorized, ordnance officials knew that the air-cooled Colt gun had serious faults. Reports of the performance of the Colt gun varied, but they did indicate that a number of commanders were not satisfied with the weapon.⁷ By 1902 the Ordnance Department had ample reason to search for a replacement for the Colt machine gun. Yet in January 1902 the new chief of ordnance, Brig. Gen. William Crozier, told the House Committee on Military Affairs that the

Maj. Gen. William Crozier, chief of ordnance, 1901-1918. *Courtesy*: U.S. Military Academy Archives.

Colt had "done very well" in field use.[8] Crozier had a good reason for delaying the purchase of a new machine gun.

In 1901 ordnance officials had expressed dissatisfaction with the design of the Krag service rifle. Weaknesses in the bolt of the rifle reduced its accuracy and prevented it from using ammunition with muzzle velocities higher than 2,000 feet per second. Engineers at the Springfield Armory began to develop a new service rifle and a companion high-velocity small-arms cartridge.[9] Procurement of a new machine gun based upon its performance with Krag ammunition would have been unwise, and selection of a standard machine gun for the army waited upon the results of the experiments at Springfield.[10]

One month after the Springfield rifle received official approval, a board of officers headed by Capt. Edwin V. Bookmiller, Ninth Infantry, convened to test machine guns. Unlike earlier boards composed of ordnance offices, the Bookmiller-Dickson Board included infantry, cavalry, and artillery officers as well as Capt. Tracy C. Dickson of the Ordnance Corps. The instructions issued to the board clearly indicated that it was to recommend a new machine gun.[11] The tests were to be:

> ... conducted and expedited in the most practicable manner for the purpose of ascertaining the following, viz.:
> First. The design of automatic machine gun *best adapted* to fulfill the requirements of the military service.
> Second. The design of mount and pack outfit *best adapted* for field service.
> Third. The *most* convenient and serviceable form in which ammunition for automatic machine guns should be packed and issued.
> Fourth. The *number* of rounds of ammunition for which pack transportation should be provided with each gun.[12]

As these orders show, the Ordnance Department had decided to end the makeshift policy pursued since 1900 and to adopt a single weapon as the army's standard machine gun. They also indicated that the Ordnance Department realized that picking a standard machine gun for the army required the selection of a substantial amount of ancillary equipment as well. Selection of these items in turn depended upon decisions concerning the type of transport system to be used, the handling properties desired in the weapon and its supporting equipment, and the amount of ammunition to be carried with the gun. In effect ordnance officials were no longer dealing with the machine gun as a weapon but rather as a weapon system; this was an important conceptual advance in dealing with the machine gun.

To a substantial degree the results of the 1903 tests confirmed previous army experience with machine guns. The 1899-1900 series of tests and field use had indicated that the air-cooled machine guns of the day had a number of serious faults. From the start of the 1903 tests these defects placed the air-cooled weapons, the Colt gun and the Danish *rifle-mitrailleuse* (an early automatic rifle), at a serious disadvantage. The Bookmiller-Dickson Board reported that after a few hundred rounds had been fired from the Colt gun, the heat radiating from the barrel seriously interfered with sighting. By the time 500 rounds had been fired, the gun was so hot it was difficult to handle, and when 1,000 rounds were fired continuously, the heat of the barrel would ignite a cartridge left in the chamber of the gun. In contrast, the water-cooled guns that the board tested exhibited none of these difficulties.[13] The work of the Bookmiller-Dickson Board was simplified by the fact that only one weapon, the Maxim water-cooled, standard-pattern automatic machine gun, survived the competition. On November 10, 1904, it was designated the standard machine gun for the American army.[14]

The second and fourth parts of the instructions received by the Bookmiller-Dickson Board reveal that by mid-1903 the Ordnance Department had decided that the army would use pack-transported machine guns. The precise date of the decision is obscure, and it appears to have been made without a thorough study of machine gun transport. According to the chief of ordnance, Brig. Gen. William Crozier, the decision was based largely upon the belief that a machine gun would probably be issued to each infantry battalion and cavalry squadron. The fact that no permanent organization had as yet been prescribed for machine guns was, in Crozier's judgment, also a factor in the decision to adopt pack transport.[15] If its origins and rationale remain hazy, some of the benefits of the decision are clear. A pack-transported machine gun was much more mobile than a carriage-mounted version of the same weapon and would have a better chance of keeping up with infantry or cavalry units operating in rough ground. It used a tripod mount which was smaller, lighter, and easier to emplace in field fortifications than a wheeled mount. This was an important advantage for what was considered to be primarily a defensive weapon. Finally, pack transport was the principal method of supplying front-line troops with small-arms ammunition and therefore a logical form of transport for a relatively lightweight weapon using this type of ammunition. The selection of pack transport for machine guns was the best choice to be made. Ironically, at the same time that the selection of pack transport appeared in the orders to the Bookmiller-Dickson Board, the army was preparing to conduct trials of a wheeled machine-gun mount.

John Henry Parker had lost none of his interest in the machine gun while serving in the Philippines.[16] Shortly after he returned to the United States in 1901, Parker asked the Ordnance Department to fund the construction of his ". . . combination carriage for machine guns and ammunition cart."[17] The cart was the solution to the problems of supplying ammunition to an infantry firing line, ". . . of getting machine guns to some point where they can be effectively used, and of supplying them with ammunition at that point."[18] It was the basis for an organization which would consist of:

> . . . a number of carts equal to the number of battalions, organized in brigade detachments, under the personal control of the brigade commander. An officer should have charge of each cart, which would carry its machine gun, of course. This solution would necessarily carry officers and men specially trained and assigned (or detailed) to this service, with the various grades necessary for suitable division of authority, responsibility and command.[19]

As Parker admitted, he had proposed the same organization for a machine-gun service in 1899.

Initially the prospects for Parker's cart seemed bright. In 1902 the War Department referred his proposal to the Board of Ordnance and Fortification; the board allocated $1,000 for the construction of the invention.[20] Work on the Parker cart began at the Colt factory in Hartford, Connecticut, in June 1902. During the next year,

Parker made several trips to Hartford to supervise the construction of the cart and a pack-saddle for it.[21] Finally the work was finished, and Captain Parker received orders to ". . . proceed to Fort Leavenworth, Kansas, for temporary duty pertaining to the organization and instruction of a detail of enlisted men in the manipulation of his ammunition cart and carriage for machine guns. . . ."[22] Organized on August 8, 1903, the detachment was manned by personnel from the First Battalion, Sixth Infantry. Parker's cart took part in a series of tests in competition with two other ammunition carts. Because the results of the initial contests were inconclusive, the War Department directed that additional field trials of all of the carts be made.[23] Ordered to march to Fort Riley, Kansas, and to participate in maneuvers held there, Parker was to report the performance of the cart during the march and maneuvers to the Board of Ordnance and Fortification.[24]

At the conclusion of the Riley maneuvers Parker and his men returned to Leavenworth to face a rigorous series of tests supervised by a new agency, the Infantry Board. This body, established on March 31, 1903, was an independent group whose advice on infantry operations and equipment could be used in the decision-making process within the War Department.[25] In a letter to the secretary of war General Crozier had suggested the establishment of the Infantry Board.

> . . . this Department instead of having to rely, as at present, on individual and often haphazard criticism and suggestions, made without responsibility and, even so, hard to secure, for improving ordnance equipment, would have an expression of opinion fron constituted authorities in the Cavalry and Infantry as a basis on which to proceed with the improvements suggested or needed.[26]

Crozier also believed that a ". . . feeling of responsibility for their particular arms would be developed in the boards and would result, it is believed, in great satisfaction to the service and improvement of material."[27]

General Crozier was correct in his assessment of the value of such an institution to the army and to the Ordnance Department and appears to have been the first chief of ordnance to advocate participation of the combat arms in the process of weapons selection on an institutionalized basis. Although he deserves credit for advancing this concept, which had been advocated for many years by various line officers, Crozier also knew that his department retained final control over the selection of all weapons and equipment within its statutory purview. When it agreed with the position of the Infantry or Cavalry boards, the Ordnance Department could use their opinions to strengthen its own case and to answer complaints if the item proved to be faulty. In case of disagreement the Ordnance Department retained the right to make the decisive, final recommendation to the secretary of war. Despite these qualifications, it is clear that the creation of the Infantry Board came as the result of General Crozier's genuine interest in institutionalizing the participation of the combat arms in the selection of the arms and equipment that they would use. This chief of ordnance was interested in reducing friction between staff and line in the Army of the United States.

As an adjunct to its test program, the Infantry Board circulated a summary of Parker's proposal for a combined machine gun and ammunition service among officers stationed at Leavenworth. Accompanying the summary was a brief of questionnaire, which asked the addressee to express his opinion concerning (1) the need for such a machine-gun service, (2) the need for such a system of ammunition supply, and (3) the desirability of combining these two functions in a single detachment. The respondent was invited to include his ideas concerning a machine-gun or ammunition supply service in his reply to the questionnaire. Of the twenty-four officers responding to this query, seventeen did not favor the establishment of a combined machine-gun and ammunition service along the lines that Captain Parker proposed. Three of the senior members of the unit conducting the test—Col. Joseph W. Duncan, Lieut. Col. Robert H.R. Loughborough, and Maj. Charles G. Morton—opposed the combination of ammunition and machine-gun services.[28] After considering the results of its tests and the answers to its questionnaire, the Infantry Board, which was headed by Colonel Duncan and included both Loughborough and Morton, reported late in 1903:

... that, in its opinion, the supply of ammunition should be considered as a separate proposition apart from the use of the machine gun, and that the [Parker] cart is not adapted to the supply of ammunition to the firing line.[29]

When the Infantry Board rejected it as an ammunition carrier, Parker's combination cart and machine-gun mount could not compete with the specialized, lighter tripod mount. Parker's campaign to persuade the War Department to adopt his ideas on machine-gun organization and ammunition supply collapsed, but his activities had contributed to the increase in military interest in the subject of machine-gun organization.

While the Ordnance Department and the Board of Ordnance and Fortification evaluated machine guns and related equipment, the military also began to consider the question of how best to use these weapons. Army efforts to determine the shape and nature of the machine-gun organization it should adopt began in March 1903. A battalion commander in the Sixth Infantry stationed at Fort Leavenworth, Maj. Charles G. Morton, asked for two machine guns to form a semipermanent machine-gun detachment within his battalion. Morton's request was endorsed by the chief of ordnance who recommended that the new General Staff work out the proper organization and tactics for machine-gun units. The First Division of the Provisional General Staff recommended that two Colt guns be sent to Fort Leavenworth to be used under the supervision of the staff of the General Service and Staff College to investigate the subject of machine-gun tactics and organization. The concept was approved, and implementing instructions were sent to Leavenworth.[30]

Upon receiving the General Staff instructions, the commandant of the General Service and Staff College asked that the investigation be transferred to the newly created Infantry Board. This was done, and the role of the Infantry Board in evaluating new items of equipment—which General Crozier had proposed only four months earlier—expanded to include consideration of who should use the new equipment and how it should be employed. Doctrinal and organizational matters were thus included in the charter of the Infantry Board.[31]

The Infantry Board used the tests of the ammunition carts and the maneuvers at Fort Riley, Kansas, as a vehicle for evaluating machine-gun organizations and tactics.[32] When the Board decided that Parker's cart and his organizational ideas were not the solution, it still had to answer the question of how the army should use machine guns.

On January 7, 1904, the Board of Ordnance and Fortification recommended that three permanent machine-gun detachments be organized in the Sixth Infantry so ". . . that the question of the most suitable organization for an automatic machine gun detachment and most suitable gun and mount therefore may be authoritatively decided. . . ."[33] The War Department approved the recommendation but limited the test objectives to the determination of a suitable organization for machine-gun detachments.[34] At the conclusion of the trials the Infantry Board reviewed the results and on December 19, 1904, issued a report which read in part:

> 5. That so far as tests have thus far been made the proper detachment and equipment for machine gun[s] is as follows:
> One non-commissioned officer and seven privates detailed from the battalion to which the gun is assigned, to be armed with revolvers, and provided with leather gloves.
> Three mules and packing outfits, one to carry the gun and its mount, and two to carry ammunition, all under the command of a commissioned officer, also of the same battalion.
> The detachment and its command, being from the battalion to which the gun is assigned, are drilled with the battalion, are a part of the battalion, and become familiar with the part they are expected to take in action.[35]

This report was forwarded to the Board of Ordnance and Fortification.

In December 1903 Maj. Montgomery Meigs Macomb had submitted an independent report on the tests of the three ammunition carts and the tactical experiments with the machine guns at Forts Riley and Leavenworth.[36] Separated by a year, both the Infantry Board report and Macomb's report advanced the same concept for using machine guns.

Macomb and the Infantry Board advocated a theory of machine-gun employment that was fundamentally different from Parker's.[37] According to Macomb, who had thirty years service as an artillery officer,

> ... the most economic and effective way of using small caliber machine guns in our service is to make them an adjunct weapon, manning them from the arm using the same caliber of ammunition and familiar with the kind of transportation required. In other words, it is unnecessary to consider these weapons as belonging to the domain of field artillery.[38]

The adoption of a relatively lightweight, tripod-mounted, pack-transported, automatic machine gun had finally resolved the question of whether the machine gun was an artillery or infantry weapon. Macomb and the members of the Infantry Board advocated assigning the machine gun directly to infantry and cavalry units instead of classifying it as a separate type of weapon manned by a distinct group of soldiers.

The structure of the machine-gun detachment and the concept of machine-gun employment recommended to the War Department in late 1904 were the products of the ideas and experience of several different men. The credit for the size and structure of the machine-gun detachment belongs to Captain Parker. Credit for the concept of incorporating the machine gun within the organization of the close-combat arms goes to the Infantry Board and to Major Macomb.[39] The commandant of the General Service and Staff College, Brig. Gen. J. Franklin Bell, supported integration of the machine gun into line units. Based on his experience in the Philippines, Bell advocated attaching one or two machine-gun detachments to each infantry battalion and cavalry squadron.[40]

> ... our future fighting is more likely to be carried on by small columns than by large ones. Under such circumstances a machine gun attached to a battalion would be more apt to be at hand when wanted than if belonging to a group under the general's orders. Who that has commanded a district or subdistrict in the Philippines has not wanted one of these guns and had to wait until it had been sent him or go without it altogether?[41]

In 1904 the experience of warfare in the Orient was fresh in the memories of many officers. The prospect of more such combat made creation of small machine gun detachments in infantry units eminently desirable.

Following the final report of the Infantry Board on machine gun organization in December 1904, the whole matter of machine-gun tactics and organization was referred to the General Staff for action. However, action was not forthcoming.

General Staff failure to act on the Infantry Board recommendations was the product of several factors. New to its business, the staff had developed neither the administrative channels for nor the habit of taking decisive action.[42] The senior members of the staff reviewed, commented upon, and then usually filed studies made by its members or by other agencies. In the case of the machine gun, selection of a course of action was complicated by the fact that the machine gun had been the subject of studies and experiments sponsored by several different agencies including the General Service and Staff College, the Infantry Board, and the Board of Ordnance and Fortification. In arriving at a decision concerning the use of the machine gun, the General Staff also had to consider the opinions of General Bell, Major Macomb, Major Morton and, of course, Captain Parker. Seldom, if ever, were the positions or opinions of these agencies and individuals in unanimous agreement on any point. In a paper written for the Army War College in 1905, Major Morton noted that ". . . while it is agreed that machine guns should not form a part of the field artillery, yet it is still undecided whether they should form a separate arm or be attached to the cavalry and infantry."[43]

Turning to Europe for ideas, the members of the General Staff found the field of machine-gun theory dominated by the work of German writers.[44] German concepts posed a serious problem for the American army. Following a short period of experimentation, the German General Staff decided to consolidate its machine guns in four and later six gun batteries. Initially these batteries were assigned to cavalry brigades and army corps.[45] The German Drill regulations of 1904 specified that "*The disposition of the machine guns, . . . rests immediately with the highest officer in command. If machine gun batteries are attached to a particular body of troops it will be possible to utilize them to their fullest extent in exceptional cases only."[46] In 1905 Major Morton reported that ". . . the [German machine-gun] batteries are to be made completely autonomous."[47] German doctrine called for the creation of separate and largely independent machine-gun units and specified that these units should be controlled by high-level commanders. The central features of German doctrine met the same resistance in the American army that Parker's theories had encountered.

American critics of the machine gun enunciated four major objections to the large-scale employment of the weapon:

1. Machine guns, unlike the infantry rifle, could not be relied upon to score a hit with each separate shot and, therefore, wasted ammunition.
2. It was difficult to determine the range from the gun to its target.
3. The weapon was mechanically unreliable as demonstrated by its tendency to jam.
4. Machine guns used large amounts of ammunition in an era when ammunition resupply was difficult.[48]

The first criticism reveals one of the major reasons for the continuing uncertainty about the machine gun. Lacking a set of performance standards developed for the machine gun, military theorists measured the performance of the weapon against standards applicable to a familiar weapon, the infantry rifle; these standards had little value for assessing the performance of the machine gun. Until the American military developed a coherent concept of machine-gun employment, it could not develop a realistic set of performance standards for the weapon.

Before the General Staff could settle upon the proper machine-gun organization for the army, it had to deal with the last three objections. The solutions to these problems would, to a substantial degree, determine the structure and type of machine-gun organization selected. Range-finders could be used to determine the range from the gun to its target. But if the target was located in terrain where the impact of the bullets was obscured, the machine-gun crew could be sure that its fire was hitting the target only if the target showed the effect of the fire. Despite their limited usefulness, range finders were issued to the first American machine-gun units.

During World War I the invention of the tracer bullet, which allowed the gunner to observe the entire path of the bullets fired by his gun, finally solved the problem of ranging on a distant target.[49]

The second problem was mechanical reliability. If jamming seriously affected the performance of the machine gun, the weapon could not be employed singly.[50] The supply of ammunition was also a major consideration. The tactical dividends of using machine guns had to be weighed against the demands that large-scale use of the weapon would make upon the ammunition supply system. Faced with major objections to the large-scale use of machine guns, General Staff planners postponed any decision on how the weapon should be used until a thorough evaluation could be made of the information contained in the reports of the observers of the Russo-Japanese War.[51]

At the beginning of the war, the Russian army possessed a small number of Maxim machine guns grouped in eight-gun batteries assigned to each division. In the Japanese army, machine guns initially were given only to cavalry brigades, but by the end of the war each infantry regiment was equipped with three Hotchkiss guns, and the Japanese were considering equipping each cavalry and infantry regiment with six machine guns. Since the Russian army fought a largely defensive war, observers accompanying the Russians gained little information regarding offensive employment of the weapon. On at least one occasion the Japanese cavalry managed to use machine guns to enfilade the flank of a Russian position, but the major offensive use of the weapon by the Japanese was in support of infantry attacks. After several battles in which attacking Japanese infantry suffered heavy losses from Russian machine guns, the Japanese began to use their Hotchkiss machine guns to provide overhead covering fire for their infantry assaults. This was, as one observer noted, a tactic that John Henry Parker had pioneered.[52]

Commentary on machine guns in the reports of American observers of the Russo-Japanese War varied widely. The War Department directed each attaché to prepare a detailed report on the Russian or Japanese arm that corresponded to the attaché's own branch of service. Attachés also received special instructions; Capt. Carl Reichmann, an infantry officer, was directed to ". . . give the

From Stepchild Invention to Standard Equipment 139

result of your observations covering the following points: . . . number of rounds of ammunition carried on person, number of rounds per man carried in train, methods of supplying ammunition to the firing line . . . the use made of machine guns, character and effectiveness of types used. . . ."[53] As neither side possessed a large number of machine guns until the winter of 1905, Reichmann and other early observers, Lieut. Walter S. Schuyler, Capt. Peyton C. March, and Capt. John F. Morrison, had little to say about the weapons.[54]

Reports filed by later observers did give some space to machine guns. Maj. Joseph E. Kuhn, an engineer, noted the popularity of the machine gun in the Japanese army and its usefulness as a defensive weapon. Lieut. Col. Edward J. McClernand, First Cavalry, reported,

> On the outbreak of the war the Japanese expected to largely limit the use of the machine gun to the defensive, but experience soon taught them to widen its field, and later it was used to great advantage on the offensive. Their rapid fire frequently silenced the fire of the Russian infantry, and caused the latter to crouch down in their trenches. When the guns stopped firing the Russians could be seen again popping their heads above the parapet. If the flanks of the line be weak, these weapons can be used there advantageously.[55]

According to the McClernand the Japanese valued machine guns highly and advocated attaching them to infantry units. McClernand's emphasis on the offensive use of the machine gun may have been overshadowed by earlier reports which focused on defensive uses of the weapon.

Only one attaché, Montgomery M. Macomb, filed a special report on machine guns. Of the attachés, Macomb was best qualified in terms of interest and experience with the weapon to comment upon it. He found that ". . . the machine gun [had] played a useful but not great part in the war" and that it could best be employed as ". . . a means of suddenly and unexpectedly increasing the volume of fire without overcrowding the firing line, thus greatly extending the scope and flexibility of the fire actions."[56] Accordingly, ". . . the best organization is that which distributes the machine guns among the fighting units so as to take instant advantage of an opportunity without making a good target for the enemy. . . ."⁵⁷ Macomb, Major Kuhn, and a senior attaché, Maj. Gen. Arthur MacArthur, all called for ". . . a careful and exhaustive investigation by the General Staff, as to the best type of gun, the organization of tactical units, and their distribution to commands."⁵⁸

As good as his report was, Macomb failed to translate his observations and experiences into concrete recommendations concerning the specific shape of future American machine-gun units and the tactics for employing these weapons. In common with his fellow attachés, Macomb failed to make a detailed report on ammunition expenditure rates for machine guns in combat and the effect of the weapon's use on the entire ammunition supply system. These oversights reflect the fact that the General Staff apparently failed to ask for this information.⁵⁹ Failure to ask the right questions robbed the attaché reports of much of their usefulness in the area of machine guns.

The reports of American observers of the fighting in Manchuria did not provide enough useful information to chart a clear and decisive course of action for the War Department. But use of machine guns in the Manchurian battles had aroused additional interest in the weapon, and the pressure to create a machine-gun organization for the army continued to mount. In April 1906 the *Army and Navy Journal* reported that War Department officials regarded the question of the proper employment of machine guns as being of ". . . the most serious and pressing importance. . . ."⁶⁰

Only sixteen days after his appointment as chief of staff, Brig. Gen. J. Franklin Bell noted that:

> The War Department is now confronted with this situation: We have adopted a type of gun, mount and pack outfit, and contracted for a considerable number [120 for field service and 75 for coastal fortifications], and actual deliveries [80 guns] are being made pursuant to this contract; but no plan for the distribution and use of these guns has been formulated. Meantime, the guns are of no value and must be stored and condemned to deterioration unless they are put in the hands of troops as fast as received.⁶¹

General Bell certainly was aware of how Congress might react if the army failed to use the 195 expensive machine guns that it had purchased. Thus Ordnance Department procurement of the new machine guns forced army headquarters to take action to create an organization to use the weapon.

Caught between continuing uncertainty and the need for action, the War Department responded in a manner designed to give it the information and the time it needed to devise a suitable machine-gun organization and doctrine. On June 19, 1906, orders were issued authorizing the creation of a machine-gun platoon in each regiment of infantry and cavalry. The platoon of three noncommissioned officers and eighteen privates was equipped with two Maxim model 1904 machine guns.[62] According to Brig. Gen. Thomas H. Barry, this was a "tentative" organization; the ". . . permanent organization and drill will be perfected after the tentative plan has been thoroughly tested."[63]

The one major conclusion about machine guns that the General Staff had drawn from the reports of the Russo-Japanese War was that the weapon was not completely reliable mechanically. One report observed ". . . that many of [the Japanese Hotchkiss machine guns] . . . became disabled through the breaking down of their delicate mechanism."[64] Reviewing attaché reports, Peyton March found that "All observers agree that machine guns should never work singly, but should be handled in pairs."[65] Employment of the weapons in pairs received added justification from the fact that the guns could support each other; it was one of the basic decisions concerning machine guns that the War Department made in 1906.[66]

Designed as an experiment, the machine-gun platoon was also a combat unit. Since the type of combat that the American army faced was the small-scale action of colonial warfare, machine guns would be most useful at the regimental level.[67]

The tactics for using the machine gun in offensive action and its effect on the system of ammunition supply were questions that the attachés had not answered.[68] While they had been asked to report on the ammunition supply system as it pertained to the individual soldier and upon machine guns, few American observers linked the two topics and commented upon ammunition consumption by machine guns. Among the few bits of information that the General

Staff received was a report by Lieutenant Colonel McClernand that the Japanese army carried forty-two hundred rounds with each gun and that the greatest number of shots he saw fired in one hour was fifteen hundred. Observing the war from the other side, Captain Morrison reported that a Russian battery of eight machine guns had fired six thousand rounds in one and a half minutes—a rate of fire that was at the limit of the practical rate of the Maxim machine gun. Morrison noted that the same battery later expended 26,000 cartridges in a two-day period. Major Morton correctly termed this data "fragmentary, and quite insufficient" for the needs of the General Staff.[69] Unable to determine the impact of the machine gun on ammunition supply, the General Staff created a machine-gun organization that would probably not tax the ammunition supply system excessively. The use of the machine gun as an offensive weapon was a subject that the War Department undoubtedly hoped to explore with its experimental platoons. Whether it could do so was questionable.[70]

Incorporation of the machine gun in infantry and cavalry formations removed the possibility of employing the machine gun in an independent role on the battlefield. The machine gun became an "organic" infantry weapon—a role recommended by the Infantry Board in 1904. In making its decision, the War Department appears to have had little choice but to follow the course outlined in 1904. Review of the elements that probably influenced the decision reveals the reasons for the failure to create more or larger machine-gun platoons.

The major factors that influenced the structure of the machine-gun platoon were certain restrictions on the number of men and guns available for creation of machine-gun units. In 1906 there were only 120 Maxim model 1904 guns available for issue. As officers on the General Staff pointed out, formation of machine-gun units equipped with more than two guns would mean that guns would not be available for equipping the Porto Rican Regiment, the Philippine Scouts, or for instructional use in military schools. Creation of a three-gun platoon would result in the employment of at least one gun singly, a practice that ran counter to the General Staff belief that machine guns should be used in pairs.[71] The desire to give weapons to every infantry and cavalry unit resulted in a machine-gun unit of limited value as an experimental vehicle. Rather than create several model units with a larger number of guns and in the process restrict the weapon to a few infantry and cavalry regiments, the War Department organized a large number of small units which could do little more than work out the details of employing machine guns on the most limited practical scale.

No less influential than the limited supply of machine guns was the severe restriction on personnel increases that the army faced. The Army Reorganization Act of 1901 classed the machine gun as an artillery weapon and explicitly authorized artillery machine-gun batteries. An escape clause provided for the use of machine guns by the infantry and cavalry, but there was no statutory authorization for the formation of machine-gun units in these branches. In 1906 this obstacle was circumvented by using sections of the 1901 law originally intended to enable the president to bring infantry and cavalry regiments to wartime strength during a national emergency. Under these provisions President Roosevelt increased the authorized strength of each regiment to allow the creation of a machine-gun platoon, an addition of a total of 943 men to the authorized strength of the army. Creation of machine-gun units on a larger scale would have required legislative approval. The likelihood of obtaining such action from an economy-minded Congress was questionable.[72] Because the War Department did not know precisely what the requirements were, it could hardly expect Congress to authorize a larger organization.

As a system for creating and evaluating small-unit drill and doctrine, the regimental machine-gun platoon had several advantages. Each platoon leader prepared drill instructions for his platoon. The instructions were reviewed and commented upon as they passed through administrative channels to the War Department. The army staff would receive the theories developed by the lieutenants who commanded the platoons and critiques of these ideas made by experienced senior officers. Thus junior and senior officers would participate in the formulation of doctrine. As two guns would probably be the basic subunit for a larger formation, some of the doctrine developed for the platoon could be used by a larger unit. Finally, creation and maintenance of the platoon would not place an excessive burden upon the personnel resources of a unit of regimental size.

The machine-gun platoon was not an ideal unit. Its size and structure had been determined by the limited number of guns available and by the desire to give platoons to all infantry and cavalry regiments rather than distributing them according to the nature of the mission of the platoon as an experimental unit. As a consequence the experiments that could be conducted were limited to platoon-level operations. Equally damaging was the fact that the machine-gun platoon was assigned to a specific battalion or squadron rather than to the regimental headquarters.[73] Only the officers and men stationed at the same post as the machine-gun platoon would have an opportunity to become familiar with the weapon.

NOTES

1. Walter Millis, *Arms and Men* (New York, 1956), pp. 154-62; Russell F. Weigley, *History of the United States Army* (New York, 1967), pp. 313-26.

2. On March 29, 1899, Brig. Gen. Daniel W. Flagler, chief of ordnance since January 23, 1891, died at Fort Monroe, Virginia. Flagler was replaced by Adelbert R. Buffington, who retired on November 22, 1901. At that time Capt. William Crozier was appointed chief of ordnance. U.S., War Department, *Official Army Register for 1899* (Washington, D.C., 1899), p. 44; *Army Register, 1900*, p. 372; *Army Register, 1901*, p. 47; George W. Cullum, *Biographical Register of the Officers and Graduates of the U.S. Military Academy*, ed. Charles Braden (Saginaw, Mich., 1910), vol V, p. 238 (hereafter cited as Cullum, *Biographical Register*).

3. U.S., War Department, *Annual Report of the War Department, 1900* (Washington, D.C., 1900), vol. III, p. 123.

4. Ibid., pp. 123-24, 147-48, 165.

5. Ibid., pp. 131-32, 156, 174.

6. Ibid., p. 39. Buffington gave three reasons for his decision: (1) the Colt could be used without a water jacket; (2) Colt guns could be manufactured immediately (they were, therefore, immediately available for use in the Far East); and (3) the Colt gun was a product of American industry; thus the army would not have to depend on a foreign source for its supply of machine guns. Ibid., pp. 39-40.

From Stepchild Invention to Standard Equipment 145

7. Endorsement of the Adjutant General, Department of the Missouri, November 7, 1901, National Archives, Record Group (hereafter, cited as NA, RG) 94, doc. 391245/C Additional E; ltr. to F. D. McKenney and reply by McKenney with four endorsements, NA, RG 156, doc. 25537, enclosure 412.

8. U.S., Congress, House, Committee on Military Affairs, *Military Appropriation Bill Hearings before the Committee on Military Affairs, House of Representatives, on H.R. 16567*, 57th Cong., 1st sess., 1902, p. 96.

9. *Annual Report of the War Department, 1901*, vol. III, pp. 12-13. This was the famous M1903 Springfield rifle and the M1903 .30 caliber cartridge.

10. In 1904 the report of the chief of ordnance stated: "As soon as the design of ball cartridge, model of 1903, was completed, all American and foreign inventors [of machine guns] . . . were invited to submit their devices for test." *Annual Report of the War Department, 1904*, vol. X, p. 19.

11. Ibid., pp. 16, 19.

12. Ibid., p. 71. Emphasis added.

13. Ibid., p. 112. The report of the 1899 tests of the Colt gun mentions overheating but does not list it as a specific defect. *Annual Report of the War Department, 1900*, vol. III, p. 153.

14. Of the four guns originally submitted for testing, two, the Danish rifle-*mitrailleuse* and the Maxim solid-action, did not complete the tests due to mechanical failures. *Annual Report of the War Department, 1904*, vol. X, pp. 19, 111. The army model incorporated several design improvements and was eventually designated the Maxim automatic machine gun, caliber .30, model of 1904.

15. Second endorsement, January 13, 1904, NA, RG 156, doc. 38356/71.

16. Parker continued to believe that his work with the machine gun would earn him an accelerated promotion. On July 2, 1902, he commented:

> But I haven't come in yet, somehow. Neither my service in Cuba, which Colonel Roosevelt, pronounced the *most deserving of reward of any officer in the army* in his "History of the Rough Riders" nor what I consider my really superior—if less prominent—service in the Philippines, nor yet my efforts to get a practical machine gun carriage made, have yet resulted in advancement by a single file. But I believe *President* Roosevelt will make it all right in the end.

Marginal comments appended to a letter from Roosevelt to Parker, May 16, 1900, Parker file, U.S. Military Academy Archives.

17. *Annual Report of the War Department, 1903*, vol. II, p. 382; NA, RG 165, Name Card Index to the General Correspondence of the Board of Ordnance and Fortification (1888-1919), entry for Parker, John H.

18. John H. Parker, "An Old Problem and Its Solution," *Journal of the Military Service Institution of the United States* XXXIII (July-August, 1903): 47.

19. Ibid., pp. 50-51.

20. *Annual Report of the War Department, 1903*, vol. II, p. 382. The board also funded the construction of ammunition carts designed by H.F.L. Allen and Maj. W.C. Manning. Ibid.

21. U.S. War Department, Special Order 142, para. 11, June 17, 1902; War Department, Special Order 253, para. 20, October 28, 1902; War Department, Special Order 141, para. 6, June 17, 1903. Parker's work at Hartford was undoubtedly facilitated by the fact that his old friend, Capt. John T. Thompson, was the ordnance inspector at the Colt's factory. Cullum, *Biographical Register*, vol. V, p. 333.

22. War Department, Special Order 162, para. 15, July 13, 1903.

23. The three carts were the Parker cart, the Manning cart, and the Allen cart.

24. Acting Adjutant General to Parker, September 16, 1903, NA, RG 94, doc. 474649/F. In 1902 Fort Riley was selected as the site for ". . . yearly autumn maneuvers to be conducted on a scale hitherto unknown in this country." *Annual Report of the War Department, 1902*, vol. IX, p. 61. The distance from Leavenworth to Riley was 135 miles. C. G. Morton, "Machine Guns In Our Army," *Journal of the United States Infantry Association* 1 (July 1904): 22.

25. War Department, General Order 45, March 31, 1903.

26. Chief of Ordnance to Secretary of War, March 10, 1903, NA, RG 156, doc. 38263-2.

27. Ibid.

28. "Copy of Correspondence of the Infantry Board Concerning the Investigation of the Use of Automatic Guns with and by Infantry Troops, and Their Proper Organization, Ammunition, Supply, Transportation, Cover, etc., dating from July 6, 1903." October 7, 1904, NA, RG 165, doc. 6844; memo Chief of Staff to Assistant Secretary of War, subject: The distribution of machine guns and the organization of detachments to serve them in the U.S. Army, May 1, 1906, NA, RG 94, doc. M.S.O. 1134830 (1906), p. 6 (hereafter cited as C/S memo on distribution of MG, May 1, 1906).

29. U.S., Congress, House, *Fourteenth Report of the Board of Ordnance and Fortification* (Washington, D.C., 1904), pp. 12-13. The Parker cart

was not immediately abandoned because of this decision. In the spring of 1904 it was tested in competition with the Vickers-Maxim tripod mount. On February 2, 1905, the Board of Ordnance and Fortification finally concurred with the conclusion of the Infantry Board that the Parker cart was not as suitable a mount for machine guns as the Vickers-Maxim tripod. Ibid.; U.S. Congress, House, *Fifteenth Report of the Board of Ordnance and Fortification* (Washington, D.C., 1905), pp. 10-11.

30. Charles G. Morton graduated with the class of 1883 from the U.S. Military Academy (twentieth in a class of fifty-two). Commissioned in the infantry, he later rose to the rank of major general and commanded the Twenty-ninth Division in the American Expeditionary Force. Charles N. Branham, ed., *Register of Graduates and Former Cadets of the United States Military Academy* (West Point, N.Y., 1964), p. 274; C/S memo on distribution of MG, May 1, 1906, p. 1; memo report, First Division Provisional General Staff, June 25, 1903, NA, RG 165, Memorandum Reports June-September 1903, doc. 432 AWC (1903).

31. NA, RG 165, "Proceedings War College Board July 1902-August 1903," doc. 839 AWC (1903).

32. C/S memo on distribution of MG, May 1, 1906, p. 5.

33. "Report of Organization to Test Machine Guns and Mounts and Organization," January 7, 1904, *Proceedings of the Board of Ordnance and Fortification*, vol. 16, p. 1, NA, RG 165.

34. War Department, General Order 16, January 22, 1904.

35. C/S memo on distribution of MG, May 1, 1906, p. 5. See also NA, RG 156, "Extract from the Proceedings of the Infantry Board," doc. 38356/109.

36. C/S memo on distribution of MG, May 1, 1906, pp. 8-10. Macomb graduated from the U.S. Military Academy with the class of 1874 (fourth in a class of forty-one). Commissioned in the artillery, he had a long and exceptionally distinguished career, which reached its zenith with his promotion to brigadier general in 1910 and subsequent service as president of the Army War College from 1914 to 1916. Macomb was one of the few outstanding staff officers in the American army during the decade prior to World War I. Branham, ed., *Register of Graduates, 1964*, p. 263.

37. C/S memo on distribution of MG, May 1, 1906, p. 5; John H. Parker *Tactical Organization and Uses of Machine Guns in the Field* (Kansas City, Mo., 1899), pp. 84-85.

38. Ibid., p. 10.

39. Major Macomb had enunciated this concept in an article published in mid-1903. M. M. Macomb, "The Armament of Field Artillery," *Journal of*

the *Military Service Institution of the United States* XXXIII (July-August 1903): 96.

40. C/S memo on distribution of MG, May 1, 1906, p. 7.
41. Morton, "Machine Guns In Our Army," p. 30.
42. Weigley, *History*, p. 322.
43. C. G. Morton, Organization, Use and Equipment of Machine Guns, April 1905, NA, RG 165, Army War College paper, serial no. 12, p. 22 (hereafter cited as Morton, AWC paper no. 12).
44. A survey of the origins of books and articles on machine guns received by the Military Information Division of the Adjutant General's Office during the period from January 1902, to September 1903, reveals the following distribution:

Germany—15	Japan—2	Switzerland—1
England—3	France—1	U.S.—1
Austria—2	Italy—1	

Fifteen additional items, mainly attaché notes, clippings, and reviews of other articles, were received from a variety of sources. Compiled from the *Index of Special Military Subjects Contained in Books, Pamphlets, and Periodicals Received in the Military Information Division*. U.S., War Department, Adjutant General's Office, for the period March 1902, to September 1903. A General Staff pamphlet on the subject of machine guns contained sixteen articles; ten were German, four were French, and there was one each of Swiss and Dutch origin. U.S., War Department, General Staff, *Selected Translations Pertaining to the Tactical Use and Value of Machine Guns* (Washington, D.C., 1906).

45. G. S. Hutchison, *Machine Guns: Their History and Tactical Employment* (London, 1938), p. 96; F. V. Longstaff and A. Hilliard Atteridge, *The Book of the Machine Gun* (London, 1917), pp. 29-30.
46. Morton, AWC paper no. 12, pp. 14-15.
47. Ibid., p. 11.
48. J. E. McMahon, "The Role of the Machine Gun in Modern War," *Journal of the United States Infantry Association* II (July 1905): 26-28. Remarks attributed to Col. James Regan, Ninth Infantry, cited in "Introductory Remarks on New Tactics—Machine Guns," John H. Parker, *Journal of the Military Service Institution of the United States* XXXV (November-December 1904): 466. E. R. Heiberg presents an extremely conservative viewpoint in an article titled "The Use of Machine or Automatic Guns for Cavalry," *Journal of the United States Cavalry Association* XV (July 1904): 251.
49. War Department, General Order 113, June 19, 1906; George M. Chinn, *The Machine Gun* (Washington, D.C., 1951), p. 305.

From Stepchild Invention to Standard Equipment 149

50. Morton noted that German regulations prohibited the individual employment of machine guns. Morton, AWC paper no. 12, p. 14.

51. Writing in April 1905, Morton concluded "That when the full details of the present war in Manchuria are known, together with the deductions of participants on both sides, many questions concerning machine guns and their use will probably be definitely settled." Morton, AWC paper no. 12, p. 23. Morton's opinion was echoed by Capt. J. E. McMahon. McMahon, "Role," p. 32.

52. Hutchison, *Machine Guns*, pp. 82, 84, 87; U.S., War Department, General Staff, *Reports of Military Observers Attached to the Armies in Manchuria During the Russo-Japanese War*, pt. 5 (Washington, D.C., 1907), p. 95 (hereafter cited as *Rpts. of Mil. Observers*). Parts 1, 2, and 3 were published in 1906 and parts 4 and 5 in 1907.

53. Capt. H. C. Hale, Acting Chief, Second Division, General Staff to Reichmann, subject: Special Instructions to Captain Reichmann, February 26, 1904, as cited in John T. Greenwood, "The American Military Observers of the Russo-Japanese War, 1904-1905," (Ph.D. dissertation, Kansas State University, 1971), p. 156.

54. Ibid., p. 446.

55. *Rpts. of Mil. Observers*, pt. 5, p. 95.

56. Greenwood, "American Military Observers," pp. 446-47.

57. Ibid., p. 447.

58. Gen. Arthur MacArthur to Maj. William Beach, October 3, 1905, NA, RG 165, as cited in Greenwood, "American Military Observers," p. 463, fn. 97.

59. The exact nature of Macomb's instructions and those given to the majority of the attachés is unclear. The War Department with congressional approval destroyed most of the pertinent documents in 1925. Copies of general and special instructions in the final reports of Col. John V. Hoff, Lieut. Col. Walter S. Schuyler, and Capt. Carl Reichmann are located in the War Department Historical Files of Military Intelligence in the National Archives. Greenwood, "American Military Observers," p. 168, fn. 119.

60. *Army and Navy Journal* (hereafter, *A-N Jou.*), April 28, 1906, p. 978.

61. C/S memo on distribution of MG, May 1, 1906, p. 17.

62. The officer in charge of the platoon was drawn from the staff of the battalion to which the platoon was assigned. Each platoon was authorized ten pack animals for transportation of the guns, equipment, and ammunition. War Department, General Order 112, June 19, 1906; *A-N Jou.*, June 9, 1906, p. 1147.

63. *Annual Report of the War Department, 1906,* vol. I, p. 558.

64. U.S., War Department, General Staff, *Selected Translations,* preface.

65. Paper entitled "Reasons for the issue of two machine-guns to one battalion of each regiment of cavalry and infantry," signed March, nd, NA, RG 94, doc. 1228217. Internal evidence indicates that this paper was probably written between March 26, 1906, and January 25, 1907. The signature as been identified by I. B. Holley, Jr., as that of Peyton C. March.

66. U.S., War Department, General Staff, *Selected Translations,* preface. Employment of machine guns in pairs meant that the organization recommended by the Infantry Board in 1904 was not acceptable. C/S memo on distribution of MG, May 1, 1906, p. 18.

67. Morton, AWC paper no. 12, p. 23.

68. In a lecture delivered at the School of Musketry, Lieut. Charles H. Mason, Nineteenth Infantry, made the following observation:

> In this country the matter [of ammunition supply] has received only occasional attention from our military writers, which, nevertheless, with the advent of the machine gun in our service, has served to bring it from practical oblivion to a nebulous state of recognition in the minds of the majority of our officers.

Charles H. Mason, "Ammunition Supply in War," *Journal of the United States Infantry Association,* VI (November 1909): 385.

69. *Rpts. of Mil. Observers,* pt. 5, pp. 94, 96; Morton, AWC paper no. 12, pp. 9-10.

70. When comparing the American platoon with machine-gun batteries used by Germany, Russia, and Japan, note that the theoretical structure of American infantry and cavalry divisions called for nine regiments. An American division would contain eighteen machine guns, which compared favorably with the number of similar weapons in European divisions. U.S., War Department, *Field Service Regulations: United States Army, 1905 with Amendments to 1908* (Washington, D.C., 1908), pp. 11-12.

71. C/S memo on distribution of MG, May 1, 1906, p. 18.

72. Ibid.; Army Reorganization Act, U.S., *Statutes at Large,* vol. 31, secs. 2, 4, and 10, 748, 750 (1901); *Annual Report of the War Department, 1906,* vol. I, pp. 7-8. Congress had allowed the authorized enlisted strength of the army to fall to 59,866 men, the statutory minimum. The actual enlisted strength of the army in 1906 was only 54,659 men. *Annual Report of the War Department, 1902,* vol. I, p. 2.

73. War Department, General Order 113, June 19, 1906.

VII

A FAILED EXPERIMENT, 1907-1909

In the years following the creation of the experimental platoons in 1906, War Department attempts to develop a permanent machine-gun organization and doctrine met with little success. Although the regimental machine-gun platoons were part of a major effort to investigate the use of this potent weapon, failure to design the experiment properly and to support it rendered its results trivial. Faced with failure, the War Department turned to a familiar figure, John Henry Parker, and a familiar device, the board of officers, to produce a machine-gun manual and organization. The result was a small handbook, which was useful only for the experimental machine-gun platoons. While staff difficulties were compounded by Parker's continued advocacy of a separate machine-gun service, the continued failure to develop adequate machine-gun doctrine resulted mainly from incomplete staff work within the War Department.

The work of creating the machine-gun platoons proceeded at a fairly rapid pace. The staff bureaus, particularly the Ordnance Department, were interested in the project and expedited delivery of the guns and associated equipment to the embryonic platoons. Staff departments did little, however, to solve the real problems that the commanders of the new platoons faced, for the army had placed the task of creating tactical doctrine for the machine gun squarely on the shoulders of its most junior officers.

According to War Department training instructions for the new platoons, the men would first learn the nomenclature and functioning of the model 1904 Maxim gun and its mount; this drill was to be ". . . persevered in until the men know each part by sight and name, and can tell at once its place and function."[1] Since the gun had eighty-eight parts, including twelve different flat and helical springs, the task was not an easy one. Next the trainees were to master the intricacies of packing the platoon equipment. A poor packing job endangered both equipment and animals, and speed in packing and unpacking was essential to rapid employment of the gun in combat; consequently, mastery of the art of pack transport became a fundamental skill for the members of the platoon.[2]

Once familiar with the intricacies of pack transport and the idiosyncracies of their animals, the neophyte machine gunners could begin to learn to use their new weapons. After each man had mastered his duties, the crews assembled for platoon drill. Finally, the platoon was ready for target practice and the chance to make its work pay off by demonstrating the proficiency of the platoon and the power of its weapons. At this point the cost-conscious mentality of the War Department intervened with crippling effect. In 1907 the annual ammunition allowance for machine guns was a thousand rounds per gun, an amount that would be expended in less than five minutes of rapid fire.[3]

Low ammunition allowances effectively prevented the machine gunners and crews from attaining a high degree of proficiency with their weapons, removed the opportunity for cross-training the members of the machine-gun crew, and robbed the platoon of what should have been the culmination of its work. The resulting frustration and attendant lowering of morale must have further complicated the platoon leader's job. In at least one case the poor marksmanship of a machine gun platoon caused the commander of the regiment to which the platoon belonged to question the usefulness of the weapon.[4]

In addition to organizing and training his unit, the platoon commander was directed by the staff to devise a "tentative" drill manual along the lines suggested by the "phraseology of commands and the mechanism of the [field artillery] drill. . . ."[5] The idea of using field artillery drill as a guide was imaginative, but the young infantry and cavalry officers could be misled if they followed the artillery regulations too closely.

Having given its most inexperienced officers the monumental task of creating drill and a training program for a new organization, the War Department required them to submit a report ". . .

A Failed Experiment

embodying your recommendations respecting needed changes in the material, personnel, organization, drill, and tactical handling of the automatic machine gun in the Army. . . ."[6] The deadline for the report was March 1, 1907, less than nine months after creation of the machine-gun platoons was authorized.

A short deadline on the reports meant that they would reflect only initial experience with the weapon and might therefore be very misleading. While the general nature of the specifications set for the report gave the platoon leader the maximum scope to express his views, the report was poorly conceived. The lack of specific and detailed questions insured that the reports that the War Department received lacked common focal points, a fact that robbed the papers of much of their usefulness. As the commander of the Rock Island Arsenal noted, the accounts ". . . are so contradictory that it is impossible to make recommendations regarding the changes required to make [the pack equipment usable]. . . ."[7] Contradictory in the concrete areas of equipment design, the reports varied widely in the less easily defined areas of drill and platoon tactics.

Poor preliminary staff work within the War Department robbed the efforts of the machine-gun platoons of much of their worth. Too much responsibility for the success of the experiment rested upon the shoulders of the platoon leaders. Due largely to a failure to understand the requirements of the experiment, the staff did little to assist the creation of the platoons beyond setting up a sketchy set of priorities for action. The Ordnance Department, a staff bureau vitally interested in the outcome of the machine-gun experiment, failed to increase the ammunition allowance of the platoon to a level that would allow proper training. Finally, the failure of the General Staff to determine the precise nature of the information that it needed and then to insure that this information was included in the platoon leaders' reports drastically limited the value of the experiment. The staff officers in the War Department clearly failed to understand the central role played by experimental design in any investigation of this type; having neglected to ask specific questions, the army received only general answers.

Creation of the experimental machine-gun platoons did generate considerable interest in the weapon. Numerous articles concerning the weapon, its organization, and tactics appeared in the professional journals supported by American officers. While a number of these articles were the work of John Henry Parker and Montgomery Meigs Macomb, after 1906 new writers appeared. Primarily machine-gun platoon leaders, these men were chiefly interested in platoon-level drill and tactics and the problems that they had encountered in their work.

The earliest article appeared in March 1908; in it Lieut. George R. Guild detailed personnel problems that prevented the machine-gun platoon from achieving maximum efficiency. Guild found that the platoon did not have enough men to handle its pack animals properly, and that because first-class soldiers were rarely detailed to machine-gun platoons, there were never enough reliable men to fill key positions. Ambitious and capable soldiers seldom joined the new units because machine-gun duty reduced their chances for promotion. These defects stemmed from the temporary nature of the machine-gun platoon. Guild's solution was the creation of a separate, statutory machine-gun organization, a solution other writers would also propose.[8]

While Guild considered the personnel problems of the new platoons, other officers argued the use of the machine gun by cavalry units. Lieut. H. R. Smalley of the Second Cavalry Regiment opened the debate in July 1908 with a copy of the report he had submitted to the War Department. Smalley noted that when his report was sent in, his platoon ". . . had not been organized a sufficient length of time to determine on needed changes."[9] Since the submission of the report his unit had marched more than 1,200 miles and in his opinion had proved itself a valuable addition to a cavalry regiment. Based upon his experience, Lieutenant Smalley recommended organization of a separate machine-gun company of four or six guns in each cavalry regiment.[10] The same issue of *Cavalry Journal* carried a less conventional article. In it Lieut. Harry L. Hodges concluded that machine-gun fire could replace the rifle fire of dismounted cavalrymen in supporting cavalry attacks. While this tactic would free more soldiers for mounted action, it would require cavalry machine-gun units equipped with a very light machine gun with an effective range of 500 to 1,100 yards. Hodges proposed that the army form cavalry machine-gun companies equipped with twelve lightweight (16.5-pound) Rexar rifles, an automatic rifle of Danish manufacture. Organized in three or four platoons and manned

A Failed Experiment

by four officers and seventy-three enlisted men, these units would be an organic source of fire support for cavalry maneuvers.[11]

Hodges continued to champion the adoption of a lightweight machine gun for the cavalry in an article on a new weapon, the Benet-Mercie. According to the young officer, tests of the weapon at Atascadero, California, had convinced Capt. John H. Parker that the Benet-Mercie had the best mechanism of any machine gun yet made—an opinion that Parker would later have cause to change.[12] Hodges' article presaged War Department action, for the Benet-Mercie eventually was adopted as the replacement for the model 1904 Maxim gun.

It is difficult to assess the impact that articles concerning machine guns had upon the position of the weapon in the army. Certainly the articles informed a wide audience of the problems encountered in attempting to use the weapon and of possible solutions for these problems. Discussions of the merits of machine guns as well as theories for their use were also aired. The articles contained little information that was new to the General Staff; indeed, many of the articles were based upon official reports that had been sent to the War Department.[13] While essays on machine guns probably had little direct influence on the War Department, they provided the officer corps with information on the machine gun that furthered its acceptance by the members of arms charged with its use.

At his request Capt. John Henry Parker had been ordered to Cuba as a member of the forces sent there in 1906. Soon he became bored with his situation on the island, and his active mind began to search for other areas in which he might gain distinction. Well aware of the state of the experiment with machine-gun platoons, Parker decided that the War Department should empanel an official board to test and evaluate tactical and organizational concepts for machine guns and then use these ideas as the basis for doctrine. Was his desire to participate in this activity another example of Parker's drive to attain recognition and advancement through association with the machine gun?[14]

The surest way to become part of the War Department effort to create machine-gun doctrine was to originate the idea for such an effort. Accordingly, Parker put together a paper describing how the machine gun had come to its present position in the army. The account was somewhat vague concerning the contribution of the Ordnance Department and omitted the work of the General Staff altogether. But it supported Parker's claim that "Every step of progress has been the direct result of the efforts of Captain JOHN H. PARKER, 28th Infantry."[15] The narrative concluded with the recommendation that the War Department establish an experimental organization to devise a standard machine-gun drill and the structure of the organization that would use it. The genuine merit of Parker's idea was tarnished by his remark that it was ". . . obviously only justice that Captain Parker should have the opportunity to do this work."[16]

Brig. Gen. Thomas H. Barry, commander of the forces in Cuba, endorsed the document with the savage observation ". . . that there are many officers alive to the necessities of this arm, and whose reports merit fully as much, if not more, consideration than this egotistical and slangy report. . . ."[17] Parker's paper seemed destined for the limbo of the adjutant general's files.[18] Fortunately for Parker, it reached the War Department at precisely the same time that the General Staff faced the incoherent mass of reports from the leaders of the new platoons.

On December 12, 1907, the War Department approved Maj. Gen. J. Franklin Bell's recommendation to organize a provisional machine-gun company at the Presidio of Monterey under the command of Capt. John Parker. Even if General Bell had not taken this action, it is quite likely that Parker would have been given the job of creating machine-gun doctrine. A copy of his chronology reached President Roosevelt on December 22, 1907, and a month later Roosevelt told Parker that he ". . . was very much pleased to give you the chance to organize that machine gun company.'[19]

Parker wanted to work at Fort Meyer, Virginia, a location close to the War Department and to his friend, the president, but the army sent him to Monterey, California, where early in 1907 the Pacific Division had reorganized a school of musketry at the Presidio. Formed from the personnel of two infantry companies and a machine-gun platoon, the school was to train selected officers and enlisted men as small-arms instructors. The only institution of its kind in the army, the School of Musketry soon received additional tasks, and in November 1907 classes were reduced from four to three annually so that the school staff could cope with the experimental work assigned by the War Department. Already the site of other experiments with small arms, the School of Musketry was the logical place for Parker's work to be conducted.[20]

Arriving at Monterey in January 1908, Parker discovered that he was to review the reports on machine-gun platoons and send a digest of the contents to the General Staff. He found that a majority of the reports favored establishment of some type of separate organization to use the machine gun. Parker interpreted this finding as support for the "absolutely independent company," which was the basic unit of his machine-gun service. His superiors did not agree with him. Col. Marion P. Maus, Twentieth Infantry, reviewed Parker's summary of the reports and found the ". . . present machine gun platoon . . . preferable in every way to the heavy machine gun companies that appear to be contemplated."[21] Maus' judgment was seconded by the commanding general of the Department of the Pacific, Brig. Gen. Frederick Funston, and the report was filed by the adjutant general.[22]

In addition to advancing his theories for machine-gun organization and tactics, Parker advocated use of indirect machine-gun fire, which envisioned employing the weapon from a covered position to strike at targets at a considerable distance from its position. The source of this idea is not clear. In 1903 Lieut. Col. Charles B. Mayne of the British army had published an article advocating indirect rifle fire. Lieut. Parker Hitt, a participant in the Monterey experiments, wrote a letter to the Ordnance Department which outlined a method of indirect fire for machine guns and described the equipment that Hitt had devised to make it work. Several months later Captain Parker sent the War Department a report which detailed methods of indirect fire, similar to those discussed by Lieutenant Hitt. Since indirect fire required special equipment, Parker also sent a letter on the subject to Gen. William Crozier, the chief of ordnance. Crozier was interested in the idea and directed that the necessary equipment be manufactured at the Watervliet Arsenal.[23]

Parker advocated two techniques that he claimed would produce accurate, long-range indirect fire from machine guns. The first method used triangulation to determine the range from the gun to the target and the precise direction of the gun-target line. Parker admitted that ". . . as a general thing, it is not practicable to explain this method so that the average enlisted man can comprehend its application; but . . . after a few demonstrations on the ground it is possible to make a sufficient number of men understand it to apply it without help from an officer."[24] The second method used a specially made aiming bar in a complicated process that involved transferring sight readings from the aiming bar to the gunsights to place the Maxim guns on target.[25] The task of evaluating both techniques was given to three officers, a cavalryman, Lieut. Col. John F. Guilfoyle, and two artillerymen, Maj. John E. McMahon and Capt. William S. McNair.[26]

A series of tests devised by McMahon and McNair proved to their satisfaction that Parker's methods of indirect fire were useless. Using the aiming bar, a machine gun fired 250 rounds at two lines of forty-five targets at a range of 1,250 yards and scored a total of four hits. Tests at greater ranges yielded even poorer results. Indirect fire by triangulation proved equally inaccurate. As the report of the board noted, ". . . the practicability of the system depends upon whether or not the points of strike of the small arms bullet, when fired from a machine gun at long range, can be observed with sufficient accuracy to enable the officer conducting the fire to adjust it on the target."[27] The target area was covered with dry grass a foot high, which obscured the strike of the bullets. The board considered the tests valid despite the effect of the grass; as its report pointed out, conditions making it possible to observe the strike of the bullet at long range—a bare, dry target area—would be exceptional.[28] The members of the board were also of the opinion that it would be extremely difficult to find machine-gun positions that were within range of the target and so located that the fire of the gun was not blocked by the hillcrest that protected the gun. Consequently, the board reported that indirect fire with machine guns was not practical.[29]

Not satisfied with the results of the Fort Riley tests, General Crozier directed that ordnance personnel test Parker's ideas and equipment at the Sandy Hook Proving Ground. These trials also proved his methods to be unsatisfactory, and Parker's concept for indirect fire—which required additional equipment costing $1,600 for each gun—was discarded. Eight years later the usefulness of indirect machine-gun fire would be demonstrated during the Battle of the Somme when British troops attacking a German position known as High Wood were supported by a group of ten guns, which fired a million rounds in a period of twelve hours. The attack succeeded, and indirect machine-gun fire was widely used in the later years of World War I.[30] In static warfare on the flat terrain of northern France large numbers of machine guns liberally supplied with ammunition were useful as indirect-fire weapons. But without these special conditions, indirect fire with machine guns was not a useful technique. War Department evaluation of Parker's system was timely and thorough and displayed a desire to obtain a fair and realistic appraisal of the military value of the concept.

Not content with official reports of his progress, Captain Parker wrote several articles that detailed the work of the experimental machine-gun company during the spring and summer of 1908. According to Parker training a machine-gun unit was a difficult, time-consuming process; the difficulties inherent in such training were in his view a powerful argument for the creation of a separate machine-gun organization.[31] Yet as his story unfolded, Parker's claims for the technical difficulty of machine-gun training began to have a hollow ring. Competing against a platoon of thirty riflemen at ranges from 1,020 to 2,000 yards, a single machine gun had scored as well as or better than individual marksmen. The results of another series of trials designed to simulate possible uses of the machine gun in combat indicated ". . . a decided superiority of the machine gun over the rifle at what we call long range."[32] Test results demonstrated that machine-gun training was not as difficult and lengthy as Parker claimed, and he admitted that the trials showed the "rapid acquirement of proficiency" by a machine-gun platoon.[33] Parker's desire to illustrate the progress made at Monterey and to counter recent attacks on the effectiveness of the machine gun forced him to admit that machine-gun training was not as difficult and time-consuming as he had claimed; this admission weakened his argument for a separate machine-gun service.

Upon completing its training at the Presidio, the provisional machine-gun company moved south to a field camp at Atascadero. Maneuvers afforded the opportunity to gain experience with the machine-gun company under field conditions and gave Parker the chance to develop a set of guidelines for assessing the employment of machine guns during field exercises.[34] Observers found the performance of the machine gun company impressive; the *San Francisco Call* reported that Parker and his guns ". . . carried off the palm for effectiveness, scoring during the day on two squadrons of Cavalry, two battalions of Infantry, and a platoon of Field Artillery."[35] Although Parker and his machine-gun company gained favorable public notice, familiarity with newsmen ultimately worked to his disadvantage. The commanding general of the Department of California, Brig. Gen. Fred A. Smith, noted with asperity that ". . . Captain Parker, from a desire not altogether unselfishly disinterested, devotes much time and correspondence in attracting attention to his personal connection with machine guns, as was exemplified at the Camp of Instruction at Atascadero, California, where he seemed to court newspaper notoriety."[36] A reputation as a publicity seeker advanced neither Parker's career nor his theories in army circles.

At the end of the summer of 1908 Parker completed his major task—the creation of a set of instructions covering machine-gun drill, rules for firing the weapons, and their care and maintenance. Parker wanted his manual to contain all of the information needed to administer, train, and employ a machine-gun company; thus, his manuscript covered such subjects as the proper care of pack animals. The idea of including all of the information that the commander of a machine-gun company would need in a single manual made good sense, but it exceeded War Department instructions.

Parker's "Manual of Machine Gun Service for Machine Guns Attached to Infantry" began with a description of a separate machine-gun company consisting of three platoons, each armed with two machine guns in peace and three guns in war. Manned by four officers and ninety-five enlisted men, the machine-gun company used 108 animals; it was a large and expensive organization. Because it was a separate unit with unique training and personnel requirements, the machine-gun company would be administered and trained by a separate corps of officers much as signal companies were handled by the Signal Corps.[37] This separate service was a modified version of the organization that Parker had advocated

A Failed Experiment

since 1899. Basing his coverage of machine-gun drill and tactics on the separate machine-gun company he proposed, Parker gave the War Department two options—either accept his manual and the organization that went with it or reject the manual and develop one suited to the existing machine-gun platoons.

While Parker's Provisional Company explored the intricacies of machine-gun employment, the General Staff reviewed the question of what type of organization the army should adopt. In June 1908 the War College Division of the General Staff submitted a lengthy memorandum addressing the reorganization of the regular army and National Guard to General Bell, the chief of staff. The War College Division recommended the organization of a machine-gun company in each regiment of infantry and cavalry.[38]

Two months later Bell received another memorandum concerning machine guns. Prepared by Maj. William H. Johnston at the direction of Colonel Macomb, chief of the First Section of the General Staff, the paper was titled "Organization of Machine Guns For the United States Army: A Discussion of Relative Value of (1) A Special Corps, (2) Regimental Detachments"; it was a response to a letter that the chief of staff had received from John Henry Parker in May 1908 suggesting a study of the "feasibility or propriety" of his ideas for an independent machine-gun service. Aided by Colonel Macomb, Parker at last succeeded in persuading the army to compare his theories with the concept of integrating machine guns into line units. Ironically, the results of this comparison would be a major factor in the final rejection of a separate machine-gun service.

Beginning with a lengthy list of "accepted principles of machine gun employment," Major Johnston laid the foundation of his critique of a separate machine-gun service. Since the machine gun was unable to contend with artillery at ranges longer than 2,000 yards and since the effect of its fire was not radically different from rifle fire, Johnston concluded that the machine gun was not powerful enough to form the basis of a separate service and that it should continue as part of the armament of the infantry and the cavalry.[39] To support his argument, he devoted approximately half of his study to an examination of the use of machine guns in foreign armies.

Because the German army was changing its machine-gun organization, the information on German machine-gun units that Johnston used was out of date. He stated that each army corps and cavalry division had a machine-gun detachment of six guns and that machine-gun companies had been added to twelve German infantry regiments, but he failed to note recent changes that had integrated machine-gun companies in all infantry and cavalry regiments and that placed separate six-gun detachments under the control of the commander of each army corps. In effect the German army had adopted a system that combined the features of both the organic and separate corps schemes for using machine guns.[40]

Use of the machine gun in the Russo-Japanese War bolstered Johnston's argument against a separate machine-gun service. The Russian army began the war with its machine-gun units organized along the lines of a separate service and had later reorganized its machine guns into four-gun detachments permanently attached to each infantry regiment.[41] In the Japanese army at the start of the war machine guns were assembled in four- or six-gun batteries and the "... *propriety of attaching them to Infantry was never questioned.*"[42]

After developing the evidence that favored the integration of machine-gun units into the existing combat arms, Major Johnston turned to Parker's theories. Noting that Captain Parker appeared to be the only military man in favor of a special machine-gun corps, Johnston proceeded to refute each of Parker's specific proposals for a separate machine-gun service. The study concluded with the recommendation that the American army employ machine guns in organic regimental units.[43]

Shortly after he turned in his draft machine-gun manual, Captain Parker submitted a proposal for legislation to create an infantry machine-gun service; the proposal reached the War Department as Major Johnston's memorandum on machine-gun organization was being circulated to the staff. Reviewing Parker's recommendation, Maj. Gen. William P. Duvall stated that Johnston's paper had demonstrated "... conclusively that a separate corps is not the proper organization for the machine gun service."[44] The concept of a separate machine-gun service appeared to be finished with the final blow delivered by a staff study that John Henry Parker had instigated.

Before Parker had placed his proposal for machine-gun legislation in official channels, however, he had sent a copy of his work directly to President Roosevelt. The president also received a "Presentation Advance Copy" of Parker's machine-gun manual, a "Chronology of Machine Guns brought down to 9 September 1908," and a seven-page memorandum entitled "Observations and Conclusion To be Submitted With the Text of Manual of Machine Gun Service."[45] With this characteristically bold act John Henry Parker neatly bypassed the General Staff and reopened the whole question of machine-gun organization just as it was about to be laid to rest.[46]

When the secretary of war, Luke Edward Wright, informed the president of General Staff opposition to Parker's views, Roosevelt did not drop the subject. Instead he suggested that the General Staff review Parker's provisional machine-gun regulations "to detect manifest errors" and that the regulations ". . . be submitted to the test of practical use as soon as possible."[47] He also asked that the War Department organize an experimental cavalry machine-gun troop. The president further stipulated that if Congress passed the bill to increase the officer corps then before it, he would issue an order creating a provisional machine-gun service along the lines that Parker suggested. Finally, Roosevelt asked the General Staff to comment upon a version of Captain Parker's proposal for a machine-gun service which the president had reworked. Roosevelt's version of the bill combined the General Staff proposal to create a machine-gun company in each regiment of infantry and cavalry with Parker's idea of using a body of field grade officers to supervise the training and operation of the machine-gun companies. This measure retained the best features of both the General Staff position and Parker's ideas and demonstrated Roosevelt's acute grasp of the essential elements of the problem.[48]

Secretary Wright and the General Staff interpreted the president's suggestions as directives. The army position on the number of weapons to be assigned to a machine-gun company was based on Roosevelt's letter:

... six guns for both peace and war seem to be a conservative mean of all the suggestions made. This number appeals to my judgement, as it would provide for two guns for use with each battalion, ... and because it is much easier to reduce each company by two guns and utilize them elsewhere, should six prove to be too many, than to add two more guns to each company, should four prove to be too few.[49]

Roosevelt's version of the bill for a machine-gun service was sent to Congress, but the legislators took no action. Since Congress did not increase the authorized strength of the officer corps, the president could not create Parker's provisional machine-gun organization.[50] As the result of his friendship with the president, John Henry Parker almost succeeded in getting the army to adopt some of his ideas concerning machine gun organization; this was, however, his closest approach to success.

Years later Parker commented bitterly on the fate of his proposed drill regulations: "The War Department treated me in a pretty shabby manner after you [Roosevelt] went out. They took my work of 1908 at Monterey, cut it down to a mere platoon basis, and then published it as the official manual *without giving me a line of credit or any recognition.*"[51] Parker had no reason for bitterness because he was not listed as the author of the manual. Published under the aegis of the General Staff Corps, the *Drill Regulations for Machine-Gun Platoons, Infantry, 1909* belonged to a class of official documents, which, unlike manuals published by army schools, seldom bore any author attribution.[52]

Parker's proposed drill regulations were linked directly to the machine-gun company, which he advocated. This organization—4 officers, 95 men, and 108 saddle, pack, and draft animals—would be equipped with six guns in peacetime and nine guns for combat service. The War Department accepted Parker's organization with two major modifications: following presidential guidance, the company was to be equipped with six guns; and because of statutory restrictions upon the size of the officer corps and a desire to establish the company ". . . in a manner uniform with other companies and troops . . ." each machine gun company would have only three officers.[53] If the War Department had secured authorization for the machine-gun companies, Parker's provisional manual would probably have formed the basis for the drill manual for these units. Congress did not act upon the War Department proposal, and the army found itself with provisional machine-gun platoons and a draft manual designed for a company-size organization.

When it became apparent that Congress would not authorize a new machine-gun organization, the War Department asked the School of Musketry to develop a manual for machine-gun platoons. In mid-summer, 1909, the commandant of the school submitted a draft, which was eventually accepted.[54]

Printed in small type on lightweight paper, the pocket-size *Drill Regulations For Machine-Gun Platoons, Infantry, 1909* was designed as a handy reference for the commanders of machine-gun platoons. "Drill"—the proper handling of the gun and its equipment—and the sections devoted to organization and ceremonies took up most of the space in the manual. In addition to platoon operations the manual discussed marches, camps, and the platoon in action; a final chapter was devoted to the vital problems of dealing with a malfunction in the gun. Although it was a useful guide, the manual had two flaws.

The writers at the School of Musketry disregarded Parker's concept of including in the manual all of the information on ancillary subjects—such as the care of pack animals and pack equipment—that the platoon commander needed to know to run his platoon. This omission became doubly serious when a list of the works that discussed these subjects was also omitted. The second major defect was that the manual contained only one page devoted to tactics. Included in a section titled "The Platoon In Action," the discussion of tactics centered upon the selection of proper positions for the gun.[55] Although adequate in its coverage of the mechanics of using machine guns, the manual failed to give a satisfactory indication of when, why, or how the guns were to be used. This omission pointed to the continued lack of agreement within the army on the subject of machine-gun tactics.

NOTES

1. Draft letter, Henry P. McCain, Military Secretary, War Department, to Commanding Officer of each machine gun platoon, nd, National Archives, Record Group (hereafter, NA, RG) 156, doc. 38356/111.

2. U.S., War Department, *Annual Report of the War Department, 1904*, (Washington, D.C., 1904), vol. X, p. 96; draft letter Henry P. McCain, doc. 38356/111.

3. In 1909 the annual allowance was raised to slightly less than 2,000 rounds per gun, a figure that was still too low. War Department, General Order 172, October 11, 1906, pp. 21-22; War Department, General Order 101, May 4, 1907, pp. 3-5; War Department, General Order 81, May 16, 1908, pp. 2-4; War Department, General Order 46, March 13, 1909, p. 4.

4. James Parker, "The Machine Gun Platoon: Should It Be Retained As Part of the Regimental Organization?" *Journal of the United States Cavalry Association* XIX (July 1908): 48-53; Frederick J. Herman, "The Machine Gun Platoon: Should It Be Retained As Part of the Regimental Organization?" *Journal of the United States Cavalry Association* XIX (October 1908): 335-47; James Parker, "The Machine Gun Platoon," *Journal of the United States Cavalry Association* XIX (January 1909): 655-59; and "Every Man His Own Machine Gun Platoon," *Journal of the United States Cavalry Association* XX (January 1910): 809-10. See also the "Editor's Table: The Machine Gun Platoon," *Journal of the United States Cavalry Association* XIX (October 1908): 455-58.

5. Draft letter, Henry P. McCain, doc. 38356/111.

6. Ibid.

7. First endorsement, Commanding Officer, Rock Island Arsenal to Chief of Ordnance, July 5, 1907, NA, RG 156, doc. 38356/383 encl. 1.

8. George R. Guild, "Our Machine-Gun Platoons," *Journal of the United States Infantry Association* IV (March 1908): 669-76. For similar views see W. P. Evans' commentary on "Our Machine Gun Platoons," *Journal of the United States Infantry Association* IV (May 1908): 953; "Defects in Machine-Gun Platoons," *Army and Navy Journal* (hereafter cited as *A-N Jou.*), June 18, 1910, p. 1251. See also the articles by Colonel Parker and Lieutenant Herman cited previously.

9. H. R. Smalley, "Machine Gun Platoon," *Journal of the United States Cavalry Association* XIX (July 1908): 158.

10. Ibid., pp. 159-64.

11. Harry L. Hodges, "The Uses of Machine Guns With the Cavalry," *Journal of the United States Cavalry Association* XIX (July 1908): 30-34, 40-42, 46. In January 1907 Lieutenant Colonel Macomb reported that the Russian army had formed cavalry machine-gun detachments each consisting of one officer and twenty-six enlisted men armed with six Rexar rifles. Montgomery M. Macomb, "Machine Guns in the Russian Army During the Campaign in Manchuria, 1904-1905," *Journal of the United States Cavalry Association* XVII (January 1907): 444-48.

A Failed Experiment   167

12. Harry L. Hodges, "The Benet Mercie or Hotchkiss Portable Machine Gun," *Journal of the United States Cavalry Association* XIX (January 1909): 511.

13. In June 1908 the War College Division of the General Staff recommended formation of machine-gun companies or troops, because machine-gun detachments were "unsatisfactory in every way." The specific problems cited were the personnel problems that Lieutenant Guild had outlined. Memo, Chief of the War College Division to Chief of Staff, subject: The Reorganization of the Regular Army and the coordination of the National Guard therewith . . . , June 1908, NA, RG 165, WCD 7448-1.

14. In July 1902 Parker had noted that his efforts to get a practical machine-gun carriage made had not ". . . resulted in advancement by a single file." Marginal comments appended to a letter from Roosevelt to Parker, May 16, 1900, Parker file, U.S. Military Academy Archives, West Point, New York.

15. "Summary Chronology of Machine Gun Organization, U.S. Army," March 19, 1907, NA, RG 94, doc. 1228217 (hereafter cited as "Summary Chronology").

16. Ibid.

17. Ibid.

18. Aware of this possibility, Parker had also sent copies of his chronology to two acquaintances, Maj. Gen. Frederick Dent Grant and Brig. Gen. William Harding Carter. Carter and Grant both forwarded the papers to Washington with lukewarm endorsements of Parker's ideas. Parker to Gen. F. D. Grant, March 19, 1907, NA, RG 94, doc. MS 1228217 Addnl. A; Parker to Gen. W. H. Carter, March 19, 1907, NA, RG 94, doc. 1230510 filed with 1228217.

19. Roosevelt to Parker, January 21, 1908, Library of Congress, Theodore Roosevelt Papers, Letterbook series 2, vol. 78, p. 3. One of the copies of Parker's "Summary Chronology" bears the pencil notation: "This chronology was submitted to the President 22 Dec. 1907; and led to orders on the subject 14 Jan. 08." How this document reached Roosevelt is not clear. "Summary Chronology," NA, RG 165, filed with doc. 5683-70; memo for Assistant Secretary of War, subject: Organization of a provisional machine gun company at Presidio of Monterey, December 21, 1907, NA, RG 94, doc. 1320473 filed with 1228217; draft letter to Commanding Officer, Presidio of Monterey, nd, NA, RG 94, doc. 1320473.

20. Ira L. Reeves, *Military Education in the United States* (Burlington, Vt., 1914), pp. 340-42.

21. Parker to Adjutant, Presidio of Monterey, July 15, 1908, NA, RG 94, doc. 1320473

22. Ibid.; memo for the Secretary of War, subject: Abstract reports by commanding officers, machine gun platoons, August 15, 1908, NA, RG 94, doc. 1320473/A filed with 1228217. The men who wrote the reports were: General officer—12 (including Arthur MacArthur, Leonard Wood, Tasker Bliss, John J. Pershing, and Funston), colonel—27, lieutenant colonel—3, major—9, captain—6, first lieutenant—27, second lieutenant—24, sergeant—1.

23. G. S. Hutchison, *Machine Guns: Their History and Tactical Employment* (London, 1938), p. 80; Memorandum on Indirect Fire for Machine Guns by First Lieutenant Parker Hitt (OCO May 4, 1908), NA, RG 156, doc. 38356/561; Parker to Adjutant, Presidio of Monterey, July 18, 1908, NA, RG 156, doc. 38356/651; Parker to Crozier, August 3, 1908, NA, RG 156, doc. 38356/656; Crozier to Maj. John H. Rice, August 11, 1908, NA, RG 156, doc. 38356/651 encl. 1.

24. Paper entitled "Indirect Methods of Machine Gun Fire," July 18, 1908, NA, RG 156, doc. 38356/651 encl. 1, p. 6.

25. Ibid.

26. "Proceedings of a Board of Officers Convened per Special Order 219, Hqs., Ft. Riley, Kas.," October 24, 1908, NA, RG 156, doc. 38356/651 encl. 2.

27. Ibid., p. 3. An earlier article by Captain Parker indicated that ranging might be a problem. Describing the results of tests at Monterey, Parker stated, "Ranges were promptly corrected by observation in all but the indirect fire problems." John H. Parker, "Progress in Machine Gun Development, 9 April 1908," *Journal of the United States Infantry Association* V (July 1908): 8.

28. "Proceedings of a Board of Officers Convened per Special Order 219, Hqs., Ft. Riley, Kas.," October 24, 1908, NA, RG 156, doc. 38356/651 encl. 2, pp. 6-10.

29. Ibid., pp. 10-11.

30. Memo, Acting Chief of Staff to Acting Secretary of War, subject: Indirect Fire for Machine Guns, May 13, 1909, NA, RG 94, doc. 1407285 filed with 1228217; Hutchison, *Machine Guns,* pp. 185-86.

31. Parker, "Progress in Machine Gun Development," p. 4. In a later article Parker expanded this argument:

> It is a fact that the necessary technical training for effective machine gun service cannot be given in the regiments as part of their routine duty. . . . that men of special aptitude, officers of special training and special talents are

necessary. . . . that taking a company of the best infantry, a selected company, and working with three selected officers for over six months, it has been found possible to make less than half of these men competent machine gunmen. . . . This experience confirms the logical view that selected men will be necessary for machine gun service, just the same as for . . . any other technical service. . . .

John H. Parker, "The Technical Side of Machine Gun Organization," *Journal of the Military Service Institution of the United States* XLIII (November-December 1908): 389-90.

32. Parker, "Progress in Machine Gun Development," p. 12.
33. Ibid., p. 7.
34. *A-N Jou.*, August 8, 1908, pp. 1349-50; October 31, 1908, p. 225; draft memo of provisional rules for judging the effectiveness of machine guns at maneuvers, August 1908, NA, RG 94, doc. 1405905; memo for Assistant Secretary of War, subject: Report of Captain John H. Parker, etc., January 18, 1909, NA, RG 94, doc. 1460770.
35. *A-N Jou.*, October 31, 1908, p. 225.
36. Report of Captain John H. Parker upon the Provisional Machine Gun Company at Atascadero Maneuver Camp, 1908, November 11, 1908, NA, RG 94, 1460770, endorsement dated December 3, 1908.
37. "Manual of Machine Gun Service for Machine Guns Attached to Infantry," manuscript, NA, RG 165, doc. 5683-70, pp. 1-5. See also Parker, "Technical Side of Machine Gun Organization," pp. 391-96.
38. This proposal was marked "O.K." and initialed J.F.B. (J. Franklin Bell). Memo for the Chief of Staff, subject: The reorganization of the Regular Army and the coordination of the National Guard therewith, etc., June 1908, NA, RG 165, doc. WCD 7448-1.
39. Memo for the Chief of Staff, subject: Organization of Machine Guns For the United States Army, NA, RG 165, doc. 3793, pp. 1, 4, 25 (hereafter cited as Memo—Organization of MG, doc. 3793).
40. Ibid., Hutchison, *Machine Guns*, pp. 96-97, 102-3, 145-47.
41. Memo—Organization of MG, doc. 3793, pp. 7-8.
42. Ibid., p. 9.
43. Ibid., pp. 13-25. Johnston's paper was later published with the addition of a section on the machine-gun organization that he proposed. William H. Johnston, "The Infantry Machine-Gun Detachment," *Journal of the United States Infantry Association* V (November 1908), pp. 391-408.
44. Parker to the Adjutant, Presidio of Monterey, September 14, 1908, with three attached documents including a memo, Acting Chief of Staff to

Secretary of War, subject: Proposed Bill for the Organization of Machine Guns assigned to the Infantry, October 12, 1908, NA, RG 94, doc. 1320473 filed with 1228217.

45. Manuscript entitled "Manual of Machine Gun Service, etc. . . ." doc. 5683-70 and accompanying papers.

46. On October 12, 1908, Major General Duvall had reported, "This subject is now being carefully studied by the First Section, General Staff, and is under consideration by the Board of Officers . . . it would be premature to ask for legislation before a carefully digested scheme has been prepared." Memo, subject: Proposed Bill for the Organization of Machine Guns, etc., October 12, 1908, NA, RG 94, doc. 1320473.

47. Letter to Luke Edward Wright, October 26, 1908, Theodore Roosevelt, *The Letters of Theodore Roosevelt*, ed. Elting E. Morison, 6 vols. (Cambridge, Mass., 1951), vol. VI, pp. 1319-20.

48. Ibid.; Acting Chief of Staff to Secretary of War, subject: Proposed Bill for the Organization of Machine Guns, etc., October 12, 1908, NA, RG 94, doc. 1320473; see attached paper headed "Memorandum 'b' " with penciled modifications.

49. The General Staff had recommended a company of four guns, whereas Parker had called for a company with six guns in peace and nine in war. Roosevelt, *Letters of Theodore Roosevelt*, vol. VI, p. 1320; memo for Secretary of War, subject: Proposed Machine Gun Organization for the Cavalry and Infantry, December 1, 1908, NA, RG 165, doc. 3793.

50. Roosevelt, *Letters of Theodore Roosevelt*, vol. VI, p. 1320, fn. 1 and 2.

51. Parker to Roosevelt, December 13, 1915, Library of Congress, Theodore Roosevelt Papers, Microfilm Reel 203.

52. Of thirty-one documents listed as General Staff Corps Regulations and Instructions in the *1909 Checklist*, only one bears an author citation. U.S., Superintendent of Documents, *Checklist of United States Public Documents, 1789-1909*, 3d ed. rev. (Washington, D.C., 1911), pp. 1225-26, 1313-14.

53. Memo for Secretary of War, subject: Proposed Machine Gun Organization for the Cavalry and Infantry, December 1, 1908, NA, RG 165, doc. 3793, p. 1. For Parker's organization, see manuscript entitled "Manual of Machine Gun Service, etc. . . ." doc. 5683-70, para. 33 and p. 5.

54. Memo for Assistant Secretary of War, subject: Drill Regulations for Machine gun platoons, August 10, 1909, NA, RG 94, doc. 5683-9; memo, office of the Chief of Staff to the Secretary, General Staff, subject: Machine Gun Drill Regulations, November 16, 1909, NA, RG 94, doc. 5683-22.

55. U.S., War Department, *Drill Regulations for Machine-Gun Platoons, Infantry, 1909* (Washington, D.C., 1909), pp. 65-66.

VIII

A MISTAKE AND ITS CONSEQUENCES: THE BENET-MERCIE, 1909-1913

Experiments with the machine gun did not end with the creation of the infantry machine-gun manual in 1909. Official interest in the weapon continued although army officers paid less attention to it. The varying degrees of interest in the weapon notwithstanding, the position of the machine gun within the American military between 1909 and 1914 was, to a large degree, determined by the status of a new model, the Benet-Mercie. Developed in France, the Benet-Mercie was a lightweight, air-cooled gun that appeared to have substantial combat potential. Following its adoption in 1909, progress in the development of machine-gun doctrine, organization, and manuals waited for delivery of the new guns—an event that did not take place until late 1911. After the Benet-Mercie arrived, army attention was diverted from doctrinal and organizational matters by serious defects in the gun. When efforts to correct these defects failed, official interest focused upon the search for a replacement for the Benet-Mercie. The entire process lasted more than four years. While American efforts to refine machine-gun doctrine and organization were hampered by problems with the Benet-Mercie, British doctrine stagnated for quite different reasons.

After 1900 the progress of integrating the machine gun in most European armies had not been impressive. Commenting upon the position of the machine gun in the British army in 1909, Col. Walter N. Congreve complained that ". . . although we have had the gun longer than any other people in the world . . . we have fallen behind foreign nations in every respect, both in thought, in mechanical devices, and in recognizing the absolute necessity for making the workers specialists."[1] At the beginning of the century, British machine-gun organization and tactics had been the most advanced in the world; however, the British army made no further advances in its organizational or tactical concepts for using the weapon. Consequently, in 1914 the British Expeditionary Force would land in France with a platoon of two guns in each infantry battalion—essentially the same arrangement it had used in 1900.

After the Boer War British neglect of the machine gun was in part the result of the effort devoted to perfecting the musketry of the British infantry. The accuracy, rapidity, and discipline of the rifle fire of the British regular soldier was so advanced that his officers saw no need to incorporate additional machine guns into infantry and cavalry formations.[2] Lack of interest in the machine gun was also fostered by the doctrine for its employment. As a keen observer noted:

> Except for a few specialists—looked upon as cranks—the machine gun was for long belittled. Few battalion commanders detailed their best officers and men to machine gun duty, which in some units was regarded as a fatigue [menial labor]. Nor was there any definite policy regarding its employment on manoeuvres. Among the many epigrammatic slogans, which though true, are so often misused to stifle thought, was that summing up the machine gun as a "weapon of opportunity."[3]

In addition to its inadequacy British doctrine for employing the machine gun also discouraged further thought on the subject.

In the early 1900s the failure of the *mitrailleuse* in 1870 remained fresh in the memory of the French army, and the French high command continued to ignore the machine gun until 1907 when it threatened to become a political issue. Questions about the lack of machine guns in French units were raised in the Chamber of Deputies; to avoid charges that it was neglecting the armament of its troops, the French government promised to equip the army with machine guns.[4] The pledge was kept, but the French high command displayed little interest in the weapon, in part because it was not easy to fit into a tactical system dominated by an emphasis on the offensive and the semimystical concept of *élan*.

Unlike its major adversary, the German army developed a strong interest in the machine gun. Plans forced the German staff to contemplate the large-scale use of reservists in front-line formations during the opening phases of a war. As a consequence, development of infantry firepower through intensive marksmanship training simply was not possible. To increase the fire effect of their infantry units, German tactical theorists began to explore the potential of machine-gun firepower. Reports of the use of the machine gun in the Russo-Japanese War sharply intensified interest in the weapon. In 1907 and 1908 every German infantry regiment received an organic machine-gun company of six guns. A separate program was undertaken to equip the frontier fortresses with machine guns; these weapons would form a reserve available for transfer to German field forces in 1914. German ordnance experts began to improve the standard Maxim gun; at a cost of 14 million marks the

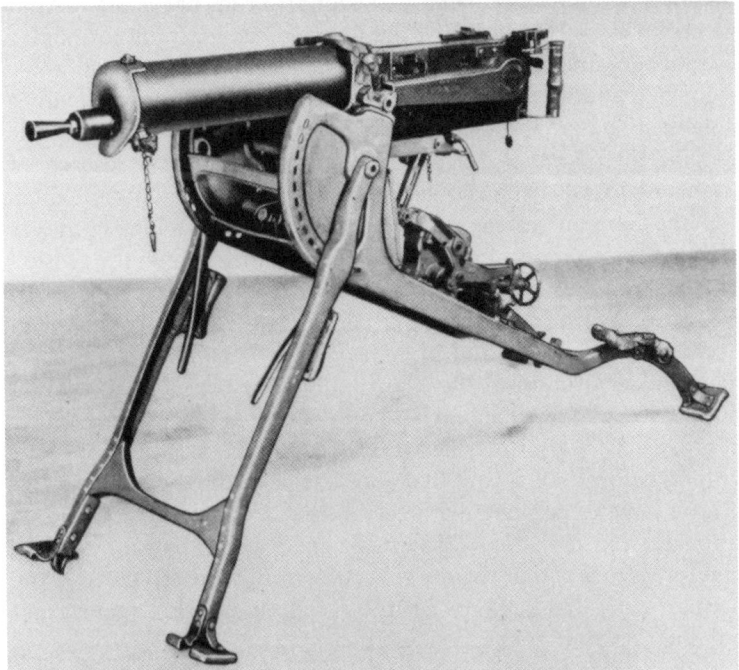

German Maxim gun, model 1908 with sled mount. *Courtesy*: George M. Chinn, *The Machine Gun* (Washington, D.C.: GPO, 1951).

combined weight of the gun and its sled mount was reduced by nearly half to 89 pounds and Zeiss telescopic sights were added to the equipment carried with the weapon.[5]

Large-scale procurement of machine guns and refinements in their design were matched by comparable developments in German doctrine. While the 1908 edition of the American *Field Service Regulations* did not mention machine guns, the *Felddienst Ordnung* of 1908, a comparable German manual, outlined a new organizational concept that greatly increased the tactical value of the weapon. Infantry regiments continued to have machine-gun companies to give the regimental commander an organic source of machine-gun fire support. In addition, a system of machine-gun detachments (*Abteilungen*), similar in composition to the regimental companies, was authorized. Placed directly under the control of the corps commander, the machine-gun *Abteilungen* were a reserve of firepower that he could deploy in support of his battle plan. After the outbreak of World War I the German army rapidly expanded the number of machine-gun detachments in each corps; the infantry regiment continued to possess a single machine-gun company.[6] Organizationally, the German army succeeded in integrating the weapon into combat formations and in creating a reserve of machine-gun units that could be shifted about the battlefield. In 1908 the German system for the employment of machine guns was far in advance of the concepts followed by other armies; the Kaiser's army would retain this lead for almost a decade.

Several factors contributed to the advanced state of German machine-gun doctrine and organization. Procurement and subsequent modernization of the Maxim gun gave the German army a modern weapon on which to base its theories and forced it to devise an organization and doctrine for the weapon. Lack of interest in the weapon before 1900 meant that concepts for using the machine gun did not have to compete with established doctrine, organizational rationale, and prejudice. Finally, the continued expansion of German forces meant that there were spaces within the structure of the German army that could be used to accommodate the organization and doctrine that the excellent German staff devised.

In the United States efforts to develop a system of organization and tactics for machine-gun units were stymied by Ordnance

Department selection of the Benet-Mercie. Less than a year earlier John Henry Parker had warned that the ". . . only danger that threatens the early solution of machine-gun organization is that attention may be diverted from the question of organization by the side issue of possible future change of equipment."[7]

Impetus for the adoption of a new machine gun came from several sources: the natural desire for a better gun, the example set by the Russian army in its adoption of an automatic rifle for its cavalry, and the low opinion of the Maxim gun common among American cavalry officers. In two articles published in early 1907, Montgomery Macomb described a lightweight (16.5-pound) automatic rifle, the Danish Rexar rifle, which the Russian army had issued to units at the end of the Russo-Japanese War.[8] Macomb believed that the work of the provisional machine-gun platoons might indicate ". . . that the Maxim automatic is not just what is wanted for the cavalry, that it is too cumbersome and too slow in coming into action, or repacking and getting out of the way."[9] Cavalry officers joined Macomb in criticizing the Maxim.[10] In a scathing critique based upon the performance of the machine-gun platoon belonging to his regiment, Col. James Parker of the Eleventh Cavalry reported that a machine-gun platoon was much slower to get into action and to move out of action than a cavalry platoon. Colonel Parker contended that the machine guns ". . . will often impede the movement of cavalry, or else be abandoned. With the machine guns cavalry must regulate by the gait of pack mules."[11] Parker's comparison ignored the different purposes of machine-gun and cavalry platoons. But his contention that machine-gun pack animals reduced the mobility of cavalry units was a problem that could be solved by the adoption of a lightweight gun carried by individual cavalrymen.

Dissatisfaction with the model 1904 Maxim was not confined to cavalry circles. Infantry officers found that the heavy gun was difficult to move by hand. Operation of the Maxim required a highly trained and skillful crew, and the delicate and complex mechanism of the gun jammed frequently. The Maxim also required a supply of water to cool its barrel; this requirement would be eliminated with the adoption of an air-cooled gun.[12]

Ordnance officials were well aware of the deficiencies of the standard army machine gun. In 1908 ordnance personnel had tested three lightweight machine guns—the De Knight, the Benet-Mercie, and a light Maxim—at the Springfield Arsenal. The Maxim gun was withdrawn from the competition, but the De Knight gun and the Benet-Mercie completed the tests successfully. The Benet-Mercie, an air-cooled weapon weighing about 22 pounds, was judged superior to the De Knight and the equal of the Maxim gun in rapidity and accuracy of fire. In April 1908 the board of officers that

Benet-Mercie machine gun, model 1909, with tripod mount added when the gun proved unstable when fired from the bipod mount. *Courtesy*: George M. Chinn, *The Machine Gun* (Washington, D.C.: GPO, 1951).

tested the Benet-Mercie at Springfield reported that it had successfully passed the tests; the Ordnance Department then asked that the gun be tested at the School of Musketry in Monterey.[13]

Maj. George W. McIver, the commandant of the School of Musketry, took the Benet-Mercie to the maneuver camp at Atascadero for an assessment of its tactical value. Under his supervision the new gun was put through a series of tests to evaluate its portability, accuracy, and rate of fire.[14] In the last test the Benet-Mercie competed with the model 1904 Maxim; both guns were fired at a group of 110 irregularly mixed prone, kneeling, and standing

A Mistake and Its Consequences: The Benet-Mercie 177

figures at a distance of approximately 1,000 yards. Each gun was allowed two minutes for firing, which favored the Benet-Mercie, since the air-cooled gun did not have time to overheat. The results of the test—40.6 percent hits for the standard gun and 43.8 percent hits for the challenger—indicated that the Benet-Mercie was as accurate as the Maxim gun at what cavalry officers believed was the maximum range from which the guns would be used.[15] Major McIver reported that (1) the new gun could be carried by one man and needed only two men to operate it effectively, (2) it was not a conspicuous target, and (3) more ammunition could be carried with the gun, since there was no need to carry water for cooling. Although the Benet-Mercie had fired only six hundred rounds continuously, the infantry major judged it to be more reliable than the Maxim and reported that the system of thirty-round brass ammunition feed strips that the gun used was superior to the 250-round canvas belts used by the Maxim. McIver closed his report with the conclusion that the Benet-Mercie was "well adapted" for use with cavalry.[16]

Major McIver's report added weight to the arguments for replacing the Maxim gun. In March 1909 the General Staff reported that in its opinion the Maxim gun was not suited to use by the cavalry and that steps had been taken to replace it with the Benet-Mercie.[17] Less than two weeks later the chief of ordnance requested authority to procure one hundred Benet-Mercie machine guns. According to General Crozier the Benet-Mercie was ". . . mechanically and tactically suitable for adoption in place of the Maxim automatic machine gun. . . ."[18] Crozier's request went a step beyond what had previously been suggested. Major McIver and the General Staff had recommended that the Benet-Mercie replace the Maxim model 1904 in cavalry units; Crozier, however, intended to replace the Maxim in both infantry and cavalry units. General Crozier told the Senate Committee on Military Affairs that the army would need fifteen hundred Benet-Mercie guns to equip its line units and the National Guard.[19] Since the army had only 282 Maxim guns, the decision to replace all of them with new guns made considerable sense.[20] Later Crozier justified the adoption of the Benet-Mercie with the remark that the weapon was chosen ". . . after exhaustive trials by two boards, both of which reported that it was the best and most reliable machine gun which had ever been before the Government."[21] Subsequent experience with the Benet-Mercie indicated that such statements greatly exaggerated the value of the gun, but in 1909 no less an authority than Capt. John Henry Parker reportedly was of the opinion ". . . that the Benet-Mercie machine gun has the most perfect mechanism of any machine gun yet invented."[22]

In his annual report for 1910 the chief of ordnance noted that the first shipment of Benet-Mercie guns would be delivered shortly but that the guns would not be issued to the service until after the adoption of pack equipment, which could not be ". . . fully developed until the guns and pertaining materials shall have been received."[23] Issue of the Benet-Mercie was delayed for almost two years.[24]

During the opening months of 1910, the War Department continued to pursue a positive course with regard to machine-gun doctrine. In late February, General Bell authorized publication of a new edition of the *Field Service Regulations*, the document that prescribed the structure and general tactical doctrine of combat units; for the first time this basic army manual contained provisions for the use of machine guns. While the topic of tactics was addressed sparingly, machine-gun organization received detailed treatment. The new regulations provided a provisional company—3 officers, 108 enlisted men, and 6 guns—for each infantry regiment and a provisional troop—3 officers, 86 enlisted men, and 6 guns—for each cavalry regiment.[25] Statutory limitations on the size of the officer corps meant that officers for these units were drawn from regimental and battalion staffs; the extra enlisted men, however, could be obtained only by increases in the authorized strengths of the regiments. Inclusion of provisional machine-gun units in the *Field Service Regulations* provided an official position on the weapon to which planners could refer.

Six months after the *Field Service Regulations* appeared, a new manual, the *Drill Regulations For Machine Gun Organizations, Cavalry, 1910*, was published by the War Department. Devised by a board of officers at the Presidio of Monterey, the new handbook followed the pattern of the 1909 infantry machine-gun manual. Although the subject of tactics occupied a few more pages than it had in the infantry manual, the discussion of the theory of machine-gun employment covered less than a page. Although longer and more detailed than its predecessor, the cavalry manual also failed to define the precise role of the machine gun in combat.[26]

With manuals for infantry and cavalry machine-gun units published and the structure of a machine-gun company established, the War Department should have asked Congress to authorize such units on a permanent basis. The army did not take this step because, as Colonel Macomb noted,

> ... the adoption of a new type of machine gun [the Benet-Mercie] differing in construction and method of operation has rendered necessary the withholding of recommendations to Congress as to the proper organization to be provided until enough of the new guns have been issued for trial and it has been determined what organization is best suited to their service.[27]

Unable to obtain a permanent organization for its machine-gun units, the army was forced to modify its recently published machine-gun manuals to fit the requirements of the new gun.

Late in 1911 the War Department finally received its first shipment of Benet-Mercie guns. A board of three officers convened at Monterey to revise the 1909 edition of the infantry machine-gun drill regulations and firing orders and to develop a structure for an infantry unit equipped with the new Benet-Mercie. At the same time the commanding general, Philippines Division, was directed to assemble a board of officers to perform similar work for cavalry units.[28] Under the supervision of Capt. William E. Welsh, the infantry board made a thorough review of the reports of the use of machine guns in the Russo-Japanese War and of the tactics and organizations currently in use in foreign armies. Using these studies as a base, Captain Welsh, Capt. Harry L. Cooper, and Lieut. Thomas W. Brown, concluded ". . . that the machine gun as an auxiliary arm is no longer an experimental weapon for which uses must be devised to suit the characteristics of the particular make of gun with which the machine gun organizations of an army are equipped. . . ."[29] Although they recognized that machine guns should be dealt with as a separate class of weapons rather than as specific items of equipment, the members of the Welsh Board viewed the machine gun as a weapon to be used mainly in defensive emergencies. Consequently the board did not devise tactics that would exploit the light weight and mobility of the Benet-Mercie, two qualities that had figured prominently in the original selection of the gun.

The Welsh Board was more farsighted in recommending the type of machine-gun unit that the army ought to adopt. The structure of the company it advocated—four officers, eighty-three enlisted men, and six guns—was adaptable to ". . . any type of gun with which the organization might in [the] future be equipped. . . ."[30] Although the Benet-Mercie could be operated by only two men, the Welsh Board found that a corporal and seven men were required for efficient operation of the gun for extended periods of time. The board also determined that the ancillary duties of reconnaissance, communications, and ammunition resupply connected with company operations required an extra platoon of men ". . . to be composed of *not less* than one infantry squad for each gun platoon. . . ."[31] Evaluating the organization it proposed, the Welsh Board found that it provided fourteen men for each machine gun—a number ". . . well within the economical limit of the relative value of its firepower."[32]

After concluding their work at Monterey, the members of the Welsh Board travelled to Sparta, Wisconsin, to observe the maneuvers of the Provisional Infantry Regiment, an experimental organization assembled to test various ideas for modernizing the doctrine and structure of the infantry regiment. Captain Welsh and his fellows did not change their concept of six-gun companies, but the officers who reported the activities of the provisional regiment concluded that a machine-gun company equipped with four guns would be adequate for American infantry regiments. Since it was the result of extensive work with the weapons and their crews under field conditions, the idea of a four-gun company carried considerable weight.[33]

For a brief period the General Staff favored the concept of a machine-gun company equipped with only four weapons. In the "Report on the Organization of the Land Forces of the United States," a major proposal for modernizing the American military

A Mistake and Its Consequences: The Benet-Mercie

system, the staff called for an eighty-one-man machine gun detachment armed with four guns. Since the detachment would be part of a new regimental headquarters company, it did not need permanent company officers; instead, members of the regimental and battalion staffs would lead the detachment in combat. Such an arrangement did not require congressional authorization of additional officers for the unit.[34]

At Sparta, Wisconsin, Captain Welsh and the other members of his board of officers witnessed a problem that would eventually nullify their work. During a prolonged test, the Benet-Mercie guns failed to develop as much firepower as a group of trained riflemen equal in number to the crew required to operate the machine gun and its equipment. The specific reasons for the poor performance of the Benet-Mercie were a low rate of fire due to the thirty-round feed strips and to frequent breakage of soft steel parts in the gun and pronounced inaccuracy during automatic fire, which was caused by the instability of the bipod mount. The report of these problems caused considerable concern. Laurance V. Benet, the co-inventor of the gun and son of the former chief of ordnance, blamed the problems with the Benet-Mercie upon the fact that neither the officers nor the men operating the weapons had received adequate training in their use. Benet was right; the troops at Sparta had received the weapons just before the maneuvers began and were wholly unfamiliar with them.[35] But the Ordnance Department began to receive additional evidence that the mechanism of the Benet-Mercie was flawed.

Ordnance Department tests determined that during prolonged firing either the firing pin or extractor would fail and cause the Benet-Mercie to jam. Ordnance experts quickly developed firing pins and extractors of improved material and design, and by early 1913 this problem had been solved.[36] However, the inaccuracy of the gun and its low rate of fire could not be remedied so easily. Designed with a bipod barrel support rather than the heavy tripod mount that most machine guns used, the lightweight Benet-Mercie was difficult to control during automatic fire. Consequently, its accuracy, particularly in the hands of an inexperienced gunner, was poor. The capabilities of the gun were further degraded by delicately made ammunition feed strips, which would jam the gun if fed into its mechanism improperly. The consequent need for extra care in loading the gun further reduced a rate of fire that was already below that of the Maxim gun. After considerable work, the Ordnance Department decided that a tripod must be provided for the Benet-Mercie. However, the problems with the ammunition feed strips were never solved.

To counter dissatisfaction with the Benet-Mercie, the Ordnance Department used a professional journal to place its case before the officer corps; the reaction assured that the attempt would not be made again. At the request of the Ordnance Department, the July 1913 issue of *Infantry Journal* carried a short piece on the Benet-Mercie written by Capt. John M. Lund, Ordnance Corps. Beginning with the reports of the official tests of the Benet-Mercie, Lund attempted to illustrate the thoroughness of Ordnance Department selection procedures and quash the idea that selection of the gun had been a hasty decision. After admitting that there had been some problems with faulty construction—a condition that had been corrected—Lund arrived at the heart of the Ordnance Department position on the problems with the Benet-Mercie. According to Captain Lund, the primary source of difficulty with the weapon lay in the fact that the gun was ". . . different both in its action and method of support and use from any machine gun previously issued."[37] Additional training and experience with the Benet-Mercie would, Lund contended, solve the problems that units had encountered in their initial attempts to use it. Commenting upon Lund's article, the editor of the *Infantry Journal* expressed hope that the defects in the gun could be corrected. If these defects were not remedied, however, the editor warned that the Benet-Mercie machine gun must be replaced with a weapon that ". . . the Infantry (the arm primarily concerned) can use with effect, and in which it has that confidence necessary to develop morale and successful battle results."[38] The War Department could not ignore such sentiments.

Initially the War Department attempted to correct the deficiencies in the construction of the Benet-Mercie; by mid-1913 it was evident that this had not reduced dissatisfaction with the weapon. Accord-

A Mistake and Its Consequences: The Benet-Mercie

ingly, Secretary of War Lindley M. Garrison asked the commanders of all infantry and cavalry regiments stationed in the United States to comment upon the Benet-Mercie. His specific questions were:

> 1. What is the opinion of the officer commanding the Machine Gun Detachment of your regiment with reference to the Benet-Mercie gun?
>
> 2. Does he consider it a satisfactory gun for field service?
>
> 3. Does he consider it to be a gun which can be handled by the average enlisted man under conditions such as would prevail in field service?
>
> 4. Can effective work be done with the gun by men who have not had careful and special training in its use?
>
> 5. Is the target work of the gun satisfactory?
>
> 6. What are its strong and weak points?[39]

From the survey army leaders hoped to discover both the exact causes for and the extent of the dissatisfaction with the Benet-Mercie. If the Ordnance Department's contention that the problems with the gun were based on lack of experience was true, additional training in the use of the gun would solve the problem. However, if the survey revealed that dissatisfaction with the gun rested on poor performance attributable to major design defects, the results of the survey could be used to justify replacement of the Benet-Mercie.

As summarized by a young General Staff officer, Capt. Douglas MacArthur, the replies to the War Department questionnaire did not favor the Benet-Mercie. Of thirty-seven respondents only eight officers found the Benet-Mercie to be fully satisfactory in field service; seventeen machine-gun platoon leaders rated it completely unsatisfactory, while twelve officers gave answers that fell in neither category. Seventeen officers believed that the average enlisted man could handle the gun in the field; twenty held the opposite opinion. Paradoxically, only four officers believed that effective use of the Benet-Mercie required special training. A total of twenty-five respondents rated the accuracy of the gun as satisfactory; only eight found it to be inaccurate.

The answers to the final question were predictable. The strong points of the gun were portability and easy concealment. The weak features of the Benet-Mercie included an extreme tendency to jam, lack of stability during firing, difficulty in traversing the gun barrel, and weak parts. One officer categorized the Benet-Mercie as a ". . . source of embarrassment and weakness instead of a strong tactical support."[40] MacArthur found that the reports expressed a ". . . unanimity of opinon that in its present form the piece cannot be regarded as satisfactory. . . ."[41] The survey resolved the questions about the Benet-Mercie: The weapon was poorly designed and of little value. Although it would be a painful admission of a mistake in weapon selection, the War Department would have to replace the Benet-Mercie. The army had adopted a weapon of radical design with capabilities that promised exceptional military usefulness; its performance, however, did not match design capabilities. In the wake of the failure of the Benet-Mercie, the Ordnance Department would proceed with deliberation in selecting a replacement.

By the beginning of 1913, word of the problems with the Benet-Mercie reached Congress. On January 9, James Hay, the chairman of the House Committee on Military Affairs, asked for all of the official reports on the Benet-Mercie, particularly the report rendered by Captain Welsh.[42] Legislators' misgivings about the value of the gun progressed to the point that in the Army Appropriation Act of June 1913 the secretary of war was authorized to spend $150,000 on more Benet-Mercie guns only ". . . if in his opinion it be for the interest of the service."[43] Despite the spur of congressional interest, the Ordnance Department search for a new machine gun proceeded cautiously.

Beginning at the Springfield Arsenal in the fall of 1913, ordnance trials followed the rigorous procedures of earlier tests. At the end of the mechanical trials, two guns—the Benet-Mercie and the water-cooled Vickers rifle caliber gun, light model—were recommended for field test.[44] Unlike the ad hoc trial of the Benet-Mercie at the Atascadero Maneuver Camp in 1908, the field-test program at Leon

A Mistake and Its Consequences: The Benet-Mercie

Springs, Texas, had as its single object the evaluation of the Vickers gun in direct competition with the Benet-Mercie. When their investigation was finished, the test board strongly recommended adoption of the Vickers machine gun.

Doubtless relieved to be rid of the troublesome Benet-Mercie, General Crozier accepted this recommendation and requested an initial appropriation of $194,000 to buy the first shipment of the new guns. Since a Vickers gun and its pack equipment cost approximately $3,000 (as opposed to $560 for the Springfield Arsenal version of the Benet-Mercie), the army could purchase only about sixty guns with the sum Crozier requested. Because General Crozier planned to procure the 361 guns that he estimated the army needed over a number of years, the annual appropriation for machine guns could continue at the $150,000 level established to procure the much cheaper Benet-Mercie guns.[45] At this rate it would take seven years to buy even the small number of guns that the chief of ordnance wanted.

Congress approved Crozier's request, but late in 1916 the chief of ordnance reported that the army had not received the new guns because of ". . . the interference of the European war, both with deliveries from abroad and with the preparation for the manufacture of this British gun in this country."[46] This delay meant that in early 1917 the American army did not have a satisfactory machine gun in its inventory.

NOTES

1. R.V.K. Applin, "Machine Gun Tactics In Our Own and Other Armies," *Journal of the United States Cavalry Association* XX (May 1910): 1196.

2. G. S. Hutchison, *Machine Guns: Their History and Tactical Employment* (London, 1938), pp. 107-8.

3. Ernest D. Swinton, *Eyewitness* (Garden City, N.Y., 1933), p. 8.

4. Hutchison, *Machine Guns*, pp. 100-101.

5. Ibid., pp. 96-97. The American Maxim model 1904 and its mount weighed 152.5 pounds with the water jacket of the gun filled.

6. U.S., War Department, *Field Service Regulations United States Army, 1905, With Amendments to 1908* (Washington, D.C., 1908); Hutchison, *Machine Guns*, pp. 102-3.

7. *Army and Navy Journal* (hereafter cited as *A-N Jou.*), October 31, 1908, p. 225.

8. Montgomery M. Macomb, "Machine Guns In the Russian Army During the Campaign in Manchuria, 1904-1905," *Journal of the United States Cavalry Association* XVII (January 1907): 443-52, and "More About Machine Guns," *Journal of the United States Cavalry Association* XVII (April 1907): 605-8.

9. Macomb, "More About Machine Guns," p. 605. Paraphrased in an article carried in the *Army and Navy Journal*, Macomb's opinion gained wide dissemination among army officers. *A-N Jou.*, June 22, 1907, p. 1164.

10. Harry L. Hodges, "The Use of Machine Guns With the Cavalry," *Journal of the United States Cavalry Association* XIX (July 1908): 46-47; Albert E. Phillips, "Machine Gun Organization, Equipment and Arms," *Journal of the United States Cavalry Association* XIX (January 1909): 544-45.

11. James Parker, "The Machine Gun Platoon: Should It Be Retained As Part of the Regimental Organization?" *Journal of the United States Cavalry Association* XIX (July 1908): 52; see also James Parker to Adjutant General, February 9, 1908, National Archives Record Group (hereafter cited as NA, RG) 156, doc. 38356/493.

12. Charles C. Crawford, "Weapons and Munitions of War," *Journal of the United States Cavalry Association* XVII (April 1907): 621-22.

13. U.S., War Department, *Annual Report of the War Department, 1908* (Washington, D.C. 1908), vol. VI, p. 60; *Annual Report of the War Department, 1909*, vol. VI, p. 29; NA, RG 156, General Correspondence 1894-1913, doc. 39153/31 encl. 1; Acting Chief of Ordnance to Adjutant General, August 22, 1908, NA, RG 156, doc. 39153/55 encl. 1.

14. Harry L. Hodges, "The Benet-Mercie or Hotchkiss Portable Machine Gun," *Journal of the United States Cavalry Association* XIX (January 1909): 511-13.

15. Ibid., pp. 513-14.

16. Report of the School of Musketry on the Benet-Mercie Portable Machine Gun, NA, RG 156, doc. 39153/55.

17. Memo for Assistant Secretary of War, subject: Organization of a Provisional Machine Gun Troop, March 11, 1909, NA, RG 94, doc. 1500967 filed with 1228217.

18. Chief of Ordnance to Secretary of War, March 22, 1909, NA, RG 156, doc. 39153/98.

19. U.S., Congress, Senate, Committee on Military Affairs, *The Army Appropriation Bill, Hearings, before the Committee on Military Affairs, Senate, on H.R. 26915*, 60th Cong., 3d sess., 1909, pp. 11-14. Only 670

Benet-Mercie guns were manufactured for the army. F.W.A. Hobart, *Pictorial History of the Machine Gun* (London, 1972), p. 94. In 1908 Congress had amended the Dick Act to require that by January 21, 1910, all National Guard units would be organized and equipped as regular army units. Amendment to Dick Act, U.S., *Statutes at Large*, vol. 35, pt. 1, sec. 2, 400 (1909).

20. Hobart, *Pictorial History*, p. 41. Since the Benet-Mercie cost only $600 compared to a price of $1,250 per Maxim gun, conversion to the new weapon could result in considerable savings. U.S., Congress, Senate, Committee on Military Affairs, *The Army Appropriation Bill, Hearings*; U.S., Ordnance Department, *Price List of Ordnance and Ordnance Stores* (Washington, D.C., 1907), pp. 8-13.

21. William Crozier, *Ordnance and the World War* (New York, 1920), p. 77. According to a later article by an ordnance officer, the Benet-Mercie was purchased because of its simplicity (specifically the ease with which parts could be replaced), rapidity of fire, and its lightness—which meant that more ammunition could be carried. J. M. Lund, "The Automatic Machine Rifle, Caliber .30, Model of 1909," *Journal of the United States Infantry Association* X (July-August 1913): 116.

22. Hodges, "The Benet-Mercie," p. 511; *A-N Jou.*, January 9, 1909, p. 508.

23. *Annual Report of the War Department, 1910*, vol. I, p. 602.

24. *Annual Report of the War Department, 1912*, vol. I, p. 914.

25. U.S., War Department, *Field Service Regulations, United States Army, 1910* (Washington, D.C., 1910), pp. 20-21, 23. The number of guns and officers in these units followed the position Roosevelt had established in late 1908. The number of enlisted men was identical with the number authorized for the line infantry company and cavalry troop.

26. U.S., War Department, *Drill Regulations For Machine-Gun Organizations, Cavalry, 1910* (Washington, D.C., 1910); Proceedings of a Board of Officers—Convened at Presidio of Monterey, California, April 10, 1910, NA, RG 94, doc. 1642464 filed with 1228217.

27. Memo for Acting Secretary of War, subject: Organization of Machine Gun Platoons, July 8, 1910, NA, RG 94, doc. 1663177 encl. 1, filed with 1134830.

28. Memo, Chief, Mobile Army Division, General Staff to Adjutant General, December 1, 1911, NA, RG 165, doc. 7949; Adjutant General to Commanding General, Philippines Division, December 6, 1911, NA, RG 156, doc. 38356/1119.

29. Proceedings of a Board of Officers convened by SO 285, War Department, December 6, 1911, dated May 22, 1912, NA, RG 156, doc. 39153/652 encl. 1, pp. 32-33.

30. Ibid., pp. 19-20, 23-24.
31. Ibid., pp. 23-24.
32. Ibid.
33. Report of Provisional Regiment Organized in Central Division in June 1912, nd, NA, RG 165, doc. 7289, pp. 58-64.
34. *Annual Report of the Secretary of War, 1912*, p. 102.
35. Proceedings of a Board of Officers convened by Special Order 285, War Department, December 6, 1911, dated May 22, 1912, NA, RG 156, doc. 39153/652 encl. 1, pp. 31-32; Laurance V. Benet to U.S. Ordnance Company, November 29, 1912, NA, RG 156, doc. 39153/688; Capt. H. L. Cooper to Adjutant General, August 28, 1912, NA, RG 156, doc. 39152/655.
36. *Annual Report of the War Department, 1913*, vol. I, p. 720.
37. Lund, "Automatic Machine Rifle," p. 115.
38. "Machine Guns," *Journal of the United States Infantry Association* X (July-August 1913): 96.
39. Memo, Chief of Staff to Adjutant General, September 17, 1913, NA, RG 165, doc. 10467.
40. Memo for Chief of Staff, subject: Benet-Mercie Gun, November 10, 1913, NA, RG 165, doc. 10467.
41. Ibid.
42. James Hay to Secretary of War, January 9, 1913, NA, RG 156, doc. 39153/697.
43. Crozier, *Ordnance*, p. 77.
44. *Annual Report of the War Department, 1914*, vol. I, p. 475.
45. U.S., Congress, House, Committee on Military Affairs, *Bill Making Appropriation for the Support of the Army for the Fiscal Year 1916, Hearings before the Committee on Military Affairs, House of Representatives*, 63d Cong., 2d sess., 1914, pp. 674-76; *Annual Report of the War Department, 1912*, vol. I, p. 927.
46. *Annual Report of the War Department, 1916*, vol. I, p. 825.

IX

AN INADEQUATE STAFF AND A MINIMAL SOLUTION, 1914-1916

During the last week of June 1917 the vanguard of the American Expeditionary Force landed in France. The regulars of the Sixteenth, Eighteenth, Twenty-sixth, and Twenty-eighth Infantry Regiments came ashore on the docks of St. Nazaire neither trained nor equipped for the fighting that had been going on in Europe for almost three years. Illustrative of this condition were their machine-gun units, which were outfitted with the Benet-Mercie model 1909 gun, a weapon that had been officially recognized as unsatisfactory in 1913 and superseded by the Vickers gun in 1914. Equipped with an outdated weapon, the machine gunners of the First Division were trained according to the tenets of a handbook designed for the Benet-Mercie, which did not adequately reflect the changes in machine-gun tactics and techniques developed in the European war. Burdened with the inadequate Benet-Mercie and ill-prepared even by the standards of their antiquated manual, the machine gunners were members of units organized according to the provisions of the National Defense Act of 1916—a major reform of army structure. These units, regimental machine-gun companies equipped with six guns, differed only in detail from the unit that President Roosevelt had advocated in 1908. Their appearance underscored the failure of the American army to keep up with European developments in the employment and organization of machine-gun units.

Many factors contributed to the army's continuing inability to make adequate provision for the machine gun in its structure and doctrine or to take advantage of the lessons of combat in France.

Reform of the military came late for want of interest in both the legislative and executive branches of government and because of a desire on the part of the majority of Americans to stay out of the European conflict. When it came, reform was aimed at the creation of a force for use in defending the United States, not for deployment to France. As important as these elements were, however, the roots of the specific problem with machine guns lay within the War Department. Restructured in imitation of the staff systems of European armies, particularly the army of Imperial Germany, the organization and efficiency of the War Department improved slowly after the passage of the legislation authorizing the Army General Staff in 1903. Like the Esher reforms in Great Britain, the Root reform program was not quite the landmark in the modernization of the American army that some have thought it to be.

While the Ordnance Department searched for a replacement for the Benet-Mercie, the General Staff continued its study of machine-gun organization and tactics. Following publication of the "Report on the Organization of the Land Forces of the United States" in 1912, the War College Division kept up its efforts to develop a modern organization for line units. Late in 1913 the chief of staff received the staff concept of a new infantry organization. The basic infantry unit, the regiment, would consist of three four-company battalions. The War College Division called for separate regimental headquarters and supply companies and a machine-gun company of two officers, fifty men, and four machine guns. Acknowledging that its recommendation had been inspired by the report of the maneuvers of the Provisional Infantry Regiment at Sparta, Wisconsin, the General Staff gave several reasons for advocating a company armed with four rather than six guns. The smaller unit would occupy less road space, a critical factor in an era of narrow roads and horse-drawn transport. It would also be easier to protect from artillery fire and observation than a six-gun unit. In the judgment of the General Staff a six-gun unit could not be controlled if it were dispersed. Justification of the four-gun company closed with a reaffirmation of the machine gun as an "arm of opportunity." The four-gun organization conformed to congressional limits on the size of machine-gun units but was unsuited for use with the three-battalion regiment that the staff also advocated.[1] More useful than the provisional machine-gun platoon, the four-gun company was

An Inadequate Staff and a Minimal Solution 191

at best an awkward compromise between congressional limits on personnel and equipment and the tactical requirements of the three-battalion regiment.

In late February 1914 the first formal table of organization for the United States Army was approved for publication. Beginning with an outline of an infantry division composed of 22,655 officers and men, the table then detailed the structure of the organizations within the division; infantry and cavalry machine-gun organizations were included. The equipment and personnel authorizations of these units reveal the effects of congressional limits on military spending. Infantry machine-gun companies were to have a war strength of four guns, two officers (detailed from battalion and regimental staffs), and forty-six enlisted men. In peacetime these units were limited to only two guns, two officers, and twenty-nine enlisted men; two additional guns would be issued when funds to pay additional enlisted men became available. The cavalry machine gun troop would have a war strength of two officers (detailed from unit staffs) and sixty-nine enlisted men, but its peacetime establishment—two officers, forty-eight men, and four guns—was not so severely reduced.[2]

The organization of the infantry machine-gun company had been proposed by the War College Division in December 1913, while the cavalry machine-gun troop was structured by subtracting one officer and two gun sections (eighteen men) from the three officers and eighty-six enlisted men of the provisional organization prescribed in the *Field Service Regulations* of 1910. As the tables of organization noted, four was the number of machine guns per company sanctioned by Congress.[3] In this area the structure of the new organizations made sense; in the main, however, the companies represented a mechanical, almost pro forma, approach to the problem of creating a useful machine-gun unit.

Intended to prescribe the proper organization for combat units, the tables of organization created an immediate problem for the War Department. Upon their receipt was each regimental commander to reorganize his unit to conform to the structure that the tables prescribed? Where were the additional men and equipment to come from? Both congressional and executive action were required before the new organizations could be adopted. Until such action was taken, the American army would continue to be organized along the lines specified in 1899 and 1901, and its machine-gun units would remain provisional organizations.[4] In August 1914 four privates were added to the infantry machine-gun platoon, bringing its enlisted strength to twenty-six—a number judged sufficient to permit the issue of the two additional guns authorized by Congress in 1912.[5] Saddled with weapons it felt compelled to issue rather than store, the army created machine-gun units with four guns manned at only half the strength believed essential by its staff.

As the tables of organization were prepared for publication, the General Staff turned its attention to machine-gun drill regulations. Although the Ordnance Department was in the process of selecting a replacement for the Benet-Mercie, the War Department decided to proceed with the development of a new manual for both infantry and cavalry units. A new test board, convened in May 1914, staged a 300-mile march from Texas City, Texas, to the firing ranges at Leon Springs, Texas, to try out pack equipment and techniques. After lengthy exercises, which tested drill and firing techniques, the board forwarded a draft of a new manual to the General Staff for review.[6] This draft represented the fifth attempt to produce a new machine-gun manual. While the tests were in progress, the Ordnance Department selected the Vickers gun as a replacement for the Benet-Mercie, but it would take at least two years to acquire the new guns; therefore, as an interim measure Brig. Gen. Montgomery M. Macomb recommended that the War Department adopt the latest set of draft regulations designed for the outdated Benet-Mercie.[7]

Despite its curious status of being nearly out of date at publication, the new machine-gun manual was a major improvement over the handbooks that it replaced. As Parker had suggested in 1908, the text gave considerable attention to the care of pack animals and to the proper techniques for using pack equipment.[8] While the bulk of the manual was devoted to the mechanics of cavalry and infantry drill with machine guns, the discussion of tactics was more detailed than that in the 1909 and 1910 drill regulations. After a conservative introduction that emphasized the role of the machine gun as an auxiliary weapon, the authors discussed the use of machine guns in various operations; particular attention was paid to the employment of machine guns from defensive positions, emphasis that fit both the conventional view of the machine gun and recent experience in Europe. The emplacement of machine guns in trenches occupied several paragraphs; discussion focused on concealment of the specific location of machine guns in defensive works—a lesson that the British and French had learned at considerable cost.[9] These locations, picked by the regimental commander, should ". . . enable the guns to command narrow approaches, cover dead spaces, and bring cross fire to bear on ground in front of trenches and other important defensive works."[10] Sited in this fashion, machine guns could accomplish their principal defensive function of paralyzing ". . . *the attack by large losses in a minimum time by sudden overwhelming and unexpected fire.* . . ."[11] Conceptually the most advanced portion of the new regulations, the sections devoted to the defensive use of machine guns were a relatively small part of the manual. Since the American army continued to emphasize the type of open warfare that the European powers had expected to wage in 1914, the manual stressed the use of machine guns in large-scale maneuver battles, which the United States forces would not fight until 1942.

The *Combined Drill Regulations* of 1915 were published before the War Department had received much information on the tactical and organizational developments that had taken place in Europe following the outbreak of the war.[12] In April 1915 Brigadier General Macomb advised Major General Scott that:

> It is highly probable that sound principles of machine gun employment will shortly be possible of deduction when a greater fund of correct information becomes available concerning the war in Europe. It will then be possible to work out an organization which will meet the needs of both sound methods of employment and of our own service. It is thought that the adoption of recommendations one by one as they are made will result in nothing, but constant readjustment. . . .[13]

A flaw in the organization of the General Staff delayed the arrival of this information for a full year.

Between 1885 and 1907 army intelligence activities had been under the direction of the Military Information Division (MID). A part of the Adjutant General's Office until 1903 when it became the Second Division of the General Staff, the MID processed a wide variety of raw data into intelligence for use by the War Department. However, in 1907, a few months after the relocation of the Second and Third Divisions of the General Staff from downtown Washington to Fort McNair, the two staff sections merged to form a new, War College-dominated Second Section of the General Staff. Operations and planning displaced the evaluation of information, and the General Staff lost its intelligence agency. When General Macomb predicted that more information concerning the war in Europe would soon become available, he was only partially right. The War Department did receive reports on the war in Europe, but it had no administrative machinery to process, evaluate, and distribute the reports to the staff agencies that needed them. Reports arrived, accumulated, and were filed haphazardly. The merger of the Military Information and War College Divisions in 1908 had resulted in the atrophy of the intelligence function within the General Staff.[14]

Destruction of the old Second Division also cut the attaché system loose. Since 1889 the information collection activities of the attachés and observers had been under the direction of the MID. In 1907 this guidance was removed and the attaché system drifted. In 1914 the War College Division proposed that eight attachés be recalled from Europe, leaving officers only in England, France, and Germany; fortunately General Leonard Wood ignored the suggestion. Wood had earlier noted that he was receiving little intelligence information and had penned a memorandum outlining the deficiencies in the handling of the intelligence function by the War College Division; however, he failed to direct corrective action, and the General Staff remained without a functioning intelligence agency. The situation did not begin to change until late 1915 when General Macomb—probably at the urging of an experienced intelligence officer, Capt. Ralph H. Van Deman—urged the creation of a separate military information section as part of a restructured War College Division. Despite its value, Macomb's proposal was rejected by Maj. Gen. Hugh Scott.[15] Thus despite the War Department need for accurate information concerning the war in Europe to aid in the modernization of the American army, the General Staff continued to lack both the ability to direct the collection of such data and the capacity to digest and disseminate the information that it received. In this respect the War Department staff in 1915 was in worse shape than it had been in 1898.

In the spring of 1915 the army was not ready to ask Congress for legislation to create machine-gun units; however, its concept of these units no longer followed the structure outlined in the tables of organization of 1914. Instead each regiment would have a six-gun company ". . . capable of subdivision into platoons corresponding in number to [the] squadrons or battalions."[16] The reason for the adoption of this more rational view is not clear, but probably the earlier four-gun regimental company represented the General Staff estimate of the unit it could get, not the unit that it needed.

Between 1906 and 1915 the combat arms came to accept machine guns as a factor in combat operations at battalion level. During this period the War Department position on the weapon oscillated from the six-gun company envisioned by President Roosevelt in 1908 to the four-gun company advocated in the report of the activities of the provisional infantry regiment and adopted in the 1914 tables of organization and then back to the six-gun organization in 1915. The six-gun company was best suited to the American army; it placed the weapon in line regiments, and it provided a pair of guns for use with each battalion—the lowest tactical headquarters that planners believed would control the guns. The six-gun unit also conformed to the pre-World War I organizations adopted by the French and German armies and gave the same number of guns per battalion as there had been in the British army in August 1914.

American interest in machine-gun tactics declined after 1910. Officers had no real chance to explore the tactical capabilities of the Benet-Mercie; when the Benet-Mercie arrived, solution of the problems encountered in operating the gun quickly became the major focus of attention. If the guns could not consistently deliver effective fire, there was little point in exploring their tactical value. After the European war began, interest in the machine gun revived; however, in the first year of the war information concerning the use of the weapon was scarce. Consequently, as the movement to update army structure gathered strength, army planners knew little about recent advances in machine-gun tactics.

Late in 1914 as a part of his final report as chief of staff, Maj. Gen. Leonard Wood called for congressional action to reform the structure of Army combat units completely.[17] No action was taken on his proposal, but Wood's successor, Maj. Gen. William W. Wotherspoon directed a committee to draft legislation for the modernization of the army. Entitled "A Bill to Increase the Efficiency of the Land Forces of the United States," the study was reviewed by Wotherspoon's replacement, Maj. Gen. Hugh Scott, and filed without action.[18] Army reform was not a dead issue, however; in January 1915 Senator George E. Chamberlain, the chairman of the Senate Military Affairs Commitee, reviewed the entire subject in a long letter to Secretary of War Lindley M. Garrison. Noting that he had recently introduced several bills concerning the army, Chamberlain characterized them as part of ". . . the system of piecemeal legislation heretofore in force looking to the improvement of individual arms and corps rather than the Army as a whole."[19] His opinion was that ". . . the time has come when a definite army policy should be adopted."[20] Chamberlain asked Secretary Garrison for a comprehensive proposal for modernizing the army and suggested basing it upon the 1912 "Report on the Organization of the Land Forces of the United States." Introduction of the War Department proposal at the start of the next session of Congress would insure that service reform was ". . . given that careful consideration which its importance demands."[21] If Secretary Garrison cared to follow the lead of a Republican senator, Chamberlain's letter appeared to provide the opportunity for modernizing the army for which the General Staff had waited since 1912.

War Department action on Senator Chamberlain's request was slow, perhaps reflecting the need to secure President Wilson's approval for the development of such a proposal. The General Staff was not directed to prepare a comprehensive plan for modernizing the army until March 11, 1915. According to the acting chief of staff, Maj. Gen. Tasker H. Bliss, the War Department program would be used in the same manner that the 1885 review of the coast defenses was used by the Endicott Board. Bliss noted that the report of the Endicott Board ". . . was never formally approved or adopted by Congress, but its tacit acceptance as a guide served to

An Inadequate Staff and a Minimal Solution 197

facilitate all legislation necessary to give effect to its conclusions."[22] He did not believe

> ... that Congress will ever by formal resolution approve and accept a broad military policy, translate it in terms of a comprehensive bill, and pass this bill with all the necessary appropriation of money to carry it into effect. Nor is it wise in the light of experience to ask it. Such a course by injecting it into the field of partisan politics tend to transform a question of policy into one of political expediency thereby tying it to the temporary fortunes of one party. It is believed that the method practiced in the case of the Endicott Board's report indicates the wise course to be followed in securing the practicable adoption of any military policy, the completion of which in the absence of an all controlling emergency must extend over a term of years and must therefore depend upon the active approval and acceptance of all parties.[23]

Bliss' estimate of the capacity of Congress to fulfill the monetary requirements of a long-term program to modernize the army was historically correct. However, during the period between 1899 and 1903 Congress had passed a body of legislation that reshaped the American army. At that time the need for such action had, admittedly, been great; under Bliss's leadership the General Staff had the difficult job of demonstrating a similarly pressing need in 1915.

Secretary Garrison directed ". . . *all* officers of the General Staff to devote as much of their time as possible to the study of this subject. . . ."[24] Consequently, the War College Division, the staff agency charged with producing a definitive statement of the War Department program for reorganizing the army, spent much of the summer of 1915 coordinating the positions of various staff agencies and did not publish its *Statement of a Proper Military Policy for the United States* until September 1915. Thoroughly Uptonian in its approach, the *Statement* outlined a program that would after five years give the country a mobile force of 500,000 trained troops (121,000 regular and 379,000 regular reserve) at the outbreak of war plus 500,000 partially trained troops ready for combat three months later.[25] A sweeping exposition of policy, the *Statement* did not contain the detailed information necessary for specific reform legislation. Such details appeared two months later in a series of appendices.

In an appendix entitled *Study On the Development of Large Calibre, Mobile Artillery, and Machine Guns In the Present European War* the staff emphasized the value of machine guns in modern warfare and proposed the assignment of eighteen guns to each infantry and cavalry regiment.[26] Although eighteen guns per regiment was a more accurate reflection of the number of machine guns needed by infantry regiments for combat in Europe, that number was not reflected in any of the proposals for legislation to modernize the army.[27]

Secretary Garrison reduced the War Department proposal to a regular army of 142,000 men augmented by a federal reserve force or "Continental Army" of 400,000 men. Just as General Bliss had predicted, Garrison's Continental Army Plan quickly became the focus of a struggle between various factions in Congress. By the end of 1915 Congress had not acted on the secretary's program, and several alternatives had appeared. As he had promised, Senator Chamberlain submitted a bill for the modernization of the land forces of the nation. The Chamberlain bill called for an infantry machine-gun company with 4 officers, 175 men, and 9 guns and for a cavalry troop with 4 officers, 182 men, and 9 guns. Staff officers believed that these companies would waste men; so they pared them down to a more economical six-gun organization with four officers, and seventy-four enlisted men for the infantry and four officers and ninety-one men for the cavalry.[28]

As Congress' attempt to restructure the national military system stretched into 1916, the legislators were exposed to lengthy testimony on a variety of topics including the ways in which the army might best employ machine guns. General Crozier noted that while current plans called for four-gun units, ". . . the existing projects need very radical overhauling."[29] General Scott told congressmen that the army needed a six-gun company, and he was supported by Col. Charles Treat of the General Staff. Charged with the defense of the Panama Canal, Brig. Gen. Clarence R. Edwards called for no less than twelve and if possible eighteen machine guns for each infantry and cavalry regiment. Major General Wood made the most radical claim of all when he stated that twenty-four guns per regiment would be a satisfactory allowance.[30]

The absence of a unified position among military experts allowed Congress to choose the machine-gun organization that best suited its ends, not those of the army. The six-gun company would be much less expensive than the proposals made by Edwards and Wood. With the exception of Senator Chamberlain's bill, which called for a nine-gun company, the proposals for military legislation—a bill submitted by Representative James Hay and a War Department draft of proposed legislation—called for units armed with six machine guns.[31]

Finally aroused to the political dangers of a continued split over military policy between his secretary of war and powerful Democratic congressmen such as Representative Claude Kitchen, the House majority leader, President Wilson withdrew his support for Secretary Garrison's program and then in February 1916 announced his support of the House bill sponsored by Representative Hay. Garrison resigned, and Wilson appointed the able mayor of Cleveland, Newton D. Baker, as his replacement.[32] Baker soon realized that additional debate on the shape of military policy would reduce the chances for the passage of any bill. Late in March the chief of staff informed the chief of the War College Division that he would not forward any more organizational changes to the secretary of war.[33]

After approval by the House the Hay bill (H.R. 12766) passed the Senate; in late April both Hay's proposal and a Senate version of it reached the General Staff. The provisions for machine-gun organization in the two bills differed only in detail. The Hay bill called for an infantry machine-gun company of three officers, seventy-one men, and six guns and a cavalry troop of four officers, ninety-two men, and six guns; the Senate revision provided for an infantry company of four officers, sixty-three men, and six guns and a cavalry troop of four officers, seventy men, and six guns.[34] Although the organizational structure contained in the Hay bill was closer to the position of the War Department and of the General Staff, the staff did not try to modify the Senate version of the bill.

Forced to take action by the crisis in relations with Mexico following the Villa raid on Columbus, New Mexico, House and Senate conferees finally produced a compromise version of the Hay bill, which passed both houses in mid-May.[35] This new law, the

National Defense Act of 1916, represented the first attempt to embody the military policy of the nation in a single piece of legislation. Reviewing the provisions of the act, the General Staff found it to be "decidedly beneficial legislation." Congress had finally given the army its first statutory machine-gun units—an infantry company of four officers, sixty-three men, and six guns and a cavalry troop of four officers, seventy men, and six guns.[36]

Legislative authorization of the regimental machine-gun company was important, yet it is quite clear that in 1916 American machine-gun doctrine and organization lagged far behind the doctrine and organization being used in France. From the start the German army exploited its superior machine-gun tactics and the flexibility of its blend of regimental and separate machine-gun companies. In late 1915 and early 1916 the Allies began to explore and exploit the tactical advantages to be gained by increased use of machine guns. The British decided that the machine gun should form the basis for a separate arm of the service; accordingly, on October 14, 1915, the Royal Machine Gun Corps was established. It would eventually attain a level of skill in handling its weapons comparable to that attained by German machine-gun units.[37]

The creation of the Royal Machine Gun Corps had no immediate impact on the American army; initially American staff planners knew nothing about the new corps beyond the basic structure of the new infantry, cavalry, and motor machine-gun units. Since it took the British army considerable time to flesh out its machine-gun corps, the American army did not begin to receive detailed information concerning the new British system until mid-1916. In late May 1916 the War Department received a lengthy, detailed, and thoroughly informative report of a *sub rosa* visit by an American officer, Capt. William A. Castle, to the Machine Gun Training Centre at Grantham, England. Widely circulated among the War Department staff agencies and army schools, the contents of Castle's confidential report were in constant demand by officers who were eager to learn the latest British methods for using machine guns.[38]

Despite its value, Castle's report arrived at least six months after the time when it could have significantly influenced War Department policy concerning the organization and employment of

An Inadequate Staff and a Minimal Solution

machine-gun units. Even had the General Staff learned the details of the British Machine Gun Corps' organization and training programs much earlier, it is unlikely that it would have adopted the British scheme, particularly since the machine-gun corps had been developed as a response to the specific needs of combat in France. However, Castle's report might have convinced the General Staff of the need to recommend the creation of more or larger machine-gun units to Congress, and the Ordnance Department might have seen the need to speed up procurement of the new Vickers guns.

Unable to get the Vickers guns that the army needed, ordnance officials refused to buy another weapon, the Lewis machine gun. Named after its American inventor, Lieut. Col. Isaac N. Lewis, the Lewis gun had been offered to the War Department in 1911. Basically a light machine gun, the 25.5-pound, gas-operated Lewis employed a sophisticated system of aluminum vanes to enhance air cooling of the barrel. Since it had recently purchased the Benet-Mercie light machine gun, the Ordnance Department was not particularly eager to test the Lewis gun. Finally tested at the Springfield Armory during the search for a replacement for the Benet-Mercie, the Lewis gun failed to perform well, apparently because of defects in its construction, and it was eliminated from the competition that led to the selection of the Vickers gun.[39]

In 1912 Lieutenant Colonel Lewis took his gun to Europe where it was eventually manufactured at Liège, Belgium, and later in Birmingham, England. The British army decided to adopt the Lewis gun shortly after the beginning of the war, and the weapon gained wide use both in line formations and with the Royal Flying Corps. Encouraged by his success, Lewis renewed his efforts to have his gun adopted by his own service. Although it was endorsed by Maj. Gen. Leonard Wood, Brigadier General Crozier opposed the Lewis gun, claiming that according to the British machine-gun expert, Christopher D'Arcy Baker-Carr, the British army had purchased the Lewis gun because it could not get enough Vickers guns.[40] Despite Crozier's opposition, a second series of trials of the Lewis gun took place in April 1916. The test board reported that the Lewis gun suffered from an excessive number of jams and malfunctions and was ". . . not equal or superior to either [the Vickers or Benet-Mercie guns]. . . ."[41] These results justified rejection of the

Lewis gun, particularly in view of the disappointing performance of a similar weapon—the Benet-Mercie, but Colonel Lewis was not satisfied, and his struggle with the Ordnance Department continued. Meanwhile, army units continued to use the defective Benet-Mercie.[42]

War Department records indicate that the General Staff received little information concerning machine-gun tactics during the first year and a half of the war. Everyone knew that both sides were using more and more machine guns, but there was a lack of details indicating precisely how they were being used. American service journals carried few articles on machine guns during the early months of the war, and the few pieces that did appear were almost exclusively translations of articles written by European officers.[43] Only after the Congress had created a new structure for the army did the War Department begin to receive concrete information on new machine-gun tactics. It is important to note that these new theories and new techniques were developed in Europe at precisely the time that the staff and Congress were working to create new military legislation. Thus, as far as new machine-gun tactics and their possible effect upon the new organization created for the army were concerned, the National Defense Act of 1916 came six months too soon.

The earliest report to contain significant amounts of new information was Captain Castle's report of his visit to the training establishment at Grantham. Although it was filled with technical information and new techniques, Castle's report did not contain a comprehensive expression of any new method of using machine guns. During the summer and fall of 1916 the *Infantry Journal* published two separate articles that described major advances in machine-gun theory in the French and German armies. One of these articles, a translation of a study by Capt. André Laffargue, contained the first detailed discussion to appear in any American service journal of the use of machine guns in offensive action in trench warfare.[44]

Even if the General Staff had possessed the most modern tactical and organizational concepts for machine-gun employment in late 1915, it is unlikely that these ideas would have been adopted or would have caused major changes in the General Staff position of a

An Inadequate Staff and a Minimal Solution

single six-gun machine-gun company per infantry and cavalry regiment. Writing to the secretary of war in midyear, Chief of Staff Scott noted the increased use of machine guns in France, which he attributed in part to the fact that the weapon was ". . . particularly adapted to advantageous use in trench warfare such as is now being carried on in Flanders."[45] Scott also observed that the expanded use of machine guns had not caused major ammunition supply problems because of the static nature of trench warfare. General Scott stressed the need for a lightweight, highly portable machine gun for use in the "more usual type of [maneuver] warfare" such as that being carried on in Poland. After summarizing the reasons behind the increase in the use of machine guns—the special nature of trench warfare, improved models of the weapon, and its great firepower—Scott stated that the American army was ". . . quite abreast if not in advance of foreign armies" in its use of machine guns. Consequently, he recommended no further action on the subject.[46]

Despite General Scott's optimism, the problem of how to make the best use of the machine gun continued to vex army planners. In February 1916 Lieut. Col. Frank L. Winn noted that there were ". . . no logical grounds, however, for determining a uniform strength in machine guns on the basis of a fixed number for each division or detachment per thousand rifles. Armies can use more machine guns in trench or position warfare than in campaigns of maneuver."[47] Winn advocated the addition of two machine-gun companies, each armed with six weapons, to every infantry and cavalry regiment and the creation of a separate machine-gun service of two six-gun companies per division.[48] He apparently intended to create a system for using machine guns in the American army similar to that used in the German army. Army leaders did not expect to engage in trench warfare; consequently, they advocated and Congress created a force designed for mobile warfare of the type taking place on the eastern front. In these circumstances the General Staff felt little need to adopt Winn's ideas.

In the years before American entry into World War I, the scope and nature of army reform was limited first by President Wilson's lack of interest in the military and then by his opposition to

American involvement in the war. Even when Wilson's administration finally recognized the need to modernize the American military system, the continued policy of remaining aloof from the European war caused army planners to design a force for mobile warfare rather than for trench combat. The view that the enormous increase in the use of machine guns in France resulted almost entirely from the "special conditions" of warfare there allowed the army to continue to support the conservative concept of adding a single six-gun company to each infantry and cavalry regiment. Since it was mid-1916 before the War Department began to receive exact information concerning the major developments made in machine-gun tactics and organization by European armies, the program of army reform that was enacted in May 1916 did not reflect the impact of these changes. The development of American doctrine and organization for using machine guns in trench warfare would occur only after Americans had begun to fight in France in 1917.

In the summer of 1916 the machine gun was a secondary issue for the army staff. Concerned with the modernization of the entire American military system, the small General Staff—which could count few really expert staff officers among its members—did not have the resources to devote to a thorough study of the subject of machine guns. Given these circumstances, the decision to stay with a single six-gun company per line regiment was the easiest and safest course to follow. A year later the army staff, with no more trained men available than there had been in 1916, had to revise completely the organization and doctrine that it had laid down in 1916.

NOTES

1. Report of Infantry Committee, General Staff, on Organization of an Infantry Regiment, December 9, 1913, National Archives, Record Group (hereafter cited as NA, RG) 165, doc. WCD 8180-1.

2. U.S., War Department, *Tables of Organization, United States Army, 1914* (Washington, D.C., 1914), pp. 3, 7, 12, 14, 19, 55.

3. Ibid., p. 12.

4. M. M. Macomb to Chief of Staff, subject: Machine gun personnel for cavalry regiments, June 23, 1914; memo for Chief, Mobile Army Division, June 27, 1914; memo from Maj. Gen. H. L. Scott, Chief, Mobile Army

An Inadequate Staff and a Minimal Solution 205

Division, June 27, 1914, all three memoranda in NA, RG 165, doc. 11205; memo for Chief, Mobile Army Division, June 27, 1914, NA, RG 94, doc. 2154767 Additional B. filed with 1228217; Brig. Gen. A. L. Miles, Acting Chief of Staff, to Adjutant General, December 29, 1914, NA, RG 165, doc. WCD 7633/12 filed with 10872. The General Staff opposed piecemeal legislation to modernize the structure of army units. Instead it wanted a single piece of legislation similar to the bill proposed by Chief of Staff Leonard Wood in his annual report for 1914. U.S., War Department, *Annual Report of the War Department, 1914*, pp. 114-21; Brig. Gen. M. M. Macomb, Chief, War College Division, to Chief of Staff, subject: Report on bills S. 6964, 6968, 6963, 6965, 6967, 6966, December 26, 1914, NA, RG 165, doc. 8481-11.

5. Memo for General Scott, subject: Status of Machine Gun Units, October 12, 1914, NA, RG 165, doc. 10872.

6. Chief of Staff to Adjutant General, March 23, 1914, NA, RG 165, doc. 7949; letter to Adjutant General, subject: Field Test of Automatic Machine Guns, June 27, 1914, NA, RG 156, doc. 94; Maj. Gen. W. W. Wotherspoon to Adjutant General, August 25, 1914, NA, RG 165, doc. 5683-68; "Machine Gun Drill Regulations 1914" (typewritten draft), NA, RG 156, doc. 94.

7. Brig. Gen. Macomb to Chief of Staff, subject: Proposed Machine Gun Drill Regulations and Machine Gun Firing Manual, March 25, 1915, NA, RG 165, doc. WCD 9069-1 filed with 7949 (1915).

8. U.S., War Department, *Combined Infantry and Cavalry Drill Regulations For Automatic Machine Rifle, Caliber .30, Model of 1909* (Washington, D.C., 1915), pp. 15-21.

9. Ibid., pp. 43, 45, 56.

10. Ibid., p. 48.

11. Ibid.

12. According to Joseph T. Dickman, the War Department began to receive this type of information in February 1915. An earlier report covered the use of machine guns at the start of the war in a brief passage and recommended a six-gun regimental machine-gun company. Joseph T. Dickman, *The Great Crusade: A Narrative of the World War* (New York, 1927), pp. 9-10; Lieut. Col. Henry T. Allen to Secretary of War, October 21, 1914, NA, RG 165, doc. 8997-1.

13. Memo M. M. Macomb, Chief, War College Division, to Chief of Staff, subject: Report of Practice March by Machine Gun Platoon, 3d Cavalry, April 1, 1915, NA, RG 156, doc. 38356/1386.

14. See Marc B. Powe, "The Emergence of the War Department Intelligence Agency: 1885-1918," (MA thesis, Kansas State University, 1974),

pp. 53-75; and Powe's "American Military Intelligence Comes of Age: A Sketch of a Man and His Times," *Military Review* LV (December 1975): 21-24.

15. Ibid.

16. Adjutant General to Commanding General, Philippines Dept., subject: Machine Gun Units, April 19, 1915, NA, RG 156, doc. 38356/1452.

17. *Annual Report of the War Department, 1914,* vol. I, pp. 114-21.

18. Maj. E. N. Jones to Chief, War College Division, subject: Interview with the Chief of Staff on draft of Bill for Reorganization of the Army, January 29, 1915, NA, RG, 165, doc. 8481-12.

19. Senator George E. Chamberlain to Secretary of War, January 26, 1915, NA, RG 94, doc. 2237877/B.

20. Ibid.

21. Ibid.

22. Tasker H. Bliss, Acting Chief of Staff, to Chief, War College Division, March 11, 1915, NA, RG 165, doc. WCD 9053-1.

23. Ibid.

24. U.S., War Department, *Statement of a Proper Military Policy for the United States* (Washington, D.C., 1916).

25. Ibid., pp. 16-17. The regular army would consist of 281,000 officers and men; a total of 160,000 would be employed in static units or overseas.

26. U.S., War Department, *Study on the Development of Large Calibre, Mobile Artillery, and Machine Guns in the Present European War* (Washington, D.C., 1916), p. 8. Bound with *Statement of a Proper Military Policy for the United States.*

27. Draft of a Bill for the Reorganization of the Army of the United States, April 5, 1915, NA, RG 165, doc. 8481-17; memo for Chief, War College Division, September 1915, NA, RG 165, doc. WCD 9053-66.

28. Russell F. Weigley, *History of the United States Army* (New York, 1967), pp. 344-46; memo Chief, War College Division, to Chief of Staff, subject: Tentative draft of a Bill "For making further and more effectual provision for the national defense, and for other purposes," December 23, 1915, NA, RG 165, doc. WCD 9054-2; memo Office of the Chief of Staff to Chief, War College Division, December 11, 1915, NA, RG 165, doc. WCD 9054-2.

29. U.S., Congress, Senate, Military Affairs Committee, *Preparedness for national defense, hearings on bills for reorganization of Army and for creation of reserve Army, before a subcommittee of the Military Affairs Committee,* 64th Cong., 1st sess., 1916, p. 529.

30. U.S., Congress, House, Military Affairs Committee, *To Increase Efficiency of Military Establishment of United States, Hearings before a*

subcommittee of the Military Affairs Committee, 64th Cong., 1st sess., 1916, p. 1133; U.S., Congress, Senate, Military Affairs Committee, *Preparation for national defense,* 1916, pp. 483-84, 908-9; U.S., Congress, House, Military Affairs Committee, *To Increase Efficiency of Military Establishment,* 1916, p. 759.

31. This comparison is drawn from various statements contained in a document WCD 9054-9, NA, RG 165. See also "A Bill for making further and more effectual Provision for the National Defense, and for other purposes," marked "This is the 'War Dept.,' Bill," January 1916, NA, RG 165, doc. 9054-13.

32. Weigley, *History*, p. 346.

33. Office of the Chief of Staff to Chief, War College Division, March 27, 1916, NA, RG 165, doc. WCD 9416-8.

34. U.S., Congress, Senate, *H.R. 12766 ordered printed with amendments of Senate, April 20, 1916,* 64th Cong., 1st sess., NA, RG 165, WCD 9054-52.

35. Weigley, *History*, pp. 347-48.

36. Memo Chief, War College Division, to Chief of Staff, subject: Report on H.R. 12766, 64th Cong., 1st sess. (as agreed to by conferees of the Senate and the House of Representatives), May 23, 1916, NA, RG 165, doc. WCD 9054-53; National Defense Act, U.S., *Statutes at Large*, vol. 39, pt. 1, secs. 17 and 18, 178 (1916).

37. For the story of the creation of the Royal Machine Gun Corps, see C. D. Baker-Carr's autobiography, *From Chauffeur to Brigadier* (London, 1930).

38. Report from Military Attaché, Lieut. Col. G. O. Squier, subject: New British Machine-Gun Corps, Nov. 1, 1915, NA, RG 165, doc. 9272-1; "The English Machine-Gun Corps," *Journal of the United States Infantry Association* XII (February 1916): 817-20; Capt. W. A. Castle to Chief, War College Division, subject: Report on a visit to the Machine Gun Training Centre at Grantham, May 24, 1916, NA, RG 165, doc. 9272-3.

39. G. W. Powell, "The Lewis Automatic Gun," *Journal of the United States Infantry Association* IX (July-August 1912): 44-48; George M. Chinn, *The Machine Gun* (Washington, D.C., 1951), pp. 278-80; W. C. Crozier to Sen. B. R. Tillman, July 15, 1916, NA, RG 94, doc. 00 4725/347 Lewis filed with 1228217.

40. Baker-Carr's memoirs support Crozier's statement. Baker-Carr, *From Chauffeur*, pp. 129-33; Leonard Wood to Chief of Staff, September 17, 1915, NA, RG 165, doc. 10467; Chief of Staff to Chief of Ordnance, September 24, 1915, with 1st endorsement October 13, 1915, NA, RG 94, doc. 2333911.

41. W. C. Crozier to Sen. B. R. Tillman, July 15, 1916, NA, RG 94, doc. 00 4725/347 Lewis filed with 1228217.

42. The controversy concerning the Lewis gun is covered in Crozier's autobiography, *Ordnance and the World War* (New York, 1920), pp. 74-203.

43. "Machine Gun Fire," *Journal of the United States Infantry Association* XI (January-February 1915), trans. G. H. Michaelson from *Streffleur's Militarische Zeitschrift*, December 1913, pp. 540-47; "Machine Guns of the German Infantry," *Journal of the United States Infantry Association* XII (July-August 1915), trans. J. M. Eager from *La Nuova Rivista di Fantera*, February 1915, pp. 111-20; editorial, "Our Machine Gun Organization," *Journal of the United States Infantry Association* XII (July-August 1915): 151-52.

44. André Laffargue, "Study on the Attack in the Present Period of the War—Impressions and Reflections of a Company Commander," *Journal of the United States Infantry Association* XIII (September-October 1916): 101-38; Friedrich V. Merkatz, "New Methods of Machine Gun Fire," *Journal of the United States Infantry Association*, XIII (July-August and September-October 1916): 1-24, 175-202.

45. Chief of Staff to Secretary of War, subject: Machine Guns and Semi-Automatic Muskets, July 27, 1915, NA, RG 165, doc. WCD 9053 filed with Envelope 4 (Special Studies [Misc.]).

46. Ibid.

47. Lieut. Col. Frank L. Winn, "Machine Guns in the Present European War, Deductions as to Desirable Organization of Machine Gun Units and Requisite Number of Guns to Accompany Our Infantry Regiment," February 14, 1916, NA, RG 165, doc. 9279-5, p. 59.

48. Each company was to have four officers and ninety men. Ibid.

X

CONCLUSION

During the five decades between Appomattox and the Zimmermann telegram the United States Army lagged far behind the armies of Europe in the modernization of its equipment, organization, and doctrine. Since the United States enjoyed the free security afforded by oceanic moats and weak neighbors, it did not need land forces comparable to those that major European powers maintained. With its shape determined by a desire for economy and a system of laws that allowed Congress to exercise control over the smallest details of military organization and equipment, the American army was little more than a collection of regiments whose administrative and logistical needs were met by technical services headquartered in Washington. Charles Darwin once defined the primary deficiency of the American military in this period when he stated that ". . . a body of well-instructed men, who have not to labor for their daily bread, is important to a degree which cannot be overestimated; as all high intellectual work is carried on by them, and on such work material progress of all kinds depends, not to mention other and higher advantages."[1] In military terms Darwin's "body of well-instructed men" was a General Staff. The American army was entirely without such an agency until 1903, and then its new General Staff was only partially operative; consequently the army failed to respond adequately to the intellectual and material forces that in fifty years brought warfare from the era of horse cavalry and smooth-bore artillery to the age of machines.

The relationship between the machine gun and the army from 1861 to the entry of the United States into World War I provides a graphic illustration of many of the organizational and intellectual inadequacies of the American military during that period. After it was offered an imperfect but promising prototype in 1861, the army for the next fifty years—as the result of technical difficulties, institutional inadequacies, overly stringent congressional control of its structure and budget, and a persistent failure of imagination—failed to create a system for using the machine gun effectively.

The early use of the machine gun by the American army is a cardinal example of the proposal that in weapons function tends to follow form. The Gatling gun resembled a fieldpiece in its physical appearance and logistical requirements. Consequently, the army considered the machine gun to be a species of artillery until combat experience and the purchase of the radically different Maxim gun in 1903 convinced military men that whatever it was, the machine gun was not an artillery piece. The machine gun, unlike the tank and the airplane, was not recognized as a new and radically different type of weapon until well after its basic physical development was complete.

Unlike the rapidly modernizing navy of the 1880s and 1890s, the army did not develop a close relationship with the armament industry.[2] Low budgets, small orders, and the high standards of quality that the Ordnance Department demanded meant that there was little chance of gaining quick or high profits in making weapons for the American military; certainly no "military-industrial complex" developed during this period. Advances in weapon design came as the result of individual inspiration and initiative, not from a desire to sell better weapons to the military.

Acceptance of the machine gun was delayed by the passive nature of the Ordnance Department's system for weapon development. Neither the inordinately conservative James Ripley nor a more reasonable chief of ordnance, William Crozier, gave serious consideration to the possibility of guiding and subsidizing civilian inventors' efforts to improve their inventions or of undertaking to improve a promising prototype in a government facility. Limited by a small budget, the Ordnance Department nevertheless could have given weapon designers and manufacturers considerable aid in developing arms that were suited to the needs of the Army.

The task of evaluating weapons that interested the Ordnance Department was usually given to a board of officers. Institutionalized in the decade following the Civil War, the board of officers was a responsive and relatively cheap device for evaluating

Conclusion

new and improved weapons. Although such boards were capable of thoroughgoing and imaginative investigation, as in the case of the Gillmore Board, the value of their work was often diminished by narrowly drawn instructions, which severely restricted the scope of their findings and recommendations. Limitation of official reports to subjects specifically delineated in the convening orders meant that information and ideas that the board developed that were not germane to these topics would not reach the army staff. Official reports also could be rendered useless when the original instructions that the board of officers received were too vague. In the case of the board that evaluated machine guns at the Springfield Arsenal in 1900, imprecise instructions led to a report that found three different machine guns suited to the needs of the service—information that did not narrow the choice of a weapon to replace the Gatling gun.

A third fault of the system for evaluating weapons was that it tended to reflect Ordnance Department requirements such as cost, durability, and interchangeable parts, rather than a concern for the operational capabilities of the model under study. Thus in 1868 a cavalry commander's criticism of the lack of mobility of the Gatling gun was rejected because the solution to the problem, a lightweight gun carriage, ran counter to Ordnance Department criteria for such equipment. As a consequence the unwieldy Gatlings played almost no part in frontier warfare in the 1870s. After the Spanish-American War, the Ordnance Department gave increased attention to operational considerations when it chose new weapons. Ironically, in the selection of the Benet-Mercie operational capabilities were a major factor in a decision that saddled the army with a poor weapon, which in turn hampered the development of machine-gun doctrine and organization in the years before American entry into World War I.

Because the machine gun was a peripheral issue for the army, individuals did most of the innovative thinking about ways to employ the weapon. One result of the lack of controversy surrounding the weapon was that—unlike Lieut. William Sowden Sims, the reformer who introduced continuous-aim firing to the United States Navy—machine-gun enthusiasts such as Edward Williston and John Henry Parker received encouragement from army officials in their work with machine guns.[3] Such encouragement was forthcoming because the machine gun did not pose a threat to established programs or interests and because the experiments were far enough apart in time for memories of earlier trials to dim and their records to be lost in War Department files.

If obscurity meant that there was little opposition to their work, it could also mean, as in Williston's case, that the results were easy to ignore. The worth of new weapons and schemes for their employment was considerably more difficult to demonstrate and to judge in the peacetime army than in the navy. Ships are machines, and their performance and capabilities can be measured and compared quite easily, but such is not the case in land forces. Military tactics is an art, not a science, and determination of the effect of new weapons upon the conduct of ground combat is extremely difficult in peacetime.

While Theodore Roosevelt was able to assist Lieutenant Sims in his crusade to improve naval gunnery, Parker's friendship with the president did not lead to acceptance of his ideas for employing machine guns. One of the main reasons for this failure was that while Sims and the navy could take action to demonstrate the correctness of his ideas, Parker could not support his concepts with concrete evidence. Improvement of naval gunnery aboard American warships depended upon the development and installation of new sighting equipment and the revision of marksmanship training; these were operations that the navy—a department under the control of the chief executive—could accomplish. Adoption of Parker's tactics and a separate machine-gun corps required action on the part of army officials and congressional action to revise the statutes that prescribed officer strength and the structure of army units. Unable to obtain legislative approval for expansion of the officer corps in 1908, Roosevelt could not implement even those portions of Parker's program that he favored.

Creation of a coherent body of tactical doctrine was not a topic of major interest in the higher echelons of the army for much of the period before World War I. Like the majority of their European counterparts, most American soldiers did not understand the extent of the changes in warfare that had occurred as the result of fifty years of rapid technological progress; consequently they failed to realize how outdated their tactical concepts actually were. Doctrine was no longer a set of relatively simple rules that prescribed how

Conclusion

men and weapons were to be maneuvered on the field of battle; it was, instead, a complex intellectual framework that enabled soldiers to conduct the intricate operations required in an arena that was increasingly dominated by the machines and techniques of modern industry.[4]

On the eve of the United States' entry into World War I, the tactical doctrine of its army remained quite rudimentary. The primary source of the official initiative to change established methods of employing weapons appears to have been the adoption of a new or improved version of the weapon. Consequently the development of machine gun doctrine was an episodic rather than continuous process. Since doctrinal changes were sparked by the introduction of new models or types of weapons, doctrine was oriented to a specific weapon such as the Benet-Mercie rather than to a class of weapons such as machine guns. For this reason American tactical concepts were restricted in scope and little or no attempt was made to develop combined arms doctrine. The Ordnance Department was the staff agency that most often stimulated doctrinal change; however, the department had only a secondary interest in tactical doctrine and organization. Until the creation of the General Staff in 1903 and the development of the system of service schools, the American army did not have agencies with a major interest in the creation and refinement of tactical doctrine and organization.

According to one of its principal architects, the General Staff was intended ". . . to do the preliminary planning for the army in order to prepare it for war and to make of its various elements a harmonious working machine."[5] Small in size, lacking both trained staff officers and established administrative routines, and hampered by the absence of a charter that clearly established its functional responsibilities and prerogatives, the new General Staff made little progress in modernizing the field army until 1916. Since its attention was focused upon the major problems posed by mobilization and war plans or upon the minor issues of daily operations, the staff devoted an inadequate amount of attention to important midrange problems such as determining the most effective method of using machine guns.

Prior to World War I, tactical doctrine occupied almost the same position in the American army that it had in the mid-nineteenth century. Tactical expertise was the product of experience rather than study; consequently, it was a subject that was understood rather than codified. Instead of a library of manuals reflecting the complex rules and concepts required to ensure the efficient operation of a modern mass army, American doctrine was contained in a heterogeneous collection of pocket-size handbooks such as the *Field Service Regulations*. Adequate for the operation of an army of separate regiments, this system would not suffice in France in 1917. Trained in a system which emphasized experience rather than codified rules of operation, the early members of the General Staff lacked the breadth of outlook and experience necessary to create a modern doctrinal system for the American army.

In its attempts to integrate the machine gun into its structure and doctrine, the American army consistently made the same key mistake: It failed to ask the right questions. Beginning with the work of the Springfield Board in 1900, continuing with the creation of the experimental machine-gun platoons in 1906 and with Parker's work at Monterey in 1908, the staff agencies of the War Department failed to tell the individuals and agencies charged with investigating the capabilities of the machine gun what types of information the army needed in order to select proper equipment, doctrine, and organization. As a consequence staff questions and the results of the trials rarely matched and the problems posed by machine-gun doctrine and organization remained unsolved. Marked by a lack of careful and imaginative thought in their preparation, army experiments with the machine gun seldom bore much fruit—a fact that underlined the lack of expertise in American staff work.

Because it had not developed answers to the difficult doctrinal questions raised by the conditions of modern war, the American army landed in France without the doctrinal and organizational framework needed to make it the "harmonious working machine" Carter had envisioned. Inexperienced and often unable to determine which problems were both important and soluble, the General Staff did not adequately coordinate and supervise the attempts to reform the structure and methods of the military. By 1917 real progress had been made in improving the American military system, but the achievements of the Root reform program in modernizing army field forces remained more potential than real.

Conclusion

NOTES

1. Charles Darwin, *The Descent of Man* (1871) as cited in John Bartlett, *Bartlett's Familiar Quotations* (Boston, 1955), p. 530.

2. See B. Franklin Cooling, "The Formative Years of the Naval-Industrial Complex: Their Meaning for Studies of Institutions Today," *Naval War College Review* XXVII (March-April 1975): 53-62.

3. See Elting E. Morison, *Admiral Sims and the Modern American Navy* (Boston, 1942), chaps. 6-15.

4. For a discussion of a similar situation in the French army prior to World War I, see Joseph C. Arnold, "French Tactical Doctrine, 1870-1914," *Military Affairs* XLII (April 1978): 61-67.

5. William Harding Carter, *The American Army* (Indianapolis, 1915), p. 205.

BIBLIOGRAPHICAL NOTES

The study is based primarily upon War Department records preserved in the National Archives, Washington, D.C., official documents printed by the Government Printing Office, and contemporary articles published in military journals of the period. Secondary works furnished technical information concerning machine-gun design as well as background on the use of machine guns by European armies. These notes cover (a) bibliographical aids, (b) manuscript sources, (c) published official sources, (d) periodicals, and (e) secondary works.

BIBLIOGRAPHICAL AIDS

There is no comprehensive bibliography focused on the specific topic of machine guns; the bibliographies of several secondary works are helpful. An article by Lieut. Robert C. Cotton titled "Machine Gun References," *Journal of the Military Service Institution of the United States* (November-December 1913), pages 467-70, is a useful bibliography for the years 1904-1910. The preliminary inventories of the records of the Adjutant General's Office, 1780s-1917 (Record Group 94) and of the Office of the Chief of Ordnance (Record Group 156), and the War Department General and Special Staffs (Record Group 165) located in the National Archives furnish the greatest assistance. The best guide to printed official documents is the *Checklist of United States Public Documents, 1789-1909.* Commonly known as the *1909 Checklist*, this useful work deserves to be in library reference collections as well as on the desk of the documents librarian where it normally resides.

MANUSCRIPT SOURCES

The records of the Office of the Chief of Ordnance (National Archives Record Group 156) were the largest single source of information used in this study. Using the collection requires negotiating the complexities of obscure filing systems manipulated by long-dead clerks and officers who were not always consistent in their record keeping. Initial confusion can turn to disgust and then despair, emotions not calculated to improve the quality of the research effort; there is, however, a partial solution to the problem. In 1964 the National Archives issued the *Preliminary Inventory of the Textual Records of the Office of the Chief of Ordnance,* Parts I and II. A descriptive listing of the groups of documents found within Record Group 156, the *Preliminary Inventory* is, in effect, a map of the terrain that the researcher must cover. In an afternoon of careful study, the student can map out the initial route; this path will, of course, be refined as work progresses and the investigator becomes more familiar with the nuances of the subject. The specific features of the various groups of documents are covered in the *Preliminary Inventory*; consequently only items of particular interest to this study are discussed.

The record of "Letters, Endorsements, and Reports Sent to the Secretary of War, 1812-89," (entry 5 of the *Preliminary Inventory*) furnishes digests of the correspondence that the secretary received concerning machine guns. Summaries of the contents of the letters as well as notes on their disposition prove valuable. The third of the chronological subseries in entry 21—"Letters received, 1812-94"—is a major source of information concerning use of the Gatling gun in the field; correspondence from Col. Nelson Miles concerning the Gatlings assigned to his command in 1876 as well as Capt. E. B. Williston's proposals for a battery of Gatlings are located in these files. Before examining the general correspondence files located in entries 28 and 29 of the *Preliminary Inventory*, the researcher should consult appendix 1 to part I of the *Inventory* for a list of the more important subjects and document numbers used in filing records in these two groups. Used carefully, this information greatly reduces the work of examining the general correspondence files while materially increasing the quality of the research effort. Records filed under document numbers 8900, 38356, and 39153 proved to be particularly valuable for this study.

Bibliographical Notes   219

   A large amount of information concerning early attempts to sell machine guns to the army is located in the "Register of Letters Received Relating to Inventions 1812-70, "Registers of Letters Received Relating to Improvements and Inventions, 1812-70," and "Correspondence Relating to Inventions, 1812-70" (entries 192, 193, and 994). Titled "Experiments with Cannon of Class 1c," the volume marked "98" of the series of "Reports of Experiments, 1826-71" (entry 201) contains reports of the tests of machine guns by the Ordnance Department as well as test reports forwarded to it by field commands; it is particularly important as a source of information for the Civil War period. The files of the activities of the Ordnance Board from 1892 to 1919 (entries 248-264) furnish information on experiments with machine guns as well as upon the general course of experimental activity in the Ordnance Department; the thirteen volumes of "Letters and Endorsements Sent, Jan. 1895-Mar. 1901" (entry 250) contain considerable information about experiments with machine guns. Boxes 80 and 81 of the "Reports and Correspondence of Ordnance Boards, 1827-70," (entry 1012) hold copies of the reports of the Maynadier Board of 1867 and the boards of officers which selected the carriages and caissons of the Gatling gun in 1868.

   Several Ordnance Department reference aids yield useful information. The "Reference Guide to Articles Published in Periodicals Relating to Ordnance Matters, 1883-89" (entry 1026) affords a partial view of the types and sources of technical information received by the Ordnance Department in the late nineteenth century. Part II of the *Preliminary Inventory* deals with the records of Ordnance Department field installations; with the exception of the "General Correspondence, 1900-15" files for the Springfield Arsenal these records were not used in this investigation.

   Since the adjutant general received all proposals for changes to tactical doctrine, the files in the records of the Adjutant General's Office 1780s-1917 (Record Group 94) contain the best record of early ideas concerning machine-gun doctrine. Entry to the files held in Record Group 94 may be accomplished through the use of the file titled "Index to Letters Received, 1890-1916," which is on microfilm M-698. Since both proper names and subjects are indexed in this file, a wide variety of topics can be addressed; the most productive headings are: Benet-Mercie; Memos—War College Division; Infantry Board; Machine Guns; Mobile Army; Macomb, M. M.; Parker, John H.; and Williston, E. B. Documents located under these headings can be requested according to their document numbers. Occasionally War Department clerks refiled papers concerning a particular topic under a single document number; records filed under document numbers 1228217 and 1320473 proved particularly useful. Located in microfilm M-727, the record of events sections of the returns of the Second Artillery Regiment provide a brief summary of the activities of F Battery, Second Artillery, during the years that Capt. E. B. Williston commanded it.

Archivist John Taylor suggests that research in the records of the War Department General and Special Staffs (Record Group 165) begin with a survey of the following files: "Name and Subject Card Index to General Correspondence, 1907-16" (series 4): "Name and Subject Card Index to Series 288, 292, 294, 296-300" (microfilm M-912), and the separate name and subject card indices to the "General Correspondence of the Board of Ordnance and Fortification (1888-1919)" (series 514 and 515). Information gleaned from these references led to examination of the following files:

"Memorandum Reports, June-September, 1903" (series 2)

"General Correspondence, 1903-06" (series 3)

"General Correspondence, 1907-1916" (series 5)

"Proceedings War College Board, July 1902-August 1903" (series 286)

"Miscellaneous Correspondence, 1903-10" (series 292)

"Correspondence deleted from series 292—on Important Subjects" (series 294)

"General Correspondence, 1903-19" (series 296)

"Monographs, Problem Reports, Army War College Studies and Committee Reports, 1906-09 (series 299)

"Journals of the First, Second and Third Divisions of the General Staff, 1906" (series 303)

Selected Documents relating to the work of the Second and Third Divisions of the General Staff, 1904-08" (series 304)

"Records of the Historical Section Relating to the History of the War Department, 1900-41" (series 310)

Bibliographical Notes

"Minutes of the Board of Ordnance and Fortification, 1888-1918" (series 511)

"General Correspondence of the Board of Ordnance and Fortification (1888-1919)" (series 516)

The collection of War College studies and reports found in series 299 "Monographs, Problem Reports, Army War College Studies, and Committee Reports, 1906-09" is particularly useful in assessing early General Staff efforts to develop machine gun doctrine and organization. Both the minutes and general correspondence of the Board of Ordnance and Fortification (series 511 and 516) help to pinpoint the role that the board played in sponsoring the work of John Henry Parker and the experiments carried out at Fort Leavenworth and Fort Riley.

The last major source of information in manuscript form is the correspondence between John Henry Parker and Theodore Roosevelt located in the Theodore Roosevelt Collection, Library of Congress. Indexed according to the last name of the correspondent, this collection is remarkably easy to use. Many of the Parker-Roosevelt letters are printed in *The Letters of Theodore Roosevelt* edited by Elting E. Morison; Morison's footnotes illuminate several of Parker's letters. The Archives of the United States Military Academy, West Point, N.Y., contain a typescript biography of John Henry Parker adapted by William Garrigus from Parker's own manuscript. Although Parker was delighted with Garrigus' "dashing style," the typescript offers little beyond a superficial treatment of Parker's exceptionally full life. Unfortunately, Parker's own manuscript has not survived.

PUBLISHED OFFICIAL SOURCES

Government publications present the researcher with a baffling array of sources; the key to solving the problem is judicious use of the portion of the *1909 Checklist* that deals with the War Department. Material listed under these headings is useful: Staff Corps, General; Adjutant General's Department; Coast Artillery School; Ordnance Department; and the Ordnance and Fortification Board. Of particular value are the indexes to the annual reports of the chief of ordnance, especially the *Index to Reports of the Chief of Ordnance, 1864 to 1912* (Washington, D.C., 1913). The reports themselves highlight those Department operations that the chief of ordnance considered important; summary in nature, they tend to paint an optimistic picture of ordnance activities. Until 1908 the government printed the detailed reports of the arsenals and armories as appendices to the annual ordnance reports. These appendices contain the records of the boards that tested machine guns.

The series of reports and papers issued as *Ordnance Memoranda, Notes on Construction of Ordnance,* and *Ordnance Notes* contain important information on experiments such as those carried out by the Gilmore Board as well as descriptions of foreign developments; volume 13 of *Ordnance Notes* contains an index to that series. Before examining the operations of the Ordnance Department, the investigator should consult the particular edition of *Ordnance Department Regulations* in effect during the period to be studied. Knowledge of these regulations greatly assists penetration of the thicket of Ordnance Department paperwork and administrative routine. Comparison of the details of succeeding editions of the regulations helps to develop a picture of the evolution of ordnance procedures and policies. Volumes III and IV of the *Collection of Ordnance Reports and Other Important Papers Relating to Ordnance Department,* edited by Brig. Gen. Stephen Vincent Benet, together with the two volumes of the *Proceedings of Court of Inquiry Convened . . . To Examine Accusations Against A. B. Dyer, Chief of Ordnance* illuminate Ordnance Department operations from 1860 to 1890. Finally, to understand the peculiar way in which the machine gun entered the structure and doctrine of the army, one must study the statutes that prescribed both unit organization and the general makeup and operation of the army. The *Statutes at Large* contain these laws, the *1909 Checklist* has consolidated indices for the *Statutes* under "Laws of United States."

PERIODICALS

Articles in the professional journals connected with the various branches of the service are a fundamental source of the information used in this study. Not only do the journals provide information on new machine guns and the American army's view of their use, but the number and type of articles indicate the amount of interest in the machine gun in the army during a particular period. Except for the work of Williston, Parker, and Macomb, few articles contain tactical and organizational concepts that go beyond the platoon and company level. Writers tended to focus upon the details of machine-gun drill and equipment, and General Staff documents and army manuals reflect this orientation.

Four periodicals are of exceptional value. With a subject index at the end of each volume, the *Army and Navy Journal* provides a large amount of information about experiments with the machine gun as well as comments concerning its value as a weapon; the *Journal* is particularly valuable as a source of information for the period from 1866 to 1900. Three professional journals, the *Journal of the Military Service Institution of the United States*, the *Journal of the United States Cavalry Association*, and the *Journal of the United States Infantry Association*, contain the bulk of the articles used. Both the *Cavalry* and *Infantry Journals* bear annual indices. Published in 1904, a separately bound subject and author index covers the first thirty-four volumes of the *Journal of the Military Service Institution*, and a separate subject index for the next fifteen volumes appeared in 1913; cumulative indices for the *Cavalry Journal* and its successor, *Armor*, appeared in 1974 as no. 12 in the Kansas State University Bibliography Series. With two exceptions, *Military Affairs* and *Military Review*, present-day periodicals are of little assistance; articles in these two magazines, however, furnish information concerning the peacetime structure and operations of the Ordnance Department and the General Staff. The *Military Review Consolidated Index* published in 1967, and the *Cumulative Indices to Military Affairs* issued in 1969 as no. 6 in the Kansas State University Bibliography Series are both useful. Periodical literature, particularly the service journals of the period, forms a major resource for those who wish to study the activities of the American army in the late nineteenth and early twentieth centuries.

SECONDARY PUBLICATIONS

Two general categories of books, works dealing specifically with machine guns and books that provide information about the army, fall under the rubric of secondary literature. G. S. Hutchison's *Machine Guns: Their History and Tactical Employment* is the single most informative work on the development of machine guns and machine-gun doctrine. While his book reflects the fact that the author was a member of the Royal Machine Corps during World War I, Hutchison devotes adequate attention to developments in equipment and doctrine made in the French and German armies. *The Book of the Machine Gun* by F. V. Longstaff and A. Hilliard Atteridge is an earlier work that contains useful information and commentary about the use of the machine gun in colonial warfare. Published a generation ago by the Navy Department, Col. George M. Chinn's superbly illustrated *The Machine Gun: History, Evolution, and Development of Manual, Automatic and Airborne Repeating Weapons*, volume I, provides a definitive discussion of the physical development of the machine gun.

A study of President Lincoln's attempts to improve the armament of the Union forces, Robert V. Bruce's *Lincoln and the Tools of War* covers the Ordnance Department system for evaluating novel weapons and equipment; in addition Bruce describes the effort to sell the Ager "Coffee-Mill" gun to the army. Additional information on Ordnance Department policies and procedures is in *Arming the Union*, a study of federal small-arms procurement during the Civil War; the author, Carl L. Davis, evaluates Ordnance Department operations in the light of personnel and administrative difficulties and presents a balanced picture of nineteenth-century army bureaucrats coping with the demands of the first modern war. A short survey of Civil War weapons, Jack Coggins' *Arms and Equipment of the Civil War* provides useful information concerning the capabilities of different types of artillery pieces and the ammunition they used. The owner of thirty-eight Gatling guns, Donald R. Toppel, and a firearms expert, Paul Wahl, wrote *The Gatling Gun*, the only book that focuses specifically upon this topic; their work contains a short but useful bibliography. Michael Howard's *The Franco-Prussian War* discusses the *mitrailleuse* and the French army's ill-starred attempt to use it in combat.

The central importance to this study of John Henry Parker's two books, *History of the Gatling Gun Detachment Fifth Army Corps, At Santiago, With a Few Unvarnished Truths Concerning*

Bibliographical Notes

that *Expedition* and *Tactical Organization and Uses of Machine Guns in the Field*, needs no amplification; Parker's *History* also forms a major resource for students of the Santiago Campaign. Brig. Gen. C. D. Baker-Carr's autobiography, *From Chauffeur to Brigadier*, is the record of the unconventional creator of the first machine-gun training school in the British Expeditionary Force; Baker-Carr had a major role in shaping the Royal Machine Gun Corps. Baker-Carr's comments upon the difficulties encountered in his attempts to convince higher authorities of the worth of the machine gun illuminate the difficulties an innovator faces even in wartime. Maj. Gen. E. D. Swinton's memoir, *Eyewitness*, provides valuable commentary on the state of machine-gun doctrine in the British army in the years before World War I. In 1920 the longtime American chief of ordnance, Maj. Gen. William Crozier, published a memoir, *Ordnance and the World War*, which contains a lengthy justification of his handling of the problem of machine-gun procurement.

Three biographies are particularly useful. Frank Vandiver's *Ploughshares Into Swords*, a masterful account of the career of the brilliant Confederate chief of ordnance, Josiah Gorgas, gives a standard against which the accomplishments of Generals Ripley, Ramsay, and Dyer may be measured. Because Confederate Ordnance procedures were to a large degree adapted from those of the prewar army, Vandiver's account is excellent background for investigation of Union ordnance operations. Russell F. Weigley's equally well-done *Quartermaster General of the Union Army*, a biography of Bvt. Maj. Gen. Montgomery Meigs Macomb, provides an account of the operations of what was the best organized of the staff bureaus supporting the Union armies. *Admiral Sims and the Modern American Navy* by Elting E. Morison holds a detailed analysis of the work of William Sowden Sims, a successful innovator whose activities paralleled those of John Henry Parker.

A number of works are unusually valuable as sources of background information. The 1885 and 1895 editions of *Farrow's Military Encyclopedia: A Dictionary of Military Knowledge* by Edward S. Farrow contain articles on the Gatling gun and other machine guns which provide a view of the position that the weapon occupied in late nineteenth century American military thought. Ira L.

Reeves' *Military Education in the United States* furnishes brief sketches of the different components of the Army school system in the first decade of the twentieth century. *The Organization and Administration of the Union Army, 1861-1865* by Fred Albert Shannon provides information useful in evaluating Ordnance Department operations during the Civil War.

For the student of the development of weapons and doctrine *Ideas and Weapons* by I. B. Holley, Jr., is an indispensible work. Not only is Holley's thesis, that peacetime development of a new weapon is largely governed by the degree to which its function has been defined, a fundamental point of departure for the study of military innovation, but in depth of research, form and style the book is the model of its kind. It is important to remember, however, that Holley's study concerns the airplane, a twentieth-century invention, and, therefore, some of his conclusions may have limited application to the creation and reception of new arms in earlier eras. Holley's book and a volume by Dennis Showalter titled *Railroads and Rifles: Soldiers, Technology, and the Unification of Germany* bracket this study in time. Showalter's work is especially valuable for the insights which it affords into the manner in which the Prussian army adopted and then adapted to the technology of the mid-nineteenth century. Anyone who investigates an aspect of army staff operations must consult Russell F. Weigley's *History of the United States Army*, which is the standard organizational history of the American military. Bernard and Fawn Brodie's *From Crossbow to H-Bomb* is the best available general account of the evolution of the weapons and tactics of warfare. Finally, Theodore Ropp's *War in the Modern World* provides both an insightful history of modern warfare and a basic bibliography on the subject.

INDEX

Adjutant General's role in doctrinal change, 56-67
Ager, Wilson, 16
Ager (Union) gun, 14-15; attempts to sell, 16-19, 21; "Coffee Mill" gun, *16*, *17*; demonstration of, 17; invented, 16
American Arms Company, 18
American Expeditionary Force, 189
Ammunition, 4; buckshot cartridge for Gatling, 43-45; center-fire primer, 52; copper cartridge for Gatling, 32-33; metallic cartridges, 32-33
Ammunition supply, 137-38; Benet-Mercie's, 177; data insufficient on, 142; large-scale use of machine guns and, 137-38; limits machine gun platoon, 152; Russo-Japanese War, 140-42
Anadarko (Indian) Agency, 80
Appropriations, 43; weapons, reduced, 36
Army and Navy Journal: Gatlings on frontier, 52; letter on Gatling, 67-68; report on machine gun employment, 140; reports of Gatlings in British army, 62-63; review of Parker's second book, 112

Army Appropriation Act of 1913, 184
Army Reorganization Act of 1901, 118, 143
Articles on machine guns, 153-55, 175, 182
Artillery, 4-5; British-made breech-loading, 5; Gatling resembles, 33; Krupp's new, xiv; machine gun classified as, 89; *mitrailleuse* used as, 61; Napoleon gun-howitzer, 5; neglect of, 83-84; Parrot rifled, 5; performance of, in Cuban campaign, 84; Rodman Columbiad, 4; smokeless powder and, 76
Atascadero maneuvers, 159-60; Benet-Mercie tested at, 176-77

Baker-Carr, Christopher, D'Arcy, 201
Banks, Nathaniel, Maj. Gen., 18, 40
Barry, Thomas H., Brig. Gen., Barry, William A., Col., 59
Barry, William F., Brig. Gen., 40
Battery F, Second Artillery, 72; experiments of, 72, 86-87; Gardner Gun tests by, 75; transfer of, 87
Baylor, Thomas A., Capt., 44-46
Beauregard, P.G.T., Gen., 10

Page numbers in italic indicate photographs

141; endorsement of Parker's
  recommendation, 156
Belknap, William W., Secretary
  of War, 64, 67
Bell, J. Franklin, Brig. Gen., 135-36;
  distribution of machine guns addressed by, 140; provisional
  machine gun company recommended by, 156
Benet, Laurance V., 181
Benet, Stephen Vincent, Capt.,
  later Brig. Gen., 43-44, 66; Gatling guns requested by, 66; test
  of center-fire cartridge by, 51
Benet-Mercie machine gun, 171;
  adoption of, delays permanent
  organization, 179; advantages
  of, 177; AEF equipped with 189;
  costs of, 185; defects of, 171,
  181-82; first shipment of, received,
  179; inaccuracy and low-rate
  of fire of, 181-82; issue of,
  delayed, 178; model, 1909, 176;
  poor design of, 184; questionnaire on, 183-84; replacement
  of, 184; sources of impetus for
  adoption of, 175; strong points
  of, 184; tests of, 176-77, 184-85,
  201; use of, continues, 202
Benton, James A., Capt., 42
Berdan, Hiram, Col., 52
Billinghurst and Requa rifle
  battery, 39-40; calibre .40, 39;
  order of, 40; test of, 41
Birkhimer, William E., 68
Bliss, Tasker H., Maj. Gen.,
  comments on army reform,
  196-98
Blunt, Orison, 16
Board of officers, 65, 210-11;
  Barry, 59; engineer, 84;
  Gillmore, 64-66; Maynadier,
  58-59; role of, in doctrine,
  56-57; tests of Gatling carriages
  by, 53; Tower, 67; value of
  work of, diminished, 211
Board of Ordnance and Fortifica-
  tion, 74; evaluation of machine
  gun by, 133; funding of Parker
  cart by, 130; Parker's report to,
  134; role of, in doctrine and
  organization, 134, 136
Bookmiller, Edwin V., Capt., 128
Boxer, E. M., 52
British Fourth Army, xi-xiii
British machine gun doctrine, 172;
  lack of progress in, 171-72;
  World War I development of,
  200
Brown, Thomas W., Lieut., 179
Browning, John M., 77
Buffington, Adelbert R., Lieut.
  Col., later Brig. Gen., 89, 117,
  127
Bureaucracy, xiv-xv; consideration
  of, in equipment design, 55;
  Parker circumvents, 99; Parker's
  lack of success dealing with, 113
Butler, Benjamin F., Maj. Gen.,
  34, 40
Butler, John G., Lieut., 52

Cambridge, Duke of, 76
Cameron, Simon, Secretary of
  War, 13; Lincoln replaces, 25
Castle, William A., Capt., 200;
  report of, 200-202
Cavalry Journal article, 154
Chaffee, Adna R., Maj. Gen., 116
Chamberlain, George E., Senator,
  196, 198-99
Cincinnati Type Foundry, 34
Civil War, 3; armament in, 3;
  lessons of, disregarded in attack
  on Santiago, 100; machine
  guns in, 39

Index

Clarke, Andrew, Lieut. Gen. Sir, 76
Colt, Samuel, 32
Colt machine gun, 126-27, 129; Maj. Gen. Otis' request for, 116-17; rejection of, 116; use of, at Las Guasimas, 99-100; use of, in Boxer Rebellion, 115-16
Columbus, New Mexico, 199
Congress, xv; action of, forced by Villa raid, 199; legislation before, 199; limits of, on machine gun organization, 190-91
Congreve, Walter N., Lieut. Col., 171
Continental Army Plan, 198
Coolidge, Charles A., Lieut. Col., 116
Cooper, Harry L., Capt., 179
Craig, Henry K., Col., 7
Crozier, William, Brig. Gen., 127; Benet-Mercie machine gun replaced by, 185; combat arms participation in weapons selection advocated by, 132; comments on machine gun organization by, 198; decision by, to replace Maxim machine gun, 177; Infantry Board suggested by, 131-32; innovation not aided by, 210; manufacture of equipemnt for indirect fire directed by, 157; purchase of Benet-Mercie machine gun requested by, 177; purchase of Lewis machine gun opposed by, 201; purchase of new machine gun delayed by, 127-28; reason for selection of pack transport of machine guns by, 129; Vickers machine gun delay reported by, 185

Custer, George A., Lieut. Col., refuses Gatling guns, 82

Dahlgren, John A., Adm., 22
Danish *rifle-mitrailleuse*, 129
Darwin, Charles, 209
Davis, Vincent, 113-14
DeKnight machine gun, 176
Derby, George M., Col., 101
Dickson, Tracy C., Capt., 128
Doctrine, xv; advantages/disadvantages of experimental platoon as a system for creating, 143-44; army mobile warfare, 203-4; attention diverted from, by Benet-Mercie, 171; cavalry manual fails to define, 179; change of, 213; decision for pack transport, 129-30; difficult to demonstrate value of new, 212; drill regulations for cavalry, 8; factors contributing to inability to change, 189-90; failure to develop, product of incomplete staff work, 151; fitted to particular equipment, 125; German, 136-37; Infantry Board develops, for machine gun, 133; lack of performance standards for machine gun, 137; lack of progress in British, 171-72; lack of progress in French, 172; machine gun, 135; new U.S. Field Service regulations provide, for machine gun, 178; not a major interest in U.S. Army, 212; objection to large-scale use of machine guns, 137; oriented to a specific weapon, 213; Parker direted to evaluate, 156; progress in German, 173-74; Provisional Infantry Regiment formed to test, 180;

229

tactical, of U.S. Army inferior, 213; tendency to use artillery concepts for Gatling, 44; trench warfare developed, 204; U.S. Army, lags behind European, 209; U.S. Army failure to keep pace with World War I developments in, 189; U.S. efforts to develop, stymied, 174-75; War Department, unsuccessful attempts to develop, 151; Welsh Board view on, 179
Douay, Charles A., Gen., 61
Downey, Fairfax, 82
Draper, Simeon, 16
Dreyse needle gun, xiv
Duncan, Joseph W., Col., 132
Duvall, William P., Maj. Gen., 102
Dyer, Alexander B., Maj., later Brig. Gen., 5, 6, 35; agreement to test Gatling by, 35; awareness of need for innovation, 36; evaluation of role of machine gun by, 90; familiarity with small arms developments of, 36; rumored to replace Ripley, 25

Eagle Iron Works, 34
Edwards, Clarence R., Brig. Gen., 198
Egbert, Henry C., Lieut. Col., 104
Endicott Board, 196
Esher reforms, 190
Expenditures, 43; decrease in, after Civil War, 72-73; influence of, on machine gun integration, 83; low level of, emphasize value of test and evaluation, 72-73

Field Service Regulations of 1910, 191
First Volunteer Cavalry, 99-100

Flagler, Daniel W., Brig. Gen., 84-85
Fortifications Appropriations Act of 1888, 78-79
Frederick the Great, 4
Fremont, John C., Maj. Gen., 19-21
Fuller, J.F.C., 3
Funston, Frederick, Brig. Gen., 157

Gardner machine gun, 75
Garrigus, William H., 115
Garrison, Lindley A., Secretary of War, 183; army reform proposal requested from, 196; Continental Army Plan sponsored by, 198; resignation of, 199; study of army modernization directed by, 197; Wilson withdraws support for plan of, 199
Gatling, Richard J., Dr., 32; demonstration of gun by, 34; fire destroys factory of, 34; first attempt of, to sell gun to army, 33; Lincoln requested by, to consider gun, 34-35
Gatling machine gun, 32, *102*; adoption of, by British, 62; battery, *81*; concentration of, in 1878, 80; demonstration of, for Maj. Gen. Hancock, 38; faults of, reported, 54; flaws in design of, 32; interest in, declines, 59; model, 1865, *37*; model of, described, 32; new model of, 33; patent model, 1862, 33; resemblance of, to artillery, 33; role of, as an auxilliary arm, 66; role of, in U.S. Army, 63-64; roles of, in 1868, 58-59; shipment of, arrives in Tampa, 98; test of, in 1865, 36-37; use of, against Indians, 80-83; use of, in

Index

Boxer Rebellion, 115-16; use of, in colonial wars, 63; use of, in Philippines, 115; use of, in Russo-Turkish War, 62; Williston's experiments with, 86-87

Geary, John W., Col., 18-19

General Service and Staff College, 133

General Staff, 126; consideration of machine gun drill regulations by, 192; continued struggle with machine gun tactics and organization by, 203; continued study of machine gun tactics and organization by, 203; continued study of machine gun tactics by, 190; creation of machine gun organization by, 142; Darwin defines, 209; directed to devote energies to army modernization, 197; directed to prepare army reform proposal, 196; does not adopt Winn's ideas, 203; does not have resources for machine gun studies in 1916, 204; early, lacks breadth of outlook and experience, 214; examination of German doctrine by, 136; failure of, to act on Infantry Board recommendations, 136-37; failure of, to ask right questions, 140, 153, 214; failure of, to coordinate reform attempts, 214; failure of, to determine information needs, 153; favors four machine gun platoon, 180; flawed intelligence organization of, 193-94; incomplete work of, 151; initial concerns of, 125; investigation of machine gun recommended by, 140; judgment of, that Maxim not fit for cavalry, 177; lack of, hampers progress, 209; lessons of Russo-Japanese War lead, to conclude machine gun not reliable, 141; not informed on British Machine Gun Corps, 200; obstacles to, creating machine gun organization, 137-38; proposal of, for first formal TO&E, 191; publication of Drill Regulation for Machine Gun platoons by, 164; reasons for, advocating four gun company, 190-91; reasons why, recommended six gun company, 202-3; receipt of bills for army reorganization by, 199; receipt of little information on machine guns by, 202; recommendation of, to develop tactics at Fort Leavenworth, 133; results of mergers of sections of, in 1907, 194; submission of memo by, 161; survey of commanders on defects in Benet-Mercie by, 183-84; unlikely to adopt British organization, 201

German machine gun doctrine, 136-37; adoption of separate machine gun companies and, 162; new concept in, 174; reasons for progress in, 173-74; superior, 200

Gibbs, Alfred, Maj., 54, 67

Gillmore, Quincy, Maj., 64-65

Gillmore Board, 64-65, 211

Goe, James B., Capt., 104

Gorgas, Josiah, Brig. Gen., 6

Grant, Ulysses S., Capt., 100

Grimes, George S., Capt., 100

Guild, George R., Lieut., 154

Guilfoyle, John F., Lieut. Col., 158

Hagner, Peter V., Col., 54-55
Haig, Douglas, Gen. Sir, xii
Hancock, Winfield Scott, Maj. Gen., 38, 73
Hawkins, Hamilton S., Brig. Gen., 96-97, 104
Hawley, Joseph R., Senator, 78
Hay, James, Representative, 184, 199
Hindersin, Gustav E. von, 60
Hitt, Parker, Lieut., 157
Hodges, Henry L., Lieut., 154-55
Holley, I. B., Jr., xiv
Hooker, Joseph S., 24
Hotchkiss machine gun, 126, 141
Howard, Oliver Otis, Maj. Gen., 6, 80
Hunt, Henry, Col., later Maj. Gen., 83, 89

Indirect machine gun fire, 157-58; use of, in Battle of Somme, 159
Infantry Board, 131-32; circulation of Parker's proposal by, 133; development of machine gun techniques assigned to, 133; doctrine added to charter of, 133; establishment, roles and value of, 131-32; recommendation of, that machine gun an infantry weapon, 142; report of, on Parker's cart, 132-33; results of, questionnaire, 133; role of, in employment concept, 135-36; tests of Parker's cart by, 131
Infantry Journal articles, 182, 202
Innovation, 210, 213; breechloaders as an, 5; changes in Ordnance Department attitude toward, 43-44; Civil War armament, 3; defect in system for evaluating, 43; inability of combat arms to influence, 55; individuals responsible for, 211; lack of, in World War I, xii-xiii; Parker as an advocate of, 112-15; reasons for failure of, in carriage design, 55; reasons for lack of, in Confederate army, 4-5; reasons for lack of, in Union army, 5; sources of doctrinal, 57-58; successful advocates of, 113-14; success of, 39; Williston's view of obstacles to, 88-89

Johnston, William, Maj., 161-62
Journal of the Military Service Institution of the United States, articles, 87-89, 107-8

Kell, Charles, 24
Kennon, Lyman W.V., Capt., 104
Kent, Jacob F., Brig. Gen., 100
Kitchen, Claude, Representative, 199
Kitchener, Field Marshal, xi
Krag rifle, 128
Kuhn, Joseph E., Maj., 139-40

Laffargue, Andre, Capt., 202
Laidley, Theodore T.S., Maj., 23
Las Guasimas, Battle of, 199-200
Lewis, Isaac N., Lieut. Col., 201-2
Lewis machine gun, 201
Light Artillery School, 90
Lincoln, Abraham, 14; asked to consider Gatling gun, 34-35; asks for Fremont's requisition, 21; attendance of demonstration by, 17; "Coffee Mill" gun name coined by, 17; order of Ager guns by, 18; Ripley urged to consider Ager gun by, 17; witness of test of Raphael

Index

Repeater by, 23
London Army and Navy Gazette, 112
London Broad Arrow, 63
Loughborough, Robert H.R., Lieut. Col., 132
Lund, John M., Capt., 182

MacArthur, Arthur, Col., later Lieut. Gen., 98, 116; call for investigation of role of machine guns by, 140
MacArthur, Douglas, Capt., 183-84
McClellan, George B., Maj. Gen., 5, 18
McClernand, Edward J., Lieut. Col., 139, 142
Machine gun, xiv; acceptance of, retarded, 15; Ager, 14-15; Bavarian, 61; cardinal example of, function following form, 210; competition of, with artillery, 44-45; criticism of, 137; difficulty in ranging with, 137-38; first self-powered, 76; French consider, a failure, 61; French experiments with, 60; Gatling, described, 33; Gravelotte-St. Privat use of, 61; ignored by Germans after 1870, 62; interest in, revives, 195; interest of Napoleon III in, 60; lack of mobility of, 80; mechanical reliablility of, 138, 141; nature of, firepower, 46; not bound to interests of traditional combat arms, 15; not recognized as radically new class weapons, 210; offered to Ordnance Department, 39; Ordnance Department fails to develop Raphael Repeater, 22; organic infantry weapon, 142; Parker's tactical theories for, 110-12; power of, demonstrated, 105; Prussian investigation of, 61; relationship between, and army, 209; resemblance of, to artillery, 44; role of, in coastal forts, 84; Russian interest in, 62; separate corps for, 110-11; supply of ammunition for, 138; use of, against American forces in Boxer Rebellion, 116; Welsh Board characterizes, as separate class of weapons, 179
Machine Gun Corps, 109-10
Machine gun platoon, 143-44; creation of, generates interest, 153; creation of, supported by staff, 151; criticism of, for slowing cavalry, 175; disadvantages of, 144; drill manual for, 152; factors influencing structure of, 142-43; leader of, charged with creating doctrine for, 151; organization and equipment of, 141; reports of, lack common focal point, 153; role of Army Reorganization Act in creation of, 143; training instructions for, 151-52
Machine gun training, 151-52; Benet comments on, 181; Lund comments on, 182
Machine Gun Training Center, 200, 202
Machine weapons, xiii, 46
McIver, George W., Maj., 176-77
Maclay, Isaac W., Lieut., 36-38
McMahon, John E., Maj., 158
McNair, William S., Capt., 158
Macomb, Montgomery M., Maj., later Brig. Gen., 134-36; article by, describes Rexar rifle, 175;

article by, on machine guns, 154; criticism of Maxim gun by, 175; quoted, 193; recommendation of, to adopt interim machine gun regulations, 192; report by, on Russo-Japanese War, 137-40; report by, on shortcomings of machine gun, 140; urges creation of military information section, 194

McWhinney, Rindge and Co., 34

March, Peyton C., Capt., 139, 141

Maus, Marion P., Col., 157

Maxim, Hiram, 76

Maxim machine gun, 75-77; German Maxim gun, model 1908, 173; use of, at Omdurman, 85; use of, in Philippines, 115

Maxim solid-action machine gun, 126

Maxim water-cooled machine gun, 129, 175

Maynadier, William, Capt., 9

Mayne, Charles B., Lieut. Col., 157

Merritt, Wesley, Bvt. Maj. Gen., 89

Miles, Nelson A., Col., later Maj. Gen., 82-83; opinion of, that Gatlings are artillery, 105; reprimand by, of Parker, 108

Miley, John D., Lieut., 101

Military Information Division, General Staff, 194

Mills, J. D., 17-19

Mitchell, W., Lieut., USN, 40

Mobility, 82-83; need for, in Indian campaigns, 82; Parker discusses lack of, 96

Montigny *mitrailleuse*, 60; British evaluation of, 65; classification of, as artillery, 60-61; improper employment of, 61

Morgan, Edwin D., Governor, 40

Morrison, John F., Capt., 139, 142

Morton, Charles G., Maj., 132; formation of machine gun detachment in battalion of, 133; reports of, 137; reports on ammunition supply termed insufficient by, 142; role of, in developing employment concept, 136

Morton, Oliver Hazard Perry, Governor, 33

National Defense Act of 1916, 189, 200, 202

Neill, Thomas H., Lieut. Col., 80

Nez Percé, 80

Nivelle offensive, xii

Norton, John, Lieut., 4

Notes On the Construction of Ordnance, 79

Ord, E.O.C., Maj. Gen., 86

Ordnance Department, 3, 6-7, 9; agency of doctrinal change, 213; attempts of, to counter dissatisfaction with Benet-Mercie, 182; Board of Heavy Ordnance, 74; Board of Ordnance, 74; Board of Ordnance and Fortification, 74; change in attitude of, toward new arms, 42; Chief of, changes twice, 126; contention of, concerning problems with Benet-Mercie, 183; criteria of, for new equipment, 211; criticism of, in *Army-Navy Journal*, 117; decision of, to adopt standard machine gun, 128; decision of, to not produce Lewis gun, 201-2; decision of, to pack transport machine guns,

Index

129-30; decision of, to replace Benet-Mercie, 184; demands on, in 1899-1901, 126; does not have close relationship with armament industry, 210; failure of, to increase ammunition allowance, 153; faults in, system for weapons evaluations, 210-11; funds provided by, for Parker's cart, 130; machine guns offered to, in Civil War, 39; misses opportunity to aid development of machine gun, 15; operations of, hindered by low funds, 72; passive nature of, system for weapons development, 210; performance expectations of, 53; proceeds slowly in replacing Benet-Mercie, 184; publication of technical information by, 79; purchases of Gatlings by, 46, 78; reasons for, domination of weapons selection, 73-74; reasons for size of, purchases in 1866, 47; role of, in creation of doctrine and organization, 125; standardization of, test and evaluation operations, 74; treatment of machine gun as a weapons system by, 128-29; weapons selection process of, 126

Ordnance Memoranda, 79

Ordnance Notes, 79

Organization, 135; AEF regimental machine gun company, 189; army experts on, 198; attempts to change army, 117-18; Benet-Mercie hinders progress in, 175; bill for change in, in 1900, 117-18; British, 171-72; cannot base, on rifle strength, 203; Chamberlain bill provisions for, 198; competing proposals for, 198; Congressional choice of, 199; Congressional proposals for, 199; Continental Army plan on, 198; coverage of, in 1910 *Field Service Regulations*, 178; creation of, in 1906, 141; decision for pack transport on, 129; defects in Benet-Mercie divert attention from, 171; defects in Parker's concept of, 110; development of, in 1903, 133; factors contributing to lack of change in, 189-90; first formal TO&E for, 191; fitted to particular equipment, 125; German concepts for, 136-37; infantry and cavalry concepts of, 191; Infantry Board develops, 134; Infantry Board report on, 134; Japanese concept for, 138; lag of, behind Europe, 200; Lieut. Guild recommends separate, 154; Lieut. Hodges proposes, for cavalry, 154-55; Lieut. Smalley recommends separate, 154; machine gun, at regimental level, 141; National Defense Act of 1916 authorizes, 200; new infantry concept for, 190; Parker proposes evaluation of, 155-56; Parker's manual describes, 160; Parker's 1901 proposal for, 130; Parker's separate corps, 109-10; progress in German, 173-74; proposed, in 1915, 198; Provisional Infantry Regiment to test, 180; Roosevelt concept of, 164; War Department does not request, from Congress, 179; Welsh Board recommends, 180; Winn's concept for, 203

Otis, Elwell S., Maj. Gen., 116-17
Otto, Augustus, Lieut., 19-20

Pack transport, 152, 175
Parker, James, Col., 175
Parker, John Henry, Lieut., later Col., 96-99, *97*; advocacy of board to evaluate concepts by, 155-56; advocacy of indirect machine gun fire by, 157-58; advocacy of separate machine gun corps by, 160; articles by, 107, 154; asks for funds for machine guns cart designed by, 130; cannot demonstrate ideas of, 212; command at siege of Santiago, *103*; comments by, on manual, 164; concept of, for separate corps, 110; controversy of, with Capt. Parkhurst, 108; creation of machine gun manual by, 160; criticism of artillery by, 107-8; difficulties of, in training provisional company, 159; direction of, to digest reports, 157; encouragement of, 211; failure of attempts to innovate by, 112-13; first book of, 106; innovations of, 114-15; machine gun manual of, 160; Major, commands in Philippines, 115; manual of, rejected, 161; orders of, to Cuba, 155; orders of, to Fort Leavenworth, 131; orders of, to Fort Riley, 131; performance of, at Atascadero maneuvers, 160; praise of, for Benet-Mercie, 178; proposal of, for regiment of black soldiers, 105-6; proposal of, for Tactical Unit of Machine Guns, 105; reasons of, for a separate machine gun corps, 109; reprimand of, 108; results of Benet-Mercie tests by, 155; role of, in developing organization, 135; second book of, 109; sends copy of report to President Roosevelt, 163; states reports support his concept, 157; submits legislative proposal of, 162; suggests study of ideas of, 161; tactical and organizational concepts of, 106, 110-12; theories of, lack evidence, 112; theories of, refuted, 162; unpublished biography of, 115; use of machine guns at San Juan Hill by, 105; War Department directs, to develop manual, 151; warning by, on delay in organizational development, 175; writes articles describing provisional machine gun company, 159-60
Parkhurst, Charles D., Capt., 108
Philippine Insurrection, 115
Philippine Scouts, 142
Pilsan, John, Lieut. Col., 19-20
Porto Rican Regiment, 142
Provisional Gatling Gun Detachment, 98-99; command of, by Theodore Roosevelt, 101; performance reports of, 101-5; support of attack on San Juan Hill by, 100-101
Provisional Infantry Regiment, 180-81
Provisional machine gun company, 155-56

Range-finder, 137
Raphael Repeater, 22-24
Rawlinson, Henry, Gen. Sir, xii
Reade, Philip, Maj., 104
Red River War, 80
Reichmann, Carl, Capt., 138-39

Index

Reno, Jesse, 6
Reno, Marcus A., Maj., 82
Rexar rifle, 175
Rifle, 4; breech-loading, 36; effect of changes in caliber of, 78; French *chassepot*, 60; Parker comparison of machine gun to, 90
Ripley, James W., Brig. Gen., 7-9, 8; advice of, on Raphael Repeater, 23; allows firing of Ager gun, 17; attempts to add machine guns to Union forces blocked by, 33; forced to retire, 25; innovation not aided by, 210; opinion of, on new small arms, 13; opposition of, to Ager gun, 22; opposition of, to Raphael Repeater, 24; prejudice of, against new weapons, 13; quotes of, 6, 13; record of, 26; relevance of experience of, 10; report on Ager gun ignored by, 20; responsibility of, for evaluation of new weapons, 12; results of devotion of, to peacetime routine, 11; sends Ager guns to Army of Cumberland, 21
Rock Island Arsenal, 153
Rodman, Thomas, Maj., 7
Roosevelt, Theodore, Col., later President, 101, 104; assistance of, to Sims, 212; bill by, 164; comment of, on Parker's second book, 172; comment of General Staff requested by, 163; personnel for machine gun platoons authorized by, 143; receipt of Parker's draft machine gun regulations by, 163; stipulation of conditions for separate company by, 163; suggestion of, accepted by War Department, 163

Root, Elihu, 116
Root reform program, 190
Rosecrans, William S., Maj. Gen., 21
Rubin, Maj., 76
Russo-Japanese War, 138-40; reports of use of machine gun in, 173; use of machine gun in, reviewed, 162, 179
Ryther, Dwight W., Lieut., 101, 104

San Francisco Call report, 160
San Juan Hill, battle of, 100-103; Parker uses, to justify theories, 106; reports on, 101, 104-5
School of Musketry, 156-57; board of officers convened at, 179; development of manual by, 165; experimental work at, 157; manual of, critiqued, 165; test of Benet-Mercie at, 176-77
Schuyler, Walter S., Lieut., 139
Scott, Hugh, Maj. Gen., 193-94; call for lightweight machine gun by, 203; opinion of, on warfare in France, 203; reform not supported by, 196; support of, for six gun company, 198
Sedgewick, John, Maj. Gen., 24
Seward, William H., Secretary of State, 16
Shafter, William, Maj. Gen., 98, 105
Sheridan, Philip, Lieut. Gen., 86
Showalter, Dennis, xiv
Sims, William Sowden, Lieut., 211-12
Sioux Campaign of 1876, 80
Smalley, H. R., Lieut., 154
Smith, Alfred T., Lieut. Col., 98
Smith, Fred A., Brig. Gen., 160
Smokeless powder, 75-76

Somme, Battle of, xi-xii
Springfield Arsenal, 214; new rifle developed at, 128; tests at, 126-28; trials to replace Benet-Mercie at, 184-85
Stanton, Edwin M., Secretary of War, 25; awareness of, of Ripley's prejudice against new arms, 14; questions of, on purchase of Gatlings, 38; test of Raphael Repeater witnessed by, 23
Statement of a Proper Military Policy for the United States, 197-98
Stockton, Howard, Lieut., 42
Strength of the army, 83
Summerall, Charles P., Lieut., 115
Sumner, Samuel S., Brig. Gen., 100
Swinton, Ernest D., Maj. Gen., 86

Tactics, xii-xiii; advantages of Benet-Mercie for, 177; army gives platoon leaders task of creating, for machine guns, 151; based on mobile warfare concepts, 203-4; early British machine gun, 62-63; factors in German development of, 174; failure of French machine gun, in 1870, 61; General Staff reaffirms traditional view on machine gun, 180; lack of concept for, 137; lessons of Civil War disregarded in, at Santiago, 100; machine gun becomes an organic weapon, 135, 142; objection to large-scale use of machine guns, 137; offensive, to be explored, 142; Parker's early theories for, 96-97; Parker's separate corps, 106-7, 109-12;

Provisional Infantry Regiment formed to test, 180; questions about offensive, not answered, 141; role of machine gun not defined, 179; roles of Gatling enunciated by Gillmore Board, 64-65; Welsh Board opinions on, 180; Williston's theories on, 87-89

Technology, xii-xiv; advance of, 4; effect of, on British tactical doctrine, 63; effect of, on metallurgy on machine gun design, 32-33

Test and evaluation, 23; Billinghurst and Requa rifle, 41; Board of Cavalry Equipments, of Gatlings, 67; board of officers, of Benet-Mercie, 176; board of officers, of indirect fire, 158; Bookmiller-Dickson Board, of machine guns, 128-30; British, of machine gun, 62; British procedure for, copied, 64-65; Browning machine gun, 77-78; buckshot cartridge, 44; comparison of Gatling, 32; considerable effort wasted, 43; demonstration, for Maj. Gen. Hancock, 38; demonstration, for Maj. Gen. Rosecrans, 21; Dyer agrees to, of Gatling, 35; failure of system for, 127; French, of *mitrailleuse*, 60; Gardner gun, 75; Gatling carriage, 53; Gatling gun, 36-38, 44-46; 86-87; Gatling gun, denied by Ripley, 33; Gillmore Board, 64-66; Leon Springs, Texas, of Benet-Mercie and Vickers machine guns, 192; Lewis gun, 201; Lincoln unwilling to order, for Union gun, 18;

Index

Maxim machine gun, 77; no direct precedent for machine gun, 15; Ordnance Department influence on, 73; pressure on, 73; Raphael Repeaters, 22-25; responsibility of Chief of Ordnance for, 12; Ripley's failure to, new arms, 11; School of Musketry, of Benet-Mercie, 176-77; standards for, 74, 77; system for, in 1852 regulations, 12; Union gun, 19; Vandenburgh volley gun, 41-42; Williston's, 72

Thomas, George W., Maj. Gen., 21
Thompson, John T., Lieut., 98
Tiffany, William, Sgt., 99-100
Tower, Zealous B., Col., 67
Tracer bullet, 138
Treat, Charles, Col., 198
Tyneside Irish (103 Brigade, 34th Division), xi

U.S. Army traditional missions, xiv-xv

Van Deman, Ralph H., Capt., 194
Vandenburgh volley gun, 39, 41-42; calibre .50, with eighty-five barrels, *41*
Veteran Volunteers, First Army Corps of, 38
Vickers machine guns, 126, 184-85, 189, 201
Vielle, Paul, 75
Villa raid, 199

Wade, James F., Brig. Gen., 98
Watervliet Arsenal, 54
Weapons, 10; need for new, 36, 116; procurement of, 10-11
Weapons development, 3-4; artillery, 76; bureaucratic considerations in, 55; effect of Franco-Prussian War on, 62; gas-powered machine gun and, 76-77; inability of combat arms to influence, 55; Rodman method of gun-casting and, 5, 7; smokeless powder, a major advance in, 75; test and evaluation and, 12
Welsh, William E., Capt., 179, 184
Wheaton, Lloyd, Brig. Gen., 115
Wheeler, Joseph, Maj. Gen., 105
Williston, Edward B., Maj., 72; critique of theories of, 89; experiments of, 86-87; proposal of, for Machine Gun Service, 87-88; theories of, 72, 86-89
Wilson, Woodrow, President, 199, 203
Winn, Frank L., Lieut. Col., 203
Wolseley, Garnet, Lord, 76
Wood, Leonard, Maj. Gen., 194, 196, 198
Woodward and Cox, 18-19
Wotherspoon, William W., Maj. Gen., 196
Wright, Horatio C., Maj., Gen., 34
Wright, Luke Edward, Secretary of War, 163

ABOUT THE AUTHOR

DAVID A. ARMSTRONG is a Lieutenant Colonel in the United States Army. He has contributed to the journal *Military Review*.